Hunting Trophy Deer

Hunting Trophy Deer

John Wootters

THE LYONS PRESS

To
My MOTHER and FATHER
who gave me a career
and the whole outdoors world
when they gave me
my first deer rifle.

Printed in the United States of America
10 9 8 7 6 5 4 3 2

Design by Desktop Miracles, Inc.
Dallas, Texas

Library of Congress Cataloging-in-Publication Data

Wootters, John
    Hunting trophy deer / John Wootters—Rev. and augmented ed.
        p.   cm.
    Includes index.
    ISBN 1-55821-601-4
    1. Deer hunting—North America.   2. Hunting trophies.   I. Title.
SK301.W6   1997
799.2'765—dc21   97-6488
                                                                                      CIP

Contents

Preface

Second chances are no more common in a writer's world than in real life. To a magazine scribbler like me, the opportunity to expand, revise, and correct something published years earlier is a rare delight. Just think—a chance to smooth those passages that seemed so clever twenty years ago (but now seem only sort of dumb), to correct the boneheaded mistakes, camouflage the former ignorance, complete the unfinished thoughts, and put in all the stuff previously omitted. At last, the chance to tell it as it really is, instead of how I thought it was twenty years ago. What joy!

It does make me wonder, though, what I'll think of this revision in another twenty years!

Birthing a book is a classic exercise in agony and ecstasy, especially when the topic is as close to the author's heart as this one is. A friend of mine, observing me in the throes of putting the final touches to my manuscript and illustrations, commented, "This book is really your life work, isn't it?" Perhaps he understood even better than I did how much the book meant to me, for at least fifty-five of my sixty-eight years have gone into its creation.

When an author is that involved with his subject, a large part of the agony is in speculating on the book's reception, especially when the target audience is a fraternity of which the author feels very much a part—in this case, the serious hunters of the nation. And even more especially when part of the contents (and, indeed, the guiding point of view) is bound to be regarded as controversial, perhaps even radical, among some of the members of that widespread and diversified fraternity.

For that reason as well as others, I have been touched and vastly encouraged by the support and assistance of dozens of people during the preparation of this manuscript. Hunters, wildlife managers, game biologists, conservationists, photographers (amateur as well as professional), editors, and friends have kept me going throughout the task with advice and counsel, suggestions, material assistance, and moral support. Their attitudes, time, and concern are appreciated beyond expression. Not one of them has attempted to impose his own point of view on the shaping of the book; they have trusted me to set down what had to be said, much of which hasn't been said before in public print.

Foremost among these has been Al Brothers, a professional game biologist and ranch manager who is the spiritual father of the quality-whitetail management concept in Texas and who has proved his concepts in actual practice over more than a decade. By applying his own management principles, he has actually produced the trophy bucks. He is also one of the guiding hands of the Texas Trophy Hunters Association.

Jerry Johnston, founding president of TTHA, was also instrumental in this book and will be more instrumental in disseminating deer-management information at the grassroots level among hunters. Robert Rogers's assistance in accumulating illustrations for *Hunting Trophy Deer* was invaluable.

Among the many other Texas people who helped in every way they could, making their talent and knowledge freely available were, in no particular order, Jerry Smith, John Lacey, Charley Jones, Murphy Ray, Amos Dewitt, Walter Elling, the late Alan Hardy, Mike Biggs, Chip Ruthven, Larry Weishuhn, Steve Nelle, and Rod Marburger. Outside Texas, I'm indebted to George Martin, Ken Elliott, and Craig Boddington, all of Petersen Publishing Co., and William Nesbitt of the Boone and Crockett Club, all who kindly helped. So did the editors of several magazines I neglected while writing *Hunting Trophy Deer*. Their contribution was more than mere patience; their active encouragment helped me over many a rough spot.

The men who began to teach me, as a boy, that there is in fact something to learn about whitetail deer beside where to stick a bullet deserve special mention, for they helped lay the foundation for this book as well as my whole career. They were my grandfather Bob Spence and former Houston mayor Richard Fonville and his nephew Palmer "Peg" Melton. Had I nvever known those three,

Hunting Trophy Deer would not have seen the light of day and I might be selling shoes or insurance.

Listing hunting buddies in acknowledgments is not superfluous when they are the kind of companions with whom I've been blessed —genuine sportsmen in the truest (and original) sense of the word; thoughtful, curious hunters; and serious students of nature, wildlife, and whitetail deer in particular. The interchange of ideas, observations, and theories with such people over years of campfires has helped me to many of the insights in these pages. I must tip my now famous camouflaged cowboy hat to Don and Penny Ruthven, Dave and Kerry Owen, Bill Shackelford, Billy Priddy, Bob Baer, Merwin Lodge, Joe Balickie, "Bear" Sitton, and others. A wise hunter never stops learning about whitetail deer, and these are a few of the people in whose company that process, for me, has gone forward.

Finally, my wife Jeannie—a dead serious trophy hunter in her own right—has doing everything that every wife of every author must do if there is to be a book at all.

With not a single exception, to the best of my knowledge, every name mentioned above is that of a dedicated *hunter*, a hunter with a deep personal commitment to the concepts of enlightened deer management. These people may have helped me partly just out of friendship in some cases, but I think their strongest motivation was genuine concern for the future of the wildlife resource and a belief that this book might have a small part in furthering it.

One thing all these people who have had so much to do with the creation of *Hunting Trophy Deer* have in common is something the anti-hunting preservationists can never hope to understand; it is simply that they love the deer. That emotion is the ecstacy part of the agony-ecstasy of writing this book, and in it lies the real reason for writing it.

John Wootters
Houston, Texas
Fall, 1997

1 Maybe Tomorrow . . .

It was a December night, the kind that hunters know better than those who pass the winter inside a house, when the cold plucks and probes at every seam in a man's clothing. Overhead, Orion blazed icily against a luminous, spark-shot cloud that was the Milky Way. Low on the western horizon, the new moon watched over the black landscape like a slitted cat's eye. One last coyote rendered one last offering to the moon, as clear and pure and lonely as a clarinet note in the night.

The five of us around the dying fire sat hushed, listening, wrapped in the splendor of the night sky. All our minds ran to the same theme: somewhere out there in the dark thickets there moved a great whitetail buck with Orion's light on his antler tips and the breath frosting in his nostrils. Each of us could see him, and felt the ancient link between the hunter and his prey. At our feet, the mesquite embers whispered softly as they drew a blanket of ash over themselves against the deepening chill.

At last, one man rose and nudged the stub of a smoking stick back into the coals, stirring a final flicker of flame. "Five a.m. comes early," he murmured. "I'm for the blankets. Tomorrow's going to be a good day to kill a deer."

"Cold, for sure," put in another figure, "and no moon and no wind. Maybe it'll be the day."

Nobody had to ask *what* day. "The day" means the day a deer hunter catches up with a good buck. Any day may be the day; that's what keeps deer hunters getting up at five a.m. on freezing mornings. We never know which day will be the day.

Another man stood up. "Maybe tomorrow's when I get my big

one. Lord knows, I'm overdue. Twenty years and I've never gotten lucky on a really good one. Maybe tomorrow . . ."

I tossed the coffee dregs from my mug into the coals and watched them sizzle away, wondering how many times I'd heard that lament around a campfire. *I hunt hard*, goes the refrain, *and I'm a good hunter. I see plenty of deer. I get my share. But somehow I never find a really big one. Just one real trophy is all I ask; we like the venison, but how I'd love to hang just one honest-to-gosh monster on the wall! But I just can't seem to get lucky.*

Have you heard it? Have you *said* it? So did I, for about the first twenty-five years I hunted whitetails. In the breast of almost every meat hunter there beats the heart of a secret, frustrated trophy hunter. Few men, however addicted to venison, will pass up an antlered buck for the better-eating doe standing beside him. And fewer still, having shot an exceptional buck, will leave the great rack in the woods and pack out only the meat.

No, almost every one of America's millions of deer hunters is at least conscious of the possibility of encountering that buck of a lifetime on any given day in the woods. They may not be holding out for him, but they'd love to find him just once—yet, somehow, they never do. They have no luck with big bucks.

The truth is that there is—almost—no such thing!

Oh, now and then a hunter, even a beginner, may stumble across a real trophy whitetail or muley and get his picture in the paper, perhaps even his name in the record book. It happens, but it's a one-in-a-million happening. Not many of us live long enough to kill a giant buck by accident. For practical purposes, I can give you an ironclad guarantee that you can hunt the rest of your life in the same places, at the same times, and by the same methods which have kept your freezer filled with the meat of ordinary bucks and *you will never take a genuine wallhanger.* In fact, those very techniques which have made you a successful hunter of run-of-the-mill deer constitute the best possible insurance against your shooting a trophy animal.

Trophy-grade bucks are different. They usually do not exist in the areas where you'd look first for deer. They live according to completely different rhythms, and they require special knowledge and skills of the hunter. There is, in short, very little luck in taking big bucks.

The dream of every deer hunter, a buck like this one, comes hard and demands the best of a hunter's woodmanship and knowledge. Luck almost never plays a part in the taking of such whitetails. *(Photo by Jerry Smith)*

Think back on the hunters you've known who have taken the biggest racks. Not many of them, I'll bet, have knocked over only *one* big one; these are the same men who show up year after year with exceptional heads, the fellows who *usually* (not occasionally) produce the biggest buck in the camp every season, or the best one killed in that particular area. They're consistent, and nobody can be that consistently lucky.

The reason is simply that these men know things most hunters haven't bothered to figure out, and they do things most hunters don't do. They know that a man can deliberately hunt a trophy deer as distinguished from ordinary bucks, that such bucks can be successfully planned for and taken. They don't go out and walk around in the woods, *hoping* for a better-than-average buck; they work at finding him, and they never rely on mere "luck."

The truth is that most hunters reading this book already have most of the know-how and hunting skills needed to nail a big buck on purpose, not by chance. They simply haven't put it all together, and they haven't adopted the attitudes of the trophy hunter. For, in fact, the difference between a trophy hunter and a meat hunter is mostly a matter of *attitude*. The latter hopes for a big set of antlers but doesn't really expect one, and settles for whatever comes along. The dedicated big-buck hunter *expects* to get a trophy, knows how to do it, and refuses to shoot until he sees what he wants.

I remember the precise moment in which I became a trophy hunter. I'd just shot a fine, fat little six-point whitetail, probably about the ninetieth buck of my hunting career. I walked up to him and stood there, looking down at my prize . . . and found myself wishing that he were still alive! It suddenly occurred to me that this wasn't the way a triumphant hunter was supposed to feel, and I promised myself that I would never again knowingly shoot a small buck.

That was about thirty years ago, and I've kept my vow as best I could. The very next buck I killed was a heavy-horned eleven-pointer with a 20-inch spread, which outweighed my little six-pointer by more than 100 percent. Since then, my kills have averaged better than ten points (eastern count, as all references to whitetails in this book will be) and about half again as heavy as the average Texas whitetail buck. Among them have been several which are, if not record-*book* trophies, at least record-*class* heads, some of which would have made the Boone and Crockett Club listings if they'd been killed a few years earlier.

In short, I already had all the basic skills to be a trophy hunter after a quarter of a century of whitetail hunting; I had only to shift my mental gears and apply what I knew to getting a really big buck, and to make up my mind that a big one was what I wanted. But when I did that, I found myself in a whole new world of whitetail hunting.

During the last few years before I popped that little six-pointer, I'd begun to grow bored with deer hunting, and had occasionally found myself considering the real possibility of giving up the sport. I'd shot so many deer since my first one, at age twelve, that I had nothing left to prove to myself or others. I knew I could kill a buck almost at will. The challenge and the throat-squeezing excitement of the hunt were gone. It's different now. Now I look forward to deer season with the same anticipation I felt as a boy, and I get the same thrill out of every buck that I got from that first one in 1941.

I've been fortunate enough to hunt most of the world's most glamorous big game, from mountain sheep in the Cassiars of British Columbia and jaguar in Central America to Cape buffalo, lion, leopard, kudu, and elephant in Africa. And I still think that a trophy whitetail is the single most exciting and most demanding animal on the face of the earth. You can't buy one, and when you hang one on the wall you can be justly proud because he's the best proof in the world that you're a *hunter.*

And that's who this book is for—hunters. Not necessarily *trophy* hunters, but all deer hunters. Because most of what is said in the following pages will give as many insights into the ways of whitetails and muleys in general as into the special ways of the big males. It goes without saying that a successful hunter must understand his game, and that means he must understand the species first. What follows will, I hope, add to the knowledge of any hunter, even those who disdainfully say, "You can't eat the horns!"

No one begins as a hunter of trophy bucks. I suppose I've shot thirty or forty whitetails which would qualify as piss-ants, little three-, five-, and six-pointers, even spikes and forkhorns, and small eight-point heads, deer not more than two and a half years old, and I'm certainly not ashamed of a one of them. That was my apprenticeship. It was on such tasty youngsters that I began to absorb the know-how and hone the hunting skills I would need to tackle the trophy bucks later on. For the taking of a big buck—which means one that has survived at least five hunting seasons—is the postgraduate course in deer hunting. Make no mistake about it; the man who has a row of giant antlers nailed up in his garage is a master hunter. He may very well knock over a forkhorn, or even a doe, now and then for the larder, but he knows something most hunters don't know about whitetails and he knows how to put that knowledge to the best use.

And he is also a conservationist in the best sense. We hear quite a lot of plain and simple baloney about hunting in general these days, and about trophy hunting in particular. People—even some hunters, to my constant amazement—condemn trophy hunting as some sort of weird exercise in *machismo.* They may say that trophy hunting strips out the finest breeding stock and impoverishes the herd's gene pool, but such critics merely reveal their own ignorance

In a herd managed for trophies, bucks like this are reasonably plentiful and perform their natural role in reproduction of the species. No such animals can ever exist in deer herds managed for *quantity* hunting.

of whitetail and mule deer reproductive mechanisms. They may suggest that it's all right to kill a deer for venison, but somehow sinful to kill him because you want his antlers, as though big antlers and good meat are mutually exclusive in the same animal.

To begin with, a real trophy hunter shoots fewer animals than the meat hunter, which, in itself, means he affects the population less. Then, his highly selective hunting is focused on very old animals, since no buck can be considered a real trophy until he is in his sixth year, at least. This means that he has already made whatever contribution to the herd that he is likely to make, and may be well past his breeding prime. My own finest whitetail trophy was more than eight and a half years old, and his molar teeth were worn down to the gums. Although he was in breeding condition when I got him, it's doubtful that this buck could have made it through the long, cold, dry winter which followed, and absolutely certain that he was within a year of his end when my bullet struck him. Which was the better fate for this animal—to die instantly and be immortalized on my den wall, or to be pulled down by the coyotes when he was sufficiently weakened by malnutrition, perhaps only a couple of months later? There is no third alternative.

And how would it have been better for the herd if I had rejected this record-class head and taken, instead, a fat young fellow with his whole breeding career before him?

The real truth is that trophy hunting and all that goes with it is biologically sound deer management. As we shall clearly see in later chapters, the incidence of trophy-class (i.e., fully mature) males in a deer population is a very good index to the health, vigor, and balance of that herd. In herds managed merely to produce some kind of a buck for as many hunters as possible, there can be few or no trophies, even though hunters may see plenty of deer in the woods. A herd which has a reasonably normal age-class distribution among the bucks, however, can be shown to be a biologically normal unit, functioning reproductively as nature intended.

This fifteen-pointer remains my finest trophy whitetail buck after fifty-five years of hunting.

A sight to warm a trophy hunter's—or a whitetail lover's—heart: three fine bucks ranging together before the rut. The presence of such animals is a sure sign of a natural, healthy, well-balanced herd. *(Photo by Mike Biggs)*

It turns out, then, that the average size of the bucks' antlers in a deer population is a pretty good index to the overall health and quality of that herd, and that any herd with animals which interest a true trophy hunter is a well-managed herd. It is also a herd, for the information of the few anti-hunting preservationists who may read this book, which most closely resembles a "natural" unhunted herd in its age and sex composition.

Deer and deer hunting have changed. They are not the same today as when I began my lifelong pursuit of whitetails, and they will not be the same in a few years as they are now. The old rules and standards don't work any more. Man's relentless alterations of the ecology have outdated them, and forced him to *manage* the deer whether he wants to do so or not.

Deer herds have to be managed within a limited and shrinking habitat, with overpopulation the ever-present specter looking over the managers' shoulders. Antlerless deer must be removed from the ranges, and this happens to be exactly in phase with the trophy hunter's management concepts. What he wishes to harvest are the geriatric cases in the herd, the tiny pinnacle of the iceberg that is a deer-herd unit, the fully mature and overmature males whose loss has no effect on the population dynamics of that herd.

As an old hunting friend of mine once said, "Even where there's *lots* of big, old bucks, there ain't very many of 'em!" It's true. Even in the finest trophy-hunting areas, a good hunter can hunt a long time without seeing a record-class buck, and, since he *is* a trophy hunter, he refuses to shoot the lesser bucks. By definition, hunting trophies is selective, restrained, discriminating hunting. So our trophy hunter cheerfully contents himself with a surplus doe or spike buck for the freezer and permits the younger bucks to live another year. He is a minority today, but he is the cutting edge of tomorrow's deer-management programs. He is ahead of his times!

That's why I say it's time to quit cowering on the defensive from the assaults of the anti-hunters and hiding behind the "I eat everything I kill" argument. I, personally, do eat most of what I kill, but I eat it because I *like* it. I hunt, however, for sport, and trophy bucks provide the grandest sport the outdoors has to offer. No ethical hunter has anything to apologize for to the anti-hunting faddists and freaks, knowing that he and his kind have been the only salvation for American wildlife to date. And we will probably continue to be the game's only friends, at least of those offering more than lip service, emotionalism, and profitable propaganda. The same men who launched the American conservation movement also founded the Boone and Crockett Club, the very mecca of trophy hunters. I regard it an honor to be called a "trophy hunter." I hope they carve it on my gravestone!

In the meantime, may there be many more starry nights around a murmuring, flickering campfire, with good companions saying, "Maybe tomorrow . . ."

2 What Is a "Trophy" Buck?

I've used the terms "trophy buck" or "trophy deer" several times, without a definition of the word "trophy." The reader may be surprised to find that I'm perfectly satisfied with the dictionary definition: a memento of a personal achievement. That dictionary says nothing about number of points, inside spread, or dressed weight, and I say that there is no single set of such specifications which can cover all regions, all hunters, and all situations. Under some circumstances, even a spike buck might qualify as a legitimate trophy, as in the case of a youngster's first kill.

Many regions simply haven't the genetic potential to produce outsized antlers, and the hunter who sets his heart on a Boone and Crockett Club record in such areas is beaten before he sets foot in the woods. Yet he still may be able to collect a trophy head there, under my dictionary definition of the word. Personal tastes and standards vary between individuals: a buck you might disdain could be the once-in-a-lifetime trophy for me . . . or vice versa. One hunter may regard great antler spread as the principal ingredient of "trophy," while another is turned on by massive beams or lots of points, and couldn't care less about the spread of a rack.

Even so, a man can be a trophy hunter anywhere, at any stage of his career. It's only a matter of deciding what constitutes a trophy in his neck of the woods, and of establishing personal standards. The one consistent factor is difficulty; a trophy is, *per se*, hard to come by, demanding patience, knowledge, and skills of a superior order. The more of each required to take a trophy buck, the greater the personal achievement.

In the eyes of many, of course, the ultimate achievement in deer hunting is to place a head in the Boone and Crockett Club Records of North American Big Game, but it must be understood that is not the definition of *trophy* that shall apply throughout this book. In the first edition, published twenty years ago, I wrote that I considered the Boone and Crockett minimum-entry scores unrealistically high. Those twenty years have thoroughly proved me wrong, however, because a veritable avalanche of record-book racks, from every corner of the whitetail range, has occurred. The minimums, in fact, may turn out to be too low. States where hunters had never dreamed of a "book" deer have produced one, or several. The old nontypical world record—which had stood since the beginning of records keeping—has been unceremoniously shoved back into third place, and the number-one typical has also been dethroned. The number of listed typical heads alone has quadrupled. Well over half the records have been collected since I first wrote this book, and it has become evident that, in trophy whitetail hunting, the "good old days" are now.

The reasons for this remarkable proliferation of trophy bucks are many. One is simply that more hunters have heard of the record book and have come to regard it as a prestigious place to be, so that big heads now come to the attention of official measurers that once would have been nailed up in a garage, perhaps, and forgotten. Another is that hunters today can and will travel across the continent and pay large sums to hunt where a record-class buck might be found. A third—and perhaps most important—reason is that the interest of landowners in big bucks has expanded, along with access to information on how to manage aggressively for such animals.

Some reviewers have been kind enough to credit the first edition of this book with sparking some interest in trophy whitetails that has brought these things to pass. I make no such claim, but agree that the trophy-buck groundswell became noticeable shortly after its original publication.

For purposes of clarity, throughout this book, I shall use the terms "record" or "record-book" buck to mean a head scoring at least 170 points under the Boone and Crockett system of measurement, and the term "record-*class*" buck to indicate one scoring between 150 and 170 points according to that system. My rationale

for this distinction is that a whitetail scoring 150 B&C points was
admitted to the record lists as recently as 1962, and there are many
heads around which appeared in fairly recent editions of the official
record book but have been dropped from the current edition.

Charlie Albertson's huge East Texas buck's teeth are inspected to determine his age: six
and a half years. The rack scored 174⅞ Boone and Crockett points after the required
sixty-day drying period, easily making the "book."

These numbers apply, of course, to whitetails in the *typical*
category; the same rationale will be used with reference to nontypical whitetails and both typical and nontypical mule deer and
subspecies of both. If a head would have qualified as a record under
the 1962 rules, I'll call it a "record-class" trophy here.

The Boone and Crockett scoring system (see Appendix) is a reasonably good one, giving credit for beam length, tine length, massiveness, inside spread, and symmetry for all deer species. If it has a
fault, it is that it penalizes lack of symmetry too severely, so that
many magnificent heads exist which cannot "make the book" but
which almost any hunter alive would instantly concede to be superior to many trophies which were accepted. Many of these unlisted
heads cannot quite make the minimum scores either way—as typical

or nontypicals—but are in no way deformed or freakish racks. It was probably inevitable that more and more hunters have come to think, and to describe heads, in terms of gross score, which is essentially the Boone and Crockett score before subtracting the so-called "deducts"—the penalties for asymmetry. It's much easier to estimate the gross score of a live buck in the field than his net, and it credits the animal with 100 percent of the antler material he grew.

Interestingly, the State of Virginia keeps whitetail records under a system which doesn't penalize abnormal points or unmatched measurements quite so harshly, but which is otherwise similar to the Boone and Crockett method, and my purely subjective evaluation of the heads which rank under Virginia's system is that they more accurately fulfill the experienced trophy hunter's concept of what makes a desirable and sought-after trophy.

The record book, whoever keeps it, will always be controversial, and so will the idea of hunting expressly "for the book." Obviously, I heartily approve of trophy hunting, or I would not be writing this volume, but there's a distinct difference between trophy hunting and record-book hunting. The latter can—often does—result in certain abuses, both legal and otherwise, of superb game animals. I personally know of trophies poached or shot illegally (at night for example), purchased, and even faked by taxidermists which today rank high in the august listings of North American big-game records.

To me, there is a subtle but essential difference between pursuing a great buck for the joy of matching one's wits and woodsmanship against his and for the deep satisfaction of winning the match and possessing him, and doing it solely for public acclaim among hunters. The former is trophy hunting, while the latter is record-book hunting.

Enough, for the moment, of records.

I've heard another theory advanced to answer the question of what a trophy buck is. It is simply that any whitetail five and a half years old or older is a trophy, regardless of the size of his antlers, based simply on the scarcity of animals in this age class. In hunted herds, not more than 2 percent of the antlered bucks will attain this age, on the average, and by the time they have survived this long they are super-wise and super-wary, so difficult to collect that harvesting one should be a high personal accomplishment for any

Although a buck's age cannot be told exactly from antler formation at any age, certain indications are reliable. The gnarled, angular, irregular appearance of this head is a good sign that the deer was extremely old and that he probably had better antlers in the previous seasons. *(Photo courtesy of Robert Rogers)*

Different types of antlers excite different trophy hunters. This is a striking example of an exceptionally widespread rack, approaching 30 inches on the insides of the beams, but it is otherwise rather undistinguished. *(Photo courtesy of Robert Rogers)*

The opposite of the wide-flaring rack is this compact whitetail head. It's still a fine trophy because of the exceptional weight, odd points, and general character. *(Photo courtesy of Robert Rogers)*

This great head, shot by Basil Dailey in Texas in 1903, ranks No. 27 in the 1991 record book. It has everything—beam length, fifteen long points, spread, and massiveness. *(Photo courtesy of Robert Rogers)*

Oddities are always fascinating, especially when they're as big as this one. Observe the double beam on the buck's right side, an extreme rarity among whitetails. *(Photo courtesy of Robert Rogers)*

For many hunters, nontypical whitetails are more interesting than typicals. Note the "drop point" on this great buck's right antler. *(Photo courtesy of Robert Rogers)*

In the first edition, I called this Texas head shot by Jeff Benson in 1892 "the unbreakable record" . . . which shows what I know! Not one but two other bucks have turned up to demote Benson's trophy ranking to No. 3. But it still remains the highest-scoring nontypical buck ever known to have been shot by a hunter; origins of the two bigger ones are unclear. *(Photo courtesy of Robert Rogers)*

Incredible massiveness in whitetail antlers! These beams would do justice to an elk, but the head also has spread and ten long points. *(Photo courtesy of Robert Rogers)*

hunter. There is merit in this argument, especially since we know that relatively few bucks have the genetic potential for exceptional racks regardless of age. Speaking for myself only, I've come to regard age as the most important criterion for trophy status. An old buck is a trophy buck in my eyes, regardless of his headgear, and I have long since abandoned the tape measure as an indicator of trophy quality. This is not to say, of course, that I don't prefer big heads to little ones, but only that I now recognize that there are lots of veteran bucks out there without the genetic programming ever to grow antlers that will make an official scorer whistle, but that are worthy adversaries for the most skilled hunter. That they are old proves their mettle, and to take one of these in fair chase is every bit as difficult as shooting any "book" deer that ever walked. Consequently, I can shoot a buck that excites me without worrying that he may not "score." If some third party decides that, by some arbitrary scoring system, the deer wasn't "shootable," that's his problem, not mine. I cannot recite the exact score of any of the hundreds of bucks I've taken. Scores simply don't enter into my shoot-don't-shoot calculations in the field. None of this, however, is meant to reflect upon any hunter who sees things differently. Nor does the fact that I will occasionally classify bucks by their B and C "point" scores in this book undermine the posture outlined above; this is simply the language we deer hunters speak, and I speak it as fluently as anyone.

As a sidelight, *age* is one of the crucial elements in the making of a trophy buck. During the first four years of a whitetail's or muley's life, he is channeling his nutritional intake in excess of his metabolic needs into adding to his skeletal and muscular development. Although he is sexually mature at eighteen months or less, he is not really grown-up until he approaches five years of age. In his fifth year, his body is as big as it will ever be and suddenly the nutritional elements which were used for skeletal development before are available for antler growth. Between a buck's fourth and fifth seasons, his antler development accelerates markedly. He may continue to grow increasingly more impressive headgear for the next three years, but if he will ever be a genuine wallhanger, it will show clearly in his fifth set of antlers.

As mentioned, he may never be such a trophy, however, because of his genetic programming, just as very few American male humans have the genetic tendency to achieve the physique necessary to play guard for a professional football team. And this is the chief grounds for the contention that *any* mature whitetail (five and a half years old or older) should be counted as a trophy for the hunter who kills him. The weakness of the argument is that a few bucks achieve relatively ancient age, nine and a half years or older, and these deer normally have very poor antlers. Most commonly, the senile bucks' racks become distorted, brittle, and frail, and may degenerate into long, thick, twisted, goatlike spikes. It would be difficult to class such heads as trophies under almost any definition.

A characteristic of very old bucks' antlers, even when they retain fairly normal configuration and size, is that they tend to appear bleached and are often badly broken, apparently from their loss of ability to assimilate the minerals necessary to grow sound antlers.

I have the antlers of one such buck, the heaviest ever shot on my small ranch in east Texas. The deer outweighed the next biggest killed there by more than 25 percent, but carried a very ordinary eight-point rack (eastern count), spindly, chalky white, and with

Big whitetails are where you find 'em. Gary Rogers killed this monstrous whitetail—No. 118 in the nontypical record book—on a small farm in east Texas, an area noted for its small deer and puny antlers. *(Photo courtesy of Robert Rogers)*

every tine broken. His teeth showed him to be more than eight and a half years old, the greatest age which can be reliably determined by tooth wear, but how much older than that is anybody's guess. He was fat, tender, and in good condition and showed no signs of rutting, even though taken at the height of the local breeding season. He was, in short, a senile old gentleman whose immediate fate was starvation if the coyotes didn't pull him down first.

Perhaps the best all-around definition of a trophy buck, and the one which will be operative throughout the rest of this book, is a five and a half year old or older buck which represents about the best antler development possible within his specific habitat and gene pool.

Biologists disagree on just how many different subspecies of the Virginia whitetail deer exist in the United States, Canada, and Mexico, the claims ranging up to about thirty or forty, with a great deal of intergradation between subspecies. For hunters, the argument is academic, of course, but there is no doubt that some of these variations on the theme do tend to much larger antlers than others, and the same is true of the various subspecies of the mule deer. The northern whitetails may be veritable giants in body size (I've seen one New Hampshire buck weighed at slightly more than 300 pounds, hog-dressed) but rarely carry racks which would qualify as trophies in other regions. By contrast, in my home state of Texas, it takes a huge buck to dress 150 pounds, and the statewide average is closer to 100 pounds, but big antlers are not uncommon, as the illustrations in this volume may readily verify.

A Texas hunter may arbitrarily define a trophy as a ten-point buck with 20-inch inside spread and a balanced rack, whereas a Maine hunter could not realistically hope for such a head. The Maine man, however, has accomplished just as great a feat by taking the biggest head his own woods are capable of producing, and cross-regional comparisons are futile. This is why I will not attempt to define a "trophy" in terms of specific antler measurements or characteristics.

The hunter who would call himself a serious trophy hunter must do so, however. This is, in fact, the essential first step in achieving that status. Years ago, an old and enviably successful hunter of big heads told me that I'd never kill a big deer "until you quit shootin' them *little* deer!" At the time, I thought he was joking, but now I know that he was imparting the most profound secret of trophy hunting. It is that if one's buck tags are filled with mediocre, underaged specimens, there is no hope of adding a monster. Since the younger deer are far easier to collect, the hunter who is willing to settle for such is almost excluding any chance he might ever have for a real trophy buck.

The way to avoid this subtle trap is to establish a set of personal minimum standards, consistent with the possibilities in your own hunting areas, and *stick to them.* If you say, "I'm not going to shoot unless its a real good head," you're defeated before you start, because under the stress of a hunting situation you have no hard guideline to go by. You'll find yourself looking at a very average rack, with only seconds to decide whether or not to shoot, and you'll crack down on him, hoping he's a good one, or talk yourself into believing it.

On the other hand, if you set your sights too high—say, a record-book head or nothing—you may spend the rest of your life without pulling the trigger. It's true that a trophy hunter must put taking a *good* head ahead of just filling the tag, and must be willing to finish the season without a deer if that's the way it turns out, but to hunt for years without taking a shot is a bit extreme. I hunt in some of the finest deer country—and big-buck country, too—in the United States, and usually pass up at least twenty to thirty legal, antlered bucks each season because they don't meet my personal standards. In recent years, I seem to be averaging a buck every two or three seasons, which is plenty for me. In fact, if a hunter can catch up with the kind of deer I like to shoot just once every other year, in even the best terrain, I'd say he was doing extraordinarily well.

Once your personal minimums for a trophy have been thoughtfully and realistically established, the next item on the agenda is to learn to judge antlers on live, wild bucks under hunting conditions— and that ain't easy! First, it takes a few extra seconds, seconds which you quite often do not have to spare, and thus it will cost you some shots at what might have been very good bucks. That's part of the trophy-hunting game. There will be more in a subsequent chapter on the niceties of judging trophies on the hoof, but for now, consider this example. You decide, as I have, that you will not shoot a buck carrying fewer than ten points, but you place no additional standards upon yourself. Even this very simple qualification will force you to learn to take that second look, to really *examine* the antlers instead of merely seeing that they're there. Sometimes that tenth point is difficult to see, especially from certain angles, and you'll discipline yourself to wait until the buck turns his head, and that's progress even if you lose the chance. If the tenth point wasn't there, you've saved yourself a disappointment; if it was, you've learned a lesson in coolness and restraint, and you know the buck is still alive and available for another engagement, perhaps.

Incidentally, there is a profound and surprising sense of satisfaction to be discovered the first time you let a buck go which you know you could have killed. One close hunting friend of mine occasionally becomes so intoxicated with this sensation that sometimes we wonder if he'll *ever* pull another trigger!

Two things are for sure: as my friend and mentor Jack O'Connor says, the *big* ones always *look* big (at first glance), and if you find yourself wondering if a buck is big enough, he isn't!

In the meantime, the establishment of personal goals in terms of antler size and the discipline to make certain they're met *before* you shoot, however great the pressure, are the two steps to insure against disappointment as a hunter accepts the challenge of the great trophy bucks.

3 Antlers—What They Are and Why They Are

Although hunters are always interested in the body size of deer and often brag about taking an exceptionally heavy buck, the *trophy* part of a deer is what grows upon his brow—his antlers.

Antlers are not only almost unique physiological appurtenances, but they have exceptional significance, to deer as well as to people. Antlers differ from horns (which are carried by cattle, sheep, goats, and the Old World antelopes, for example) in that they are made of solid bone. Horns have a bony core covered by a sheath composed of a substance called keratin, the same substance of which your fingernails are made. Horns are never shed (with the exception of the American pronghorn), and grow throughout the bearer's life. If a horn is broken (that is, if the bony core breaks), it is a permanent loss, never to be replaced, and may place the owner at a severe and probably fatal disadvantage in coping with his environment. Horns (again, the pronghorn is the exception) are never branched.

Antlers, on the other hand, are shed annually and regrown within a few months. If one is broken, the loss is temporary and of little consequence to the owner. Most antlers are branched in mature specimens of the species. With the exception of the caribou, no American deer exhibit antlers on the females, and the antlers of cow caribou are very small and insignificant.

Many species of horned game have horned females, and in some species (the African oryxes, for example) the cow's horns are longer and more impressive than the bull's. In these species, horns are a distinctly useful defensive weapon; there are records of female Cape buffalo, oryx, and sable antelope, for example, having actually killed lions.

A buck's antlers are not primarily defensive weapons; otherwise, he'd have them the year round. They're secondary sexual adornments, erotic stimulants to does, and the symbol of his dominance status during the rut.

Antlers are not primarily defensive weapons; if they were, the logic of biology would furnish the animals with their weapons the year round, instead of just during the mating season, and the does would probably have developed them as well as the bucks. A buck will occasionally use his antlers to defend himself against dogs, coyotes, or men, however. I've seen it happen, and I know at least one hunter who carried the scars of a whitetail's antler tines on his midriff for half his lifetime. However, antlers are predominantly an expression of sexual dimorphism, a visible distinction between the sexes which is useful to the animals themselves (as well as to hunters). The size and development of the antlers also serve to rank the buck on the dominance scale—the "pecking order"—of males in his locality. Finally, the antlers are used as weapons against other bucks in fights of greater or lesser seriousness during the reproductive rituals of the species.

Antlers are status symbols, helping locate a buck within the dominance hierarchy. The buck at left has a pretty good head, but he readily yields to the much bigger fellow at right. Note the laid-back ears and erected hair on the right-hand buck, clear-cut threat displays. *(Photo by W. A. Maltsberger)*

The annual cycle of antler growth, maturation, and shedding is controlled by the level of the male sex hormone, testosterone, secreted by the testes. These levels are controlled by the activity of the pituitary gland located at the base of the brain, and the pituitary, in turn, is at least partially stimulated by changes in the length of daylight periods as the seasons change, although other factors are known to exist. In about mid-April, in most of the range, the new set of antlers begins to grow from pedicels on the buck's

Antlers have always seemed to fascinate mankind, from prehistoric times until today. Cast antlers can give useful hints on the size, survival, and home range of trophy bucks, and today there's even a "shed" record book!

Hunters call extra tines like those on this fourteen-pointer, bagged by the author's wife, "kickers," "cheaters," or just "trash," and they tend to appear with advancing age. One year earlier, although almost as big, this buck carried only ten points.

brow. The antlers are an outgrowth of the skeleton, composed mostly of such minerals as calcium and phosphorus, and are nourished by a covering of skin which hunters call velvet, containing a rich supply of blood vessels. Antlers are said to be the fastest-growing bony tissues known in the entire animal world, and make tremendous demands upon the buck's metabolism during their period of growth. Some estimates are that as much as 50 percent of a mature buck's nutritional intake goes into antler development during the four months or so of growth, and it has been said that these demands on a buck's body fully equal the demands producing young make on the body of a doe.

During this period, a big buck's principal business seems to be growing his crown, and he is extremely retiring, moving about no more than necessary to satisfy his hunger and thirst, and taking great care of his expanding antlers. They are relatively soft and the velvet is easily damaged during this period, and the owner seems to

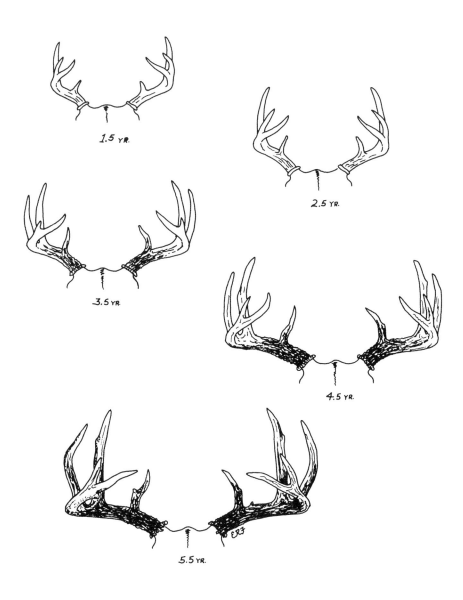

1.5 YR.

2.5 YR.

3.5 YR.

4.5 YR.

5.5 YR.

The progression in antler development through the years is evident in these drawings of the same buck's racks throughout his life span. He was a very promising yearling, with a tiny eight-point rack at age one and a half. By age three and a half it was apparent that he would forever be a ten-pointer (at least as far as *normal* tines are counted). A good head at four and a half, this buck came into his own during the hunting season of his fifth year. At this age he was physically mature, and his system could concentrate nutritional intake on antler growth.

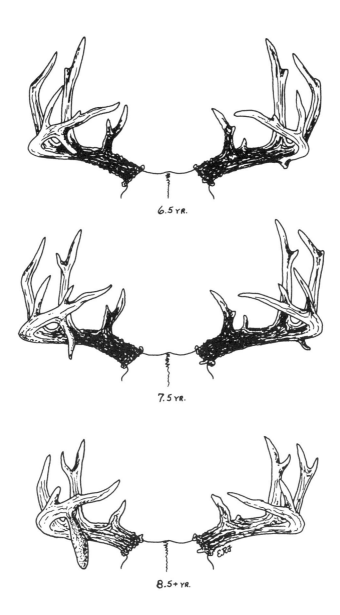

6.5 YR.

7.5 YR.

8.5+ YR.

The buck had his finest antlers at six and a half and seven and a half years. By now a marked tendency to nontypical formations has appeared, each rack accurately predicting the development of the next year's set. At age eight and a half plus, the buck obviously began to descend into senility, with a smaller rack than he had four years earlier. If he survived another year or two, he might have only grotesquely heavy, deformed spikes. *(Reprinted from* Producing Quality Whitetails *by Brothers and Ray)* know it. Occasionally, in spite of his best efforts, some injury will occur to a buck's new antlers, and the result is usually what hunters call "acorn horns," tines which remind one of minaret spires.

The antlers are fully developed by late August or early September, depending on the latitude. Note that the growing season coincides with the lushest period of the year, spring and summer, when forage is not only most plentiful but also has the highest protein content. This is a point of some importance to the trophy hunter, as we shall see further on.

When development is complete, still controlled by the pituitary clock, the velvet's blood circulation becomes restricted, and something causes the buck to rid himself of it. He rubs the velvet away against shrubs and small trees, and it's a fascinating process to watch. A buck seems to know by intuition exactly where each part of his antlers is, even though that part may be outside the range of

Look carefully just above where this buck's right ear joins his head, and you'll see the stub of a deformed antler, contrasting with the normal one on the other side. This type of deformity usually results from an injury to the animal's body on the opposite side from the malformation, commonly to a foot or leg. *(Photo by Walter Elling)*

his vision. I once watched a mature captive buck cleaning up his new antlers against a woven wire fence, and was astonished at the deftness with which he could flick away a clinging tatter of velvet. There seemed to be nothing random about it; his total control of his antlers in space was so obvious that I could believe that he could have picked up a given leaf on the tip of any particular tine, if he had chosen to.

In the process of cleaning the velvet away, the animal damages the bushes, creating what hunters call "rubs," but this antler cleaning is a very unemotional, businesslike process, and the rubs so made are quite different in appearance from those the same buck makes later on during the peak of the rut. Not only are the antler-cleaning rubs obviously old and dried out by the time hunting season rolls around, they are not nearly as explosive.

Contrary to common hunters' beliefs, the dark, walnut-colored stain which the antlers of major bucks exhibit during hunting season is a product of the hemoglobin in the blood supply of the velvet. The bigger the antlers, the more velvet and the more blood, and thus the darker the apparent color of the by-now-dead bone which composes the antlers. Some staining occurs during rubbing, from sap from the saplings and bushes rubbed, but, in vigorous bucks, this is not the chief source. As the season wears on, the blood stain may bleach out from exposure to the sun, and by the time the antlers are shed, they may be distinctly whitish.

At about the same time that the buck feels the urge to strip the velvet, certain other physiological changes occur in his body. His testicles enlarge, descend, and begin to produce mature sperm, and his neck swells visibly. Also, the tarsal glands, on the insides of his hocks, begin to secrete a rank, musky-smelling fluid which seems to function as an erotic attractant and stimulant for does. This secretion increases greatly as the herd gets into the rut, eventually turning the tufts of hairs of the glands tarry-black and running down the buck's legs.

The antlers not only function as a badge of the bearer's masculinity and breeding condition, but they also serve to give him what humans would call "status" within the herd. Deer are obviously aware of antlers and antler size, just as hunters are. In a gathering of whitetails of both sexes, before the rut proper, the buck with the biggest antlers is the unquestioned boss, and all the lesser bucks and does give way to him. He can go where he pleases, eat the choicest forage, and lie down wherever he chooses. There is even a gesture of submission, seldom photographed, in which a lesser buck or doe will approach the dominant male in a cowering crouch, neck extended, and very respectfully touch noses for an instant. The action is uncannily reminiscent of a human subject bowing deeply before his king.

In most cases, the mere presence of a big-antlered buck is sufficient to gain him this deference. However, when two bucks of nearly equal antler size happen to inhabit the same area, they may disagree as to which is dominant. The disagreement is settled by a passage at arms with locked antlers, pushing and straining, until the stronger buck wins. These fights are unlike those later in the mating season, being entirely shoving matches, without the real savagery the same two bucks might reveal later on. They are meaningful to the deer, however, serving to establish the local pecking order to the satisfaction of all.

The serious battles which take place during the rut will be discussed in another chapter, but they, too, are a part of the reason nature has endowed the male deer with antlers.

The rut will be finished, and the biological need for antlers ended for the year, by December or January in more northern climates, January or February in the south and southwest, and even later in tropical Mexico, where I've seen antlered bucks in May. Testosterone levels ebb, the testicles contract and cease to produce mature sperm, and the antlers are sloughed away, leaving only the pedicels to form the bases for the next season's set.

An odd sidelight on deer antlers—all species of deer, both Old and New World—is that they are the only known example in nature of dead bone normally and firmly retained adjacent to living bone tissue. Almost universally, the body sequesters and sloughs away dead tissue of any kind as rapidly as possible. The connection between the dead bone of antlers and the living bone of the buck's pedicels, however, is solid and lasts as long as the antlers are biologically useful. Then a layer of special cells in the pedicel forms to create a clean fracture plane along which the antler separates, after which another kind of special bone cell quickly grows over the raw

Whitetail antlers are sometimes shed close enough together so that both sides can be found with a bit of searching. Those at left are one year old, those at right, two seasons.

pedicel to seal it against invasion by bacteria or parasites. Shedding the antlers is timed by changes in the buck's blood testosterone level, activated in turn by the changing photoperiod, but we do not understand how his body "knows" it's time to slough off the now-useless antlers.

Both antlers usually drop at about the same time, and sometimes can be found quite close to each other with a little searching. I've seen both shed antlers lying close to a fence often enough to believe that they may have been jarred loose when the buck jumped the fence. Once, I watched a small buck who was still wearing only one side of his rack casually reach up with a hind foot and kick the antler off just as he might have scratched his ear with a rear hoof!

Under some circumstances, antlers are never shed. Damage to the buck's testicles while the antlers are in velvet stops any further development and he will carry the velvet-clad antlers for the rest of his life. If castration occurs after his antlers are stripped, he will shed them immediately, and never grow another set.

Certain fairly well-defined regions exhibit an unusually high percentage of so-called "stag bucks," bucks with permanent, velvet-covered antlers. The gonads of these animals will be nonfunctional, but with no sign of physical injury. Such an area, for mule deer, is in the northeastern portion of New Mexico, along the Colorado

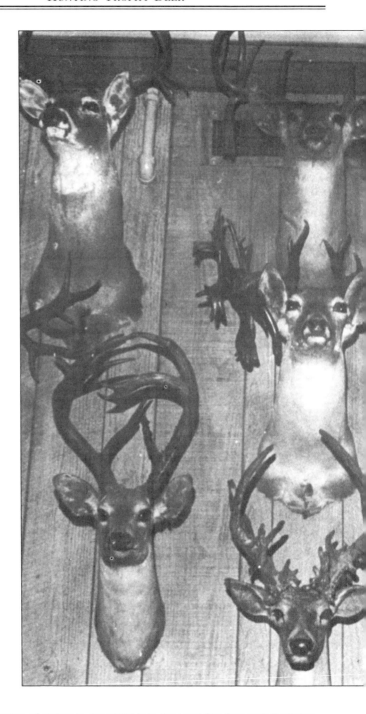

The greatest collection of antlers in the world is in the Lone Star Brewery's Buckhorn Saloon Hall of Horns in San Antonio, Texas. A very few of the hundreds of freak heads

displayed are shown here. The world record nontypical whitetail and several record-book typical heads are part of the display.

border. Researchers have not been able to identify the causes of this phenomenon, but it is known that it occurs disproportionately among whitetail bucks living on strongly granitic soils.

Does of both whitetail and mule deer occasionally produce an abnormal quantity of the male hormone testosterone and may grow antlers. These are rarely fully developed and usually do not lose the velvet, and these animals are capable of producing young. It's a bit disconcerting, to say the least, to see a pair of healthy spotted fawns lustily nursing what appears to be a young buck in velvet!

Does whose testosterone levels are high enough to carry their antlers throughout the cycle, to the polished stage and then through shedding, are usually incapable of reproduction. Antlered whitetail does are more common than most hunters believe, about one doe in 10,000 having these male characteristics. In Texas's whitetail herd, that figure suggests that there must be about 250 or so antlered does running around the woods at any one time. I've seen several such animals shot for bucks in my thirty-five years of deer hunting, but not one of them even remotely approached anything that could be called trophy status.

Shed antlers in the woods may be common or very rare, depending upon climate conditions, the number of bucks left in the herd after harvest, and the number of rats and other rodents in the area, as well as the nature of the vegetation covering the ground. Many animals, including deer themselves as well as cattle and other domestic livestock, chew the shed antlers, presumably for the mineral content. Nothing is wasted in nature.

Within three to four months of shedding the antlers, the bucks' pedicels begin to swell and the annual cycle—at least ten million years old—begins again.

Primitive man was interested in and impressed by antlers, and used them as a symbol of virility and masculinity in various religious and cultural rites. He also used antlers or parts of antlers in a myriad of ways as tools, especially for pressure-flaking flint into projectile points, knives, and other weapons. Archaeologists seem to have uncovered an uncommonly large number of artifacts of prehistoric humanity which were bits and pieces of antler decorated with mysterious scribings and symbols, the meanings of which we do not know.

Perhaps the beauty of deer antlers held some special fascination for early man, hunter that he was; certainly they still exert such a hold on modern hunters. I know men who study the great whitetail heads as chess players study the masters' games, men who can identify a photograph of one of the top record heads at a glance, as to who killed the deer, in what year, where, and the Boone and Crockett score, just as a kid can quote all the statistics on his favorite athlete.

Famous whitetail heads may be sold for prodigious amounts of money, and a few hunters of my acquaintance actually collect the mounted heads of super bucks. There is almost a modern "cult of the antler": one wonders if we are really very different, for all our technology and sophistication, from our hairy ancestors who seem also to have been moved by the symbolism of deer antlers.

4 Field-Judging Heads

In Chapter 2 I emphasized the importance of learning how to make quick evaluations of trophy quality under hunting conditions. My observation is that most hunters do not master the knack until they've seen quite a few bucks, and reach a point at which they're no longer stricken with almost overpowering excitement at the mere sight of deer antlers.

Since relatively few of us are privileged to see that many live bucks in the field, most of the process of learning to evaluate trophies must necessarily be carried out on mounted heads or photographs. The advantage of mounted heads is that the hunter can make his estimates and then check himself with a tape measure, something that's a bit tough to do on living deer.

Even on photographs, it's often possible to check such linear measurements as inside or outside spread and the lengths of tines, at least on pictures in which the buck is looking straight at the camera with his ears in a normal, alert position. The trick is to compare the measurements of the ears to the dimension of the rack about which we're guessing. On a mature buck, the length of the opening in the ear will be very, very close to $5\frac{3}{4}$ inches, and the ear from its tip to the smallest diameter (an inch or so away from the head) is almost exactly 6 inches in whitetails. If this measurement is made carefully on the photo, preferably with a micrometer caliper, and the spread, say, is measured in the same way, then the following formula will give the actual spread, usually within a half-inch or less.

$$\frac{\text{spread measurement in photo}}{\text{ear-opening measurement in photo}} \times 5.75 = \text{actual spread}$$

Size him up for yourself. Uneven tines, 18 to 19 inches inside spread, short beams, and a bit spindly. This buck looks good at first glance, but a hard look shows him to be below most trophy standards. Give him another year. *(Photo by Taft Morrow, Maltsberger Ranch)*

The only pitfall in this system is judging exactly where the ear opening begins; in some pictures it's impossible to be precise.

Another method, somewhat less reliable in pictures but more useful in the field, is comparing the total tip-to-tip spread of the ears—again, in a fully alert position—to the antler spread. Taxidermists' forms are deliberately designed to minimize apparent ear spread, in order to make the rack look as wide as possible, and the ear-tip spread of mounted heads is rarely much more than 14½ inches, often less. But my measurements on dead deer indicate that the spread is much closer to 16 inches as a national average (big bucks) and possibly as much as 18 inches on a big northern white-tail.

I haven't measured nearly as many muleys as I have whitetails, but those I have measured ranged from 18 inches eartip to eartip on desert mule bucks, up to a full 22 inches on big Rocky Mountain deer.

Again, ear position is highly variable, and you must be careful to make spread estimates only from the full-alert frontal aspect, which, of course, is usually not difficult to get on a wild deer.

Tip-to-tip spread of a buck's ears in the full-front, alert position is the quickest index to linear dimensions of the rack. This animal's ear-tip spread is close to 16 inches, and a glance is enough to show that the inside curves of his beams are a couple of inches outside the eartips, giving him perhaps a bit more than 20 inches on the inside. From this, the length of the longest points can be estimated. Look also for the space between the tips of the antler beams as an index to beam length. *(Photo by Taft Morrow, Maltsberger Ranch)*

If the massiveness of a set of antlers is exceptional, it will be the first thing you notice. I compare circumference at the bases to the pistol grip of my rifle. This buck's bases are far thicker than that, and actually become heavier at midbeam. The gnarled formation suggests that this is a very old buck. *(Photo by Jerry Smith)*

With practice, a hunter should be able to estimate maximum inside spread very quickly in the field. Take $15\frac{1}{2}$ or 16 inches as the eartip spread (on all except the Coues and other small subspecies of whitetails) and figure how much wider the inside spread is. With this figure in mind, it shouldn't be too difficult to grab a quick estimate of the longest tines, and to make an eyeball guess as to whether there is a great difference in tine length on each side or whether the points are fairly near the same length. I usually find myself arriving at a quick *average* tine-length figure, excluding the brow tines or eyeguards, rather than trying to estimate each one separately. In the process, I have automatically counted at least the normal or "typical" points, and noted the presence or absence of nontypical tines.

The only other elements to be figured are beam thickness and beam length. Beam massiveness is self-evident; if the head is particularly heavy, it will be the first thing you notice. About the only clue I can offer for making a really serious guess at circumference is to note that the average rifle's pistol grip (most common, current models) is about $4\frac{1}{2}$ to 5 inches around at the smallest point. It happens also to be at about that circumference at the bases that white-tail heads begin to get into the most commonly accepted "trophy" category. With some sort of comparison to your rifle's pistol grip established (at least whether you think the antlers are bigger or smaller than the grip), you can check in an instant to see whether the antlers carry their massiveness at the base well out toward the tips or whether they tend to taper rapidly.

Beam length is the most difficult of all measurements to estimate on a live buck in the field, and it happens also to be the single most important measurement for the Boone and Crockett score. I know of no way except simple experience to even guess about beam length, but there are a few tips which may be helpful. If the head has great inside spread—say, 20 inches or more—and the tips of the beams come close together in front, beam length will probably be greater than 25 inches, and maybe much greater. This much can be seen when viewing the deer from the front. If you can see him from a side perspective as well, try to notice how close his beam tips come to touching a vertical line drawn upward from his nose. If they're close, his main beams will be respectable, and may be very long; if they're well out in front of his nose, they're surely long, unless the head is freakishly narrow in spread.

Another clue is the spacing of the fighting tines (all normal points between the eyeguards and the beam tips) along the main beam. If they give the impression of being crowded, especially on an eight-pointer, the beams may not be particularly long. If they seem well spaced out, especially on a ten-pointer, the beams are probably very good.

There are some more general hints to take into consideration. First, a buck's spread always appears deceptively great when seen from the rear; always go slow on shooting if this is the only view you have. A buck seen from above will fool you, too, but in the other direction; it'll look smaller, overall, than it really is. This is a problem in mountain hunting, and sometimes when hunting from tree stands or from elevated towers.

A buck seen at long range in very good sunlight coming over the observer's shoulder always seems bigger than he is, and, conversely, if the light is bad, or the deer is backlighted, he may score much

Go slowly in judging any deer head from the rear; the spread always looks greater than it is and the other relationships are distorted from this angle. This is a wonderful old buck, but he won't score as well as this view suggests. *(Photo by Mike Biggs)*

higher than first impressions may suggest. On any really big buck, the antlers will be by far the widest part of the body when viewed from directly in front or directly behind.

These comments apply as much to mule deer as to whitetails, by the way, but there is a characteristic of mule deer antlers which is unmistakable on trophy-grade bucks, and it is a sort of "boxy" appearance to the rack, which will seem to be about as high as it is wide whether viewed from the front, side, or rear. This effect, together with massiveness and a lack of obvious freakishness, almost always guarantees a good mule deer trophy.

In the case of either species, however, there is not a hunter alive who can make even a reasonable guess as to the possible score of a real nontypical head until the buck is dead. Some are so complicated that no two official Boone and Crockett scorers will get the same measurements, and on a few I doubt that the same scorer could come up with the same total, even roughly, twice in a row.

Some hunters are fascinated by nontypical racks, or by some particular abnormal characteristic. I've always wanted to shoot a big whitetail with a matched pair of "drop" points, nontypical tines extending downward from the main beams, often in the form of parentheses, but I've only seen one such head in all my years in the woods. He was a tremendous buck with everything else—massiveness, plenty of long points, and good spread—but he was on private property on which I didn't have permission to hunt. He bounded across a country road in front of my car, ran about 200 yards, and stopped to look back at me. That moment sorely tested my soul, since the season was open, I had an unfilled buck tag, and I had a rifle, but I let him go. Sometimes, I'll admit, I still wish I hadn't!

About all that can be said about nontypicals, relative to field-judging, is if you see one you like, shoot him. Except for a general impression of size, not much real judging is possible.

For the trophy hunter who relishes the idea of a record-book whitetail, I once did an analysis of the top hundred typical heads in the current Boone and Crockett lists in an effort to discover which element of a rack was most important. The answer will surprise most hunters. There are heads in the top hundred which have little more than 17 inches inside spread, and there are ten-point racks in that select group. There are heads which are not outstanding for massiveness . . . but there are *no* heads there with short main beams! The *average* main-beam length, in fact, is $27\frac{1}{2}$ inches, an almost unbelievable measurement.

A composite head, made up of the average measurements of those top hundred typical record-book whitetails, would look like this: main beams, $27\frac{1}{2}$ inches; inside spread $21\frac{1}{2}$ inches; about thirteen points; and a base circumference of about 5 inches. Naturally, this composite head would be perfectly symmetrical except for that extra tine. Tine lengths are not given in the Records of North American Big Game, but you can bet that most of them were very long. In fact, it's possible to demonstrate mathematically that the thirteen tines on this hypothetical "average" rack must average about $4\frac{3}{4}$ inches long, which means that the longest points would be about 10 inches and the shortest points about 3 inches.

Choosing which one to shoot from a pair of bucks like these is a wonderful dilemma for any hunter. Both are fine trophies, but the deer on the left is actually a six-by-four while his companion is an eleven-pointer. Both are wide and fairly heavy, with weak brow-tines. Although he may not score as well, I like the left-hand buck because he looks older. *(Photo by Mike Biggs)*

In terms of percentages, this composite rack gets 70 percent of its total score from beam length and aggregate tine length, no more than 18 percent from massiveness, and only 12 percent from inside spread. Of course, this composite "record" also scores about 185 points, since he represents only the top hundred out of some 290-plus whitetails in the records, but those *percentages* may be expected to apply also to a 170-pointer which barely makes it into the listings. In other words, if the buck you're looking at in the field is notably deficient in one of those departments (say, he's a ten-pointer instead of a twelve or thirteen), he must make up the difference somewhere else, perhaps in extra length of the tines. By the way, it's not impossible to make the book with an eight-pointer—there are several in the record lists—but it would have to be a truly awesome eight-point head. I've scored three phenomenal eight-pointers, and only one broke into the record *class* at 150-plus scoring points.

Even a hunter who couldn't care less about placing a buck in the records may benefit from a thoughtful study of these facts and figures, if only because they'll condition him to think in terms of and to look for specific elements of a trophy rack, rather than merely an overall impression of bigness.

The one thing which cannot be taken into consideration is the rare circumstance of an unusually small-bodied buck with well-formed antlers. He may appear tremendous, and be very ordinary. This happened to a hunting friend of mine once; he shot what he believed to be a very fine, mature buck and was astounded at how small the antlers were until we weighed the deer in camp. He pulled the scales down only to 85 pounds, dressed, and this in an area where the average mature buck weighs more than 125 and those hefting as much as 150 to 180 are not terribly rare. We'll have more to say about this later on, when we discuss judging a buck's age on the hoof, but there is really no protection against it if the small-bodied deer is alone when seen.

Nor is there any protection against the tricks your eyes will play on you at times. One afternoon I was hunting in an area known to be inhabited by a very large whitetail. I saw his big, splayed tracks and his breeding rubs, smoking fresh, on large saplings. All afternoon I had the sensation of being very close to this trophy buck, but he did not appear in the flesh. At dusk, I started the long

Despite the author's caution about judging bucks from behind, this one really is as good as he looks—or better! He lacks mass but he's a rare basic six-by-six frame with few visible deducts, lots of beam and tine length, and startling spread.

walk back to my car, but I had gone only about half a mile before a buck burst out of a thicket very close to me and galloped 50 yards before turning to look back at me. Through the scope, and in the afterglow from the western sky, I could see heavy antlers, at least 25 inches wide, and I fired. It was so dark that I had to search for the deer with a flashlight, but he'd gone only a few yards before dying.

When I found him, I refused to believe that it was the same buck I'd shot. He had a very small eight-point rack, no more than 15 inches wide, and was a three and a half year old deer. What had happened, of course, was that I had been so intent on the big fellow in that area for so many hours that my mind was programmed to see a big buck. When this one bounced out, I simply saw, in the poor light, what I expected to see, instead of what was really there before my eyes. It can happen to any hunter, regardless of his experience or coolness, and I suppose can only be avoided by never shooting until one has had the chance to evaluate *all* elements of the rack (taking nothing for granted, as I did on this unfortunate little deer, regarding number of tines, tine length, and beam length) and never shooting in bad light.

The real shame of it was that this buck had the potential to become a nice trophy within two or three more seasons. But he taught me an important, if ego-bruising, lesson, and his venison was tasty.

Painful as that experience was, it was nothing compared to what I've come to call "the agony" of the trophy hunter. The agony comes about when a hunter holds a rifle on a fine buck, trying to decide whether he's fine enough, and knowing that he's probably the best trophy the hunter is going to see that season. It's easy for a case-hardened trophy hunter to pass up the two and a half and three and a half year old bucks which make up the majority of his sightings in

A great trophy buck? Well, that depends on where you're hunting, but he's only two and a half years old. We'll never see how good he can be unless he's part of a population hunted by trophy hunters.

good hunting country. What really gets tough is the effort to decide whether a big buck is only a four and a half year old which is just before becoming a real record-class head, or a fully mature one which probably won't get much if any better in the antler department. "What if I shoot this one and see a record head on the way back to camp?" one agonizes. "But what if I *don't* shoot? Will I have another chance?"

There is no way out of this dilemma for the hunter who's really serious about *big* heads. It's a part of the game, like the loneliness of the long-distance runner. You get used to it. But a trophy hunter never settles for second best, and he never shoots until he sees the one he wants, even if that means he never shoots.

The difference between the trophy hunter and the ordinary hunter can be seen in this imaginary situation. It's the last day of the season and you have no meat. Suddenly, you find yourself looking at two bucks standing side by side, within easy range. One is a smallish eight-pointer which you judge to be about a three year old, while the other is a spike. Which do you shoot?

Most hunters today would unhesitatingly shoot the eight-pointer, because he is the "better" buck. A genuine trophy hunter would shoot the spike, knowing that neither deer is in any sense a trophy and that both will be good eating. His reasoning is as follows. The eight-pointer is only a couple of years away from possible trophy status, and the habitat already has three years of forage "invested" in him. The spike is a genetic defective which has no hope of ever becoming a superior buck, but, even if he could become a trophy someday, he's a full four years away from that status and the habitat has invested only eighteen months in his growth.

With the trophy hunter, it's not so much a question of which buck should be *shot*, but which should be *spared*.

That's what makes him different from the general run of people with guns and licenses in the woods.

5 Big Bucks Are Different

If big-buck hunters are different—and usually better—than run-of-the-mill deer hunters, so are the animals they seek. Every deer-hunting book ever written has stated that bucks are not like does in their habits and behavior, and that's true. But mature bucks—remember, that means five year olds and older—are so different from the younger males that they might as well be a separate species. What this chapter will attempt to do is to examine how, to what degree, and how they get that way.

The most obvious difference is simply that a mature buck has survived at least five hunting seasons. He has experience that a younger buck cannot have. Various sensory perceptions have more meaning for him, and his lifestyle must necessarily have been altered by his experiences, or he would not have lived to maturity in most areas today. He lives according to different rhythms.

For background, let's review a few facts about whitetail natural history and plug in some observations. Whitetail fawns are usually born as twins, with the sex ratio almost exactly one male to one female. Buck fawns reveal a different personality almost as soon as they're big enough to follow their mothers. The word is spooky; they seem to come into the world more alert and wary, and they become continually more so as time goes by. Early fawns, born in early May, may have tiny antlers in their first year of life, and are called nubbin bucks by some hunters. Male fawns born as late as August are still babies during the following hunting season, although they won't have spots and may show slight velvet-covered protrusions where their antlers will be. With or without antlers, the little bucks will not be permitted to follow their mothers during the dam's heat

This young fellow—probably just a very good yearling—has little or no chance of partic-ipating in the breeding rituals of a biologically balanced herd, at least for two or three more years. By then he will have earned his spurs—and antlers—as a dominant male. In many U.S. whitetail herds today, however, he would rank as a "trophy buck," sadly enough. *(Photo by W. A. Maltsberger)*

period; either the doe will drive them away, or her lover will do it for her, for a breeding buck will not tolerate the nearness of any other male. It's the first of many hard lessons to be learned by the buck fawn if he is to survive. I have witnessed a doe entering estrus driving away her youngster, and that was the most forlorn little deer I ever hope to see, standing in the gathering dusk and watching his mother disappear into the thickets. His whole world had just collapsed around his ears, and he was utterly bewildered. I wanted to go and gather him up in my arms and comfort him, but of course it was not possible.

The young buck usually grows his first real set of antlers in his second year, so that they are hard and polished during hunting sea-son when he is about eighteen months old. This timing is the reason that the age of bucks is usually given as, say, four and a half or five and a half years old. If the young buck is healthy and vigorous, on good range (12 to 18 percent protein content), he should have at least four points at this time. We now have good evidence that at least some spike bucks are genetically inferior animals which don't have the potential to become outstanding trophies. Small eight-point racks are not at all uncommon on long yearlings, and a few eighteen-month-old bucks will sport perfect, though tiny, ten-point racks.

It is while the buck has this first set of antlers that he must somehow begin to learn to deal with the hunter, and the majority of such bucks do not learn quickly enough. In many states, the average age at death for whitetail males is about eighteen months.

Those who do survive this first hunting season are infinitely wiser, and the odds begin to turn a little in their favor, for they have already begun to establish successful escape patterns.

Although physically capable of breeding in this period, yearling bucks have few opportunities to do so. The efforts of spikes and little forkies around does which are about to come into heat are as comical as the fevered fumblings of high-school boys. In the buck's second full year of life, however, his luck is likely to change. If he happens to be part of a well-balanced whitetail population with a normal age-class distribution among the bucks, he will be at the very bottom of the dominance chain, save only for the yearlings. The mere presence of fully mature males in the area produces in the two and a half year old an effect called psychological castration, and prevents him from becoming sexually active. He will always give way to a bigger buck, never engaging his superiors in combat. If, however, he is a member of a herd in which there are few or no four or five year old bucks, he may find himself able to dominate enough of his juniors to breed the does. In such herds, the ratio of antlered bucks to does is usually very low, from one in five to as few as one in ten or fifteen. This is a result of bad herd management, with too much unselective pressure on the males and no culling of surplus does, and every sexually mature buck in the herd must make his contribution to the next season's fawn crop.

It's important to note that the young-middle-aged buck is not prevented from breeding by actual, physical intimidation or punishment from the big bucks, but merely by his acceptance of their dominant status within the local society. If the dominant buck in a herd is harvested by a hunter, say, halfway through the rut, the two

Above, the Waltz of the Warriors, a stately, menacing circling, bodies always broadside and hair erected to make each animal seem larger. Ears are laid back and drooped and chins tucked in to display the antlers. Cocked tails complete the posturing, which, if neither rival can be intimidated, precedes actual combat.

Below, as a buck reaches maturity, his main biological function is breeding. Dominance is all he has to live for, even if he must engage in physical combat to prove his status and his right to a breeding territory. *(Photos by Mike Biggs)*

and a half and three and a half year old bucks which were inactive until then will immediately begin to breed the available does.

In the meantime, the local buck herd is combed out once more by the hunters' rifles, and the survivors are the wariest, most cunning, and probably luckiest.

One year later, the buck is no longer an adolescent. At three and a half years, he shows his potential for body size and antler pattern. His skeletal growth is nearly complete and his musculature is developing into heavy shoulders, blocky hams, and a powerful neck to wield the antlers which are beginning to be taken seriously by the other deer in the herd. During this season's rut, he is likely to be a definite factor. And if he makes it through this third full hunting season, he has been awarded a sort of master's degree in evasive tactics. For the rest of his life, he will be very, very difficult to catch in a set of rifle sights.

In his fourth full year of life, the buck is, for all practical purposes, mature. Depending on the composition of the herd, he may well be *the* dominant buck in his neck of the woods, with the

These yearling bucks are only sparring, testing themselves while carefully avoiding antagonizing each other. They are not angry, and there's no winner or loser in this match . . . but in a few more seasons they'll be trying to kill each other!

Bucks are sedentary and retiring during the antler-growing period. A great deal of energy and nutrition go into antler development, and bucks are excessively careful with the tender velvet. Velvet antlers feel hot to the touch, but even gentle bucks dislike having them handled.

An unusual photo of a buck that has already shed one antler. Shedding occurs from late December to late February, depending upon latitude. *(Photo by Walter Elling)*

Before the rut, even mature bucks are quite amiable toward one another and often hang out in "bachelor clubs." But such associations are short-lived once the velvet comes off and the racks are polished. *(Photo by Mike Biggs)*

younger animals warily deferring to him as he once did perhaps to his own father. If there are older, bigger bucks in the area, he may now challenge them boldly, and win his share of the battles. During this breeding season and the next two, he will be fearfully busy and will make his greatest contribution to the gene pool of his herd, fathering as many as forty to fifty fawns in *each* of his three peak seasons. During the rut, his nutritional intake will be reduced by as much as 50 percent, and he may lose a full one-fifth of his total body weight.

By now, his antlers are big (though they will continue to improve somewhat over the years) and their characteristic pattern will be very obvious. Tendencies toward extra-wide spread, many points or abnormal points, great weight, or whatever will be clear in this fourth set of antlers. Find his shed horns this January, and you will be able to recognize him at once if you see him next October.

By now, too, his lifestyle is well established. He has learned that certain patterns of movement, certain bedding areas, and certain hours offer him fewer frantic alarms and greater serenity. He probably has retreated to terrain into which few hunters penetrate, and where none *can* penetrate without his knowing long before he is in danger and from which two or more well-tested escape routes exist. He has gained courage and cunning, and knows how to stand motionless, controlling his nerves, as an unseeing human passes within yards, crashing through the woods and spreading his nauseating scent about. In his first year, the buck might have broken and run, but now he knows that hiding is safer. Unconsciously, he has begun to order his daily routine more toward the hours of darkness, and to route himself to avoid openings; now he leaves the trail to skirt the margins of a meadow in the shadows at the edge of the forest, rather than follow his companions blithely across the sunlit center of the clearing.

His armor has become almost complete. He has learned to take nothing for granted and to pay attention to every sound, sight, and odor that reaches his sensors. He sleeps lightly and feeds briefly. He moves to water like a shadow among the shadows of dusk, dips his nose reluctantly and jerks his head erect, with water drops splashing from his chin, every few seconds. He does not linger.

He may have, by now, become completely unkillable. There are such bucks, deer whose chosen habitat protects them so perfectly that no legal hunting technique can take them. I've hunted several such, together with many other veteran hunters of proven skill, and been defeated year after year. There was one, a monstrous ten-pointer, which could be seen on almost any day, with binoculars, but simply could not be approached within rifle range. He lived in a broad, shallow draw on the side of a rocky hill, and any daytime approach skylined the hunter for many minutes long before he could try even a desperately long shot. An approach before daylight was inevitably so noisy, in the loose rocks, that the buck was alerted. We tried big, noisy drives, and slow, subtle, one-man drives with a gun on each of the buck's known escape routes. We attempted to install brush blinds, and he never came near them. We tried to rattle him up, without success. Not only did we never kill that deer, but none of us ever fired a rifle at him, even though we could see him on almost any day. He was more than a match for the most cunning efforts of half a dozen of Texas's best deer hunters, season after season.

That is the sort of animal the trophy hunter seeks by choice. There have been two or three other such bucks in my hunting career, and I remember each of them with respect and with love. They beat me, but every glimpse I got of them, alive and wild and challenging, remains etched in my mind, long after I've forgotten what scores of the bucks I've killed even looked like. The big bucks can capture a man's imagination as no other American animal.

Trophy hunters count very small victories as precious. I've heard variations of the story around a hundred campfires: "I had the big fellow figured perfectly! I guessed right where he'd be and worked the wind just right, and got within 100 yards of him. Even got him in the scope for a second, but then he just vanished before I could shoot!"

By the time a buck has survived enough seasons to acquire a set of antlers like this one, he has also acquired a habit of incredible alertness and caution, plus a level of awareness of his surroundings that is incomprehensible to humans. *(Photo by W. A. Maltsberger)*

An old buck can literally starve to death in the midst of plenty after his teeth are worn out so that he cannot chew his cud. Note this animal's pathetic body condition, with ribs, hips, and vertebrae showing through his rough coat. If he survives another winter, the chances are he will never have another head as good as this one, and a hunter's bullet now would be a kindness as well as collection of a very nice trophy. (Photo by Jerry Smith)

Perhaps in no other aspect of hunting do serious hunters take such pleasure from their failures!

We tend, however, to give such animals too much credit for sheer, human-type intelligence. In fact, they are not really smart, but rather superlatively clever and wary, and absolute masters of their habitat. A big buck behaves as he does because that's the way he was programmed by nature. He reacts so effectively precisely because he cannot think in the way that we do, and he therefore never suffers from the indecision that consideration of several alternatives can present. He doesn't move mostly at night because he knows that sportsmen cannot legally hunt him then, but because his experience has been that he is less often disturbed during the hours of darkness. He doesn't select a bed-ground after an intellectual appraisal of the surrounding terrain and wind direction. Instead, he lies down in an impregnable spot simply because he has learned, in his dim animal mind, that this is a good place and a safe place; he goes there because he prefers tranquil surroundings.

An old buck's evasive tactics are not really creative, no matter how frustrated and futile they may make us feel. He's incapable of reasoning out new and ever more devious tricks to play on hunters;

his choices of action are nothing more than repetitions of those which have worked before. He only wants to be where there are no sudden, deafening explosions and no human odor, and if he finds himself in the presence of a human being, his heredity and experience have taught him how to rid himself of that presence most effectively. We can handicap ourselves psychologically by believing that a trophy buck is invulnerable, with supernatural abilities, whereas, in fact, some of these characteristics can actually be used against the old fellow by a hunter who knows what he's about.

I said earlier that a mature buck's armor is *almost* complete, but there always remains one chink in it. That chink occurs during rut, and I shall devote a full chapter to making the most of it.

The remainder of a whitetail's life cycle, assuming he has arrived at age five, is less dramatic but just as interesting. Between the ages of four and a half and seven and a half years, as mentioned, he is the unquestioned king of his particular neck of the woods. By now his body has assumed a chunky, blocky, heavily muscled appearance and he appears shorter-legged than he really is because of the depth of his torso. Even his gait has changed; he no longer bounces daintily along like a doe or young buck, but gallops, almost seeming to lumber a bit. His antlers are at their lifetime best during these three years, assuming reasonably good forage during spring and summer. He may not be a record-book trophy (only a tiny percentage of even mature bucks will ever be), but his rack is as good as it will get. He is in the prime of his strength, confidence, and sexual vigor.

But, in his mouth, he already has the beginnings of his downfall. His molar teeth, at this age, will reveal much wear, more or less depending upon the soil on which he lives and the protein content of his forage. He can still chew his cud, but it takes a little longer each year. When he's eight and a half years old, almost anywhere in the whitetail range, the hand of death is already upon him, tightening its grip as the teeth inexorably wear down toward the gumline. He may still be sexually active, but his rack has begun to show the signs of senility, growing smaller than his last season's antlers, perhaps, and more gnarled and angular, probably with the addition of one or more random tines. By deer standards, at this age he is an ancient patriarch. Only a tiny percentage of bucks ever reach this age, even in unhunted herds, and even fewer go on to their ninth and tenth seasons.

If he does, he will be senile. He will not usually take part in the rutting rituals of autumn, and his body loses condition as he fights to get enough to eat, even in the midst of plenty. He becomes under-nourished, and finally may starve, usually during the hardest weeks of late winter or during a prolonged drought. Actually, not many whitetails actually starve to death, because predators, parasites, or disease attack them as soon as they become sufficiently weakened. The end is never gentle, but it's the way nature works. The anti-hunting preservationists don't like to think about these things, but hunters actually see them. And sometimes shed a private tear in the seclusion of the forest, standing over the coyote-torn carcass of an ancient buck.

This buck's age proved to be six and a half years, which means he'd fulfilled his biologi-cal role in the whitetail herd; it was time for him to go.

6 Mule Deer and Whitetails

The life cycle of a mule deer buck is not so very different, in most ways, from that described for a whitetail in the previous chapter. The facts of his birth and development to maturity are similar, with the same events occurring at about the same ages. A muley, too, is a trophy at age five and a half (and seldom before), if he is ever to be one, and he rises through the dominance ranking as he grows older at about the same general rate.

Muleys seldom have spikes, most yearlings sprouting forked horns, at least. The second rack of a good-quality buck should be a four-point head, by western count, except that the eyeguards are usually undeveloped. From then on, the typical mule deer will always be a four-pointer (plus brow tines), his rack merely becoming higher, wider, and heavier with age. Nontypicals may occur at any age, and, as in whitetails, this tendency can be identified by the time the buck is approximately three and a half years old.

There are two major differences in the muley's lifestyle, compared to his whitetail cousin. First, he is not territorial. The whitetail usually spends his entire life within a square-mile area, often much smaller. This permits him to learn that territory with an uncanny thoroughness, understanding all the subtle relationships of contours and knowing every trail, shrub, rock, and tree.

An example of just how alert whitetails are to their surroundings was shown to me one evening as I watched some deer feeding on a crop of winter oats on my own small ranch. I invariably kept a block of mineralized stock salt in that clearing for my cattle, always in exactly the same place, but I had allowed a few weeks to pass before replacing the previous block after it was used up. The deer, of course, enjoyed the salt lick, too, and knew exactly what it was. The fresh block had been put in place on the afternoon in question.

A doe and fawn appeared in the clearing and began to nibble at the oats, but they had not been there more than a minute or two before the fawn spotted that salt block. For those who haven't seen one, a mineralized salt block is about a foot square and of an earthy, reddish-brown color. The fawn instantly knew that the block hadn't been there on the day before, and began to snort and whistle and stamp, flagging her tail, and generally making so much fuss that she made her mother too nervous to continue feeding. Within a few minutes, they fled.

Now bear in mind that the salt block was not a large, conspicuous, or suspiciously shaped object, and further that an identical salt block normally occupied that exact position the year around. Not only did the whitetails not regard the salt as a threat, but they actually ate it. Yet, because this was a *new* block, the deer instantly became aware of it. That's what I mean when I say that a whitetail is intimately familiar with every smallest detail of his accustomed surroundings. I might add that I saw *no* bucks on the oat patch that evening, although there were three which habitually fed there.

A mule deer, however, covers a lot more ground during his annual wanderings and, although he certainly knows his range better than any hunter could ever hope to, he cannot have the familiarity of the whitetail with his home territory. I believe this is why mule deer bucks tend more to *run* for safety, in contrast to the whitetail, which relies much more on *hiding*. It is also why the hunter will occasionally see a mule buck make what seems to be a simple blunder in trying to escape, sometimes boxing himself into a canyon or rim-rocking himself.

The other chief difference between muleys and whitetails is that the former are migratory, at least to some extent. There are records of mule deer herds regularly migrating more than 100 miles, twice each year. Much more common, however, is a relatively short migration in the vertical plane. The summering grounds are high up in the mountains, often above timberline, sometimes at elevations of more than 11,000 feet above sea level. The onset of winter, however, eventually drives the herds down into the valleys, away from the impossibly deep snows at high altitudes, and this descent

A major different between mule deer and whitetails is in habitat, especially the muley's vertical migrations as the seasons change.

often involves horizontal movement of a dozen miles or more even in the most sedentary herds.

In past years, the mature bucks tended to migrate downward somewhat earlier than the does and fawns, it seemed to me. But over the years a distinct change occurred in the habits of the animals, presumably because of heavier and more pervasive hunting pressure. The major bucks seem to be the very last to leave the high country and furthermore that they can endure the alpine winter and deep snow even longer than the longer-legged, bigger elk which share their ranges. I do know that it takes real, honest-to-gosh *winter*, and not just a few snow flurries, to bring the big bucks down in certain heavily hunted regions.

The hunter, therefore, has an extra dimension to contend with: he must not only find the deer, and then the bucks, but he has to try to figure at what elevation they'll be tomorrow or next week, whereas the whitetail hunter can be confident that a big whitetail will almost always be within a half-mile radius, the year around.

The breeding mechanisms of the whitetail will be dealt with at length in another chapter, but can be summed up here by saying

Mule bucks do fight during the rut, but not as frequently or as savagely as whitetails. Muleys gather a small, loose-knit harem, while whitetail males attend to only one doe at a time. This is a picture of a battle looking for a place to happen.

that a buck consorts with only one female at a time, and remains with her only a few hours at most. The muley, by contrast, collects a harem—if he's dominant enough—of three or four does, on the average, and defends his breeding rights to these females from other males. The ladies have much more to say about the permanence of this relationship, however, than do cow elk, for example. If a doe wanders away to take up with another buck, the herd buck never tries to bully her back into line. If the other buck comes too close, however, and the two males are reasonably well matched, there may be a battle.

Muleys are by no means as aggressive as whitetails, and serious fights between bucks are neither as frequent nor as savage as those between whitetails. Mule deer antlers are quite often damaged in these late-winter battles, however, apparently because the extreme cold makes the antler material brittle and more easily broken.

Bucks of both species tend to shun the company of females except during the mating season or when the animals are drawn into proximity by the availability of choice forage, such as an alfalfa field. From antler-shedding time until the velvet is stripped from the new rack, the bucks form bachelor clubs and may be seen in groups of three or four, up to as many as eight, in my own experience. The animals seem to prefer the company of other males near their own age, and this is especially true of the fully mature bucks. Thus, it's not uncommon to find two big bucks of nearly equal size and status as almost inseparable companions. The association is much too regular to be mere chance, and the old boys appear to really enjoy the company of their peers . . . until the rut approaches, at which time they become bitter enemies. During the rut, the only association between bucks that I have observed is between youngsters of not more than two and a half years, or, occasionally, between a big, mature male and a yearling. In either situation, there can be no significant sexual competition between the individuals involved.

Although it is true of whitetails, it is even more true that mule bucks' life patterns are so different in summertime that a hunter cannot gain much information at that time of year which will be used during the hunting season. In both species, the animals are seeking entirely different kinds of browse during the different seasons, and going to different areas to find it. This renders scouting in late summer and early autumn considerably less productive than is sometimes suggested in the outdoors magazines, and this is doubly true of mule deer. Except for the joy of being among the deer and perhaps coming to understand their personality and reactions, such scouting is largely futile unless conducted during the few days immediately before opening day of the hunting season.

Whitetails' patterns change, too, often rather radically in a very few days, but at least the animals will still be within their basic, limited home territory, and tracks and sign may be of use in locating a decent buck. An example is to be seen when a day or two of windy weather at just the right time produces an abrupt mast fall. Suddenly, the deer will seem to desert the feeding grounds where they could reliably be found for the last several weeks. Look for them then in the beech, oak, and other nut-tree stands within their known home territories, and if the mast is still on the ground when the season opens, they'll still be there. In this sense, whitetails are more predictable than mule deer.

Mule deer are, on the whole, much easier to see in their natural habitat than whitetails. The journals of Lewis and Clark suggest that these animals were once plentiful far out on the plains, wher-ever a few breaks and coulees offered them a bit of cover. Today, of course, we think of mule deer as mountain animals, but they still retain their fondness for open country and still rely on herding for mutual protection from predators much more than the solitary whitetail. Because they now stick to the mountains, mostly, muleys depend on their eyes as their principal early-warning system, since wind currents are notoriously fickle in mountain terrain. Not that a mule deer doesn't have good senses of hearing and scent; he does, but they are more corroborative than primary in warning him of potential danger. His whitetail cousin, by contrast, places at least as much reliance on his ears and nose as he does on his vision. A white-tail may see a hunter and wait for confirmation from his nose, for example, before he takes action. In the brushy country inhabited by most whitetail herds, this is really not surprising, but many hunters of my acquaintance seem not to have noticed the difference. It's a difference that can be crucial in developing hunting tactics.

Finally, there are distinct differences between the two species in general personality. The mule deer has had a reputation for

Big whitetail bucks specialize in being unseen, hiding rather than fleeing from danger, while muleys usually frequent more open country, are easier to observe from a distance, and often depend upon flight as a main defense. *(Photo courtesy of Robert Rogers)*

The whitetail tends to be solitary, except for the relationship between a doe and her fawns of the year, whereas mule deer have a stronger herd instinct.

dumbness for many generations, while the whitetail has always been conceded a high ranking on the IQ scale. I believe that the mule deer is a bit more trusting, overall, than a whitetail, but I'm not sure the difference is really one of intelligence. After all, the white-tail has about 400 years of experience with white men armed with guns, whereas the real pressure on the muley has developed only since the end of World War II. Before that, the muley's range was relatively sparsely populated and sportsmen did not travel as much for their hunting then as is common now.

There is also no doubt that the modern whitetail has changed his tactics; he relies much more on hiding than on flight than the older books tell us he once did. I know old-time hunters here in Texas who can confirm this out of their own memories. Perhaps hunters have helped evolve a skulking, burglar-bold breed of white-tail deer by combing the runners out of the breeding herd with the rifle. Or maybe the deer are simply adaptable enough to learn the tricks of hiding within a few generations. In any case, being unseen is the whitetail's best tactic today, whereas the mule deer is cer-tainly much less skillful at the game.

Perhaps he'll get that way in time; I seem to note an increasing tendency on the part of muley bucks, particularly big ones, to duck and dodge and avoid the open, straightaway flight these days, and hunters who have spent more time with that species than I have heartily confirm this impression.

But the real trophy-class mule bucks are almost as distinct in their habits from the other deer in the herd as big whitetails are, and the hunter who counts heavily on stupidity in record bucks of either species to put his trophy on the wall is going to have a long wait for a taxidermist's bill. Except in herds which have been totally protected from hunting, the biggest trophy deer simply didn't get that way by being stupid.

If forced to state my opinion, I'll concede that I think that, age class for age class, whitetail bucks are cleverer and tougher to catch up with in any kind of cover, but that's not to say a big muley is a pushover. One ground for my opinion is the fact that it seems to be possible to strip most of the record-class heads out of a mule deer herd when a new area is opened to hunting for the first time pretty quickly, whereas it's almost impossible to do that in a whitetail herd.

A hunting camp in the Colorado Rockies, with three outstanding mule deer bucks on the meatpole.

A fine muley of the desert subspecies, taken by the author in Mexico's beautiful Sonoran Desert.

About the only way trophy-class bucks can be eliminated from good whitetail habitat is excessive shooting of the younger bucks, so that no replacements are coming along to fill in the mature age class as the old bucks are lost. This is, in fact, exactly the reason that large areas of the United States have so few real trophy whitetails—not overshooting of the deer, but *shooting the wrong kind* of deer, a subject about which I'll have a lot more to say in another chapter.

7 Where and When

Contrary to the average hunter's idea, it *is* quite possible to hunt specifically for trophy bucks. It is *not* merely hunting in the usual manner and hoping to see a better than average head. As mentioned earlier, in fact, that process offers a reasonably good guarantee against stumbling across a trophy, simply because most hunters' usual manner of hunting is geared to show them the most deer of any size or sex for the time and effort spent. We have seen that by the time a buck is truly mature and therefore possibly in the trophy class, his habits and patterns of movement have become so different from those of ordinary deer that he evades common hunting methods effortlessly.

If you doubt that statement, let me tell you a couple of stories. Michigan wildlife officials once tried an experiment in which thirty-nine whitetail deer were released in one square mile—just 640 acres—of typical good whitetail habitat which was surrounded by a deerproof fence. Nine of the deer were bucks of various ages. Six veteran Michigan hunters were allowed to hunt this captive herd. Conditions were ideal, with a nice tracking snow and good hunting weather. Bear in mind that the deer population of this area was known to be one to every 16 acres, roughly. But the hunters were hard pressed even to see a deer, and it took the six of them *four days* before glimpsing one of the bucks. Fifty-one hours were required to actually kill a buck, even though the animals were unable to escape the enclosure.

I do not know whether any of the bucks in this experiment were mature, trophy animals, nor whether these deer had come from heavily hunted areas and had had experience with hunting pressure but the conclusion that any whitetail can make himself eerily absent when the heat is turned on is inescapable. Big bucks have this ability honed to the highest degree.

South Dakota conservation researchers carried out an even more amazing experiment when they live-trapped a mature whitetail and fitted him with a radio transmitter and long orange ribbons in his ears. He was released in an open hunting area, but escaped hunters for an entire week. The biologists, who were able to maintain an exact radio fix on this buck's location at all times, noted that some hunters actually passed within 40 yards of the deer without ever suspecting his presence. During the second week of the experiment, a team of expert hunters was directed to the marked buck's area. They knew where he was, but the most careful searching failed to produce even a single sighting (remember the orange ear streamers!). Finally, one of the hunters jumped the buck by almost stepping on him, and, even then, the deer escaped safely!

Three factors must all be present to produce big bucks—adequate nutrition for optimum growth, a population managed for normal age-class distribution so that the bucks may attain at least five and a half years of age, and the local genetic tendency to grow large antlers. Look for an area with all three if you want a wallhanger.

That's what you're up against, in spades, when you set forth after a trophy whitetail, and I say again that ordinary hunting tactics and techniques will not bring him under your gun. The only things which will, if anything can, are careful planning and skillful hunting.

The planning step is crucial. The first problem, obviously, is ferreting out and gaining access to an area where trophy bucks are known to exist. Such areas must have all three ingredients for big bucks: (1) hunting must be regulated in such a way that deer in the mature age classes are present; (2) adequate, high-protein forage must be available (which often means a fairly low population density); and (3) the genetic tendency to big antlers. If any one of these elements is missing, there will be no trophy bucks.

Western Canada is justly famous for big whitetails, with Saskatchewan and Alberta leading the parade. U.S. hunters, however, are not always eligible for deer licenses in the area of Saskatchewan producing most "book" heads—the farming region of the southeastern quadrant, including the towns of Weyburn and Estevan. During the last twenty years, the bush country north of the Saskatchewan farmlands has begun turning out some impressive trophies, and deer licenses for alien (American) hunters are now sold. West-central Manitoba is now producing a few extraordinary racks, too. The prairie grain fields, especially south and east of Edmonton, Alberta, are a mother lode of big racks. Alberta also enjoys a very well-developed outfitting industry. In the last decade, a few knockout whitetails have started turning up in southeastern British Columbia, and this may be a big-whitetail sleeper region.

Grain fields explain the bucks coming out of the American midwestern prairies, too, although it's corn rather than Canada's wheat, barley, and rye. As this is written, Iowa may be the hottest hot spot in the midwest, but west-central Illinois (which only recently offered nonresident licenses), Kansas (ditto for out-of-state licenses), and Nebraska are all premier areas for corn-fed monsters. I made special mention of Missouri in the first edition of this book twenty years ago as a leading midwestern producer of exceptional racks. In the meantime, Missouri has broken the nontypical world record, which, in that same edition, I declared "unbreakable."

Around the edges of the Corn Belt, western Kentucky, northern Arkansas, and eastern Colorado must be taken very seriously these days by big-buck hunters. The farm country of Indiana and Ohio regularly produce record-class heads, as well.

Texas boasts by far the largest deer herd in the nation (more than 3.5 million animals, not to mention desert mule deer in the Trans-Pecos), and has always delivered great trophy heads, especially in the south Texas brush country. Antler quality varies widely from season to season in this semi-arid landscape, but in 1992, for example, Texas produced no fewer than thirteen whitetail bucks attaining the Boone and Crockett minimum scores for record-book entry. Considering that these brutes came out of an area comprising no more than one fifth of the state's total rural acreage, there may be no other place in North America offering Texas's concentrated combination of sheer numbers of bucks plus antler size. The state's production of great herds actually seems to be increasing, after an apparent decline during the 1970s, probably because of a new and enlightened emphasis on management of ranch lands for big-antlered whitetails.

To the north, Wisconsin, Minnesota, and Michigan still dominate the American record books, but Montana, especially Flathead County, seems to be furnishing more big heads these days. South Dakota, around Rapid City, and Wyoming near Sundance, are overlooked venues for the trophy hunter. So is northern Idaho's Snake River drainage. Whitetails in all these northern states west of Ohio are of the big northern woodland subspecies, *O. v. dakotensis*, as are the giants of western Canada. *Dakotensis* bucks can dress out three hundred pounds or more, and such a deer makes even big antlers look small. Farther east, from upstate New York through Maine to New Brunswick, is found the other big northern whitetail subspecies, *O. v. borealis;* I have personally seen a New Hampshire buck on reliable scales weighing 324 pounds dressed. The record books hold a scattering of enormous racks from *borealis* country, but seemingly not as many, per capita, as from *dakotensis* range, even though the animals are of similar body size.

In the deep south, Virginia (the state for which the whitetail deer was originally named) towers over its neighbors in trophy production, with the seaboard area leading the way. Georgia is a solid producer, and Alabama is the comer on the Gulf Coast.

The reader may be interested to learn that this entire geography section of *Hunting Trophy Deer* needed a total rewrite for this edition because so much has changed, so rapidly, during the last two decades.

This points out the fact that prime trophy areas come and go. An area may turn hot for five or ten years and then the production tapers off, while some new trophy area is discovered somewhere else. This phenomenon results from the maturation of a "new" whitetail herd. The major bucks in a region recently restocked will attain trophy age and the word will get out. Hunters flock in, but, for the most part, they have not the skills to take many of the older bucks. Instead, they shoot the two and a half and three and a half year olds, never allowing replacements to reach maturity. Abruptly, the production of real trophy heads diminishes, although there may be plenty of deer, even an overpopulation, in the area. Again, it's not a matter of overharvesting the old bucks, but of harvesting the wrong kinds of bucks. This process may be slowed down where the herds live on private property and some sort of management can be practiced because the harvest can be carefully controlled. In some states, however, the main effort of the professional game managers on public lands must be to deliver *quantity*, rather than quality, and trophy hunting is the epitome of quality hunting for quality game. Sadly, in many states the biologists know exactly how to manage the herds for quality, but the politics of the game commissions are such that they cannot do it, at least not until the sportsmen of those states demand it.

It's easy to blame the wildlife department, but the reality is simply that the blame lies squarely on the shoulders of the citizens who are shouting the loudest. More of this in the chapter on management.

Although I have pinpointed certain states known to be capable of producing trophy whitetails, it must be remembered that an outstanding buck may turn up in nearly any state. Actually, the 1991 edition of the Boone and Crockett Club record listings notes thirty-eight states, seven Canadian provinces, and one Mexican state as having originated record typical or nontypical racks. Of the remaining ten states which have this species (only Alaska and Hawaii do not), some have surely produced record-*class* heads, if no record-*book* trophies, and a few may have produced true records which have never been officially measured for the book. I know of not fewer than twenty heads which would easily make the B&C minimum score, nailed up in barns or hanging in offices, private homes, service stations, or greasy-spoon restaurants in south Texas, which have not and will never be entered in the Boone and Crockett competitions. Their owners either don't know about the record book, or don't care, and this must also be true in many other regions of the United States.

Within every big-buck state there are vast areas where there are no big bucks, of course, and even in the big-buck regions of these states, the distribution of major trophy bucks will always be extremely spotty. In the very best trophy-deer counties of south Texas, for example, are many ranches (all hunting here is on private land) which have been so badly managed that you have no more chance for a real trophy buck there than you do in New Mexico, which has never produced a record head. The adjacent ranch, however—with identical genetics, terrain, and forage—can be a fine spot for a super buck. So the serious trophy hunter must do a lot of research to place himself on exactly the right piece of ground, ground that is producing the big fellows *now* and not during the last decade, even after he has located the most promising general areas in his chosen state.

This research will involve contacting anybody and everybody you think may be of help. County chambers of commerce may be a source of information, as are the outdoors editors of local newspapers. So are the information offices of the various state game departments, local game wardens, taxidermists, other hunters, landowners, rural mail carriers, and REA linemen, among others.

Taxidermists located in fairly large cities are particularly good sources, since the nature of their business allows them to see trophy heads from a fairly wide region. Small-town taxidermists may get mostly local trade and, while they may have detailed knowledge of their immediate vicinity, chances are they won't have the statewide picture that their metropolitan competitors do. Both are useful, at various stages of the search.

Be warned that many people, even those who live on the land and see many deer, may not know what a really big whitetail buck looks like. They'll tell you that there's a hell of a buck living in Smith's woodlot and crossing the crick near the bend in the road,

Whether the big bucks deliberately choose the most protective cover or the cover happens to make bucks big is a question that will never be answered, but there's no doubt that's where they'll be . . . in the roughest places you can find. *(Photo by Jerry Smith)*

but the deer will merely be big according to *their* standards, or perhaps big of body but not of antler. It pays to do a little subtle and courteous cross-examination to satisfy yourself that you and your informant mean the same things by "big buck." Sometimes photographs are extremely useful in this process.

Landowners will often welcome a hunter who can convince them that he's interested only in trophy bucks and will shoot nothing else, whereas they may not permit the run-of-the-mill hunter on their property. They recognize that a real trophy hunter cannot, by definition, be a trigger-happy, bloodthirsty lout; trophy hunting carries about it an aura of superior skills, ethics, and restraint, and quite rightly so.

Having located the specific grounds upon which you are convinced you have some sort of chance to see an older buck, you still have a lot of scouting and planning to do. My favorite time to explore a new hunting area is a few weeks after the close of the hunting season, and before the bucks begin to drop their antlers.

Deep snows make this impossible in many states, of course, unless the hunter is willing to do his scouting on skis or snowshoes. Snowmobiles, at this time of the year, should be kept strictly out of the deer woods; the animals simply don't have the energy reserves, during the depths of winter, to survive being harassed by a noisy machine.

In my own exploring, of course I'm keeping an eye out for a glimpse of antlers, as well as for tracks, old breeding rubs, and browse marks, but my principal effort is to learn the lay of the land itself. I try to get a feel for how the contours flow into one another, where the prime cover is (thickets, swamps, etc.), and how the major game trails connect with all features of the terrain. I look particularly for out-of-the-way pockets of cover, places it's easier to go around than through, spots far from vehicle access. Most of all, I'm looking for the roughest, most remote, hardest-to-hunt spots I can find, the places where a hunter has to get up earliest, walk the farthest, and work the hardest just to reach, places in which the very idea of trying to get a dead deer out curls my hair! Chances are, these are the most undisturbed pockets in the county, for the simple reason that ordinary hunters either don't know what they hold, or won't exert that much effort. What they hold, of course, are the biggest buck deer in the vicinity. They're big because they've had time to grow to maturity there, and that's because these strongholds of theirs are just too difficult to hunt.

One of the most intriguing questions about trophy whitetails which has ever occurred to me—and which I cannot answer—is this: are the big bucks to be found in these inaccessible pockets because they're smart enough to select such places, or because of the accident of birth? We know whitetails never travel very far from the spot on which they're born. Is it possible that the big ones seem to hang out in the tough coverts merely because they were born nearby and the habitat has protected them well enough to allow them to grow up? Did the buck choose the cover or did the cover make the buck big? I don't suppose we'll ever know the answer.

Whatever the answer may be, it's a cinch that the biggest bucks *are* to be found in the most remote and difficult areas, as a rule. I can almost pinpoint the most promising spots on a topographic map of an area, or even more easily on an aerial photograph, provided

I'm familiar enough with the general characteristics of the terrain and vegetation to interpret what the maps show me. With practice, I think any experienced hunter can save himself a lot of time and random walking in a new area by doing the same thing. U.S. Soil Conservation Service offices in most county seats can help you find sources of topos and aerial photos of any area of interest.

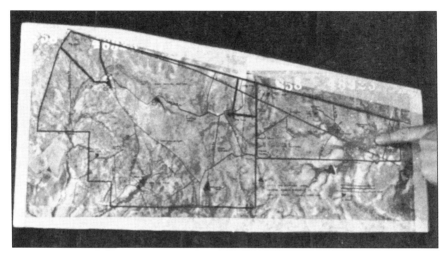

When a region with the big-buck requirements is found, topographical maps and aerial photographs like this one save a lot of exploring by pinpointing the thickest, most remote, hardest-to-hunt spots in the area.

Once I've made my basic survey of the area, I try to stay out of it—and hope others will—until about September. By then, most bucks will have stripped the velvet from their new antlers and left the rubs for me to see. There is a theory that the bigger the sapling rubbed, the bigger the buck which rubbed it. I can't verify this as an absolute fact, but I suspect that it holds pretty well true as a general rule. Then, of course, in September I should be able to see tracks and other signs to help me shape the specific tactics I'll use on and after opening day. I look for the relative abundance of known favorite whitetail foods and try to spot places with a lot of certain particular goodies, such as acorns or mushrooms.

I also plan certain still-hunting routes, with the prevailing winds of the hunting season in mind and with morning and afternoon sun angles figured in advance. I note landmarks, visibilities, and distances. Throughout this process, I'm still not looking specifically for bucks. I've long since decided where I expect to find the bucks, and I'm developing strategies and approaches now. Hunting seasons are all too short for the trophy hunter, even in states where they're most generous, and the more groundwork I can accomplish before the season opens, the more time I'll have for the dead-serious hunting effort during the legal shooting days.

It will be seen from this description that hunting a trophy whitetail can be, probably *must* be for success, a year-round activity. Most of the hunting is done in the hunter's mind and not with his feet and eyes. It begins almost as soon as one season is finished, and continues through the changing seasons, planning, inquiring, exploring, and more planning, until the next season closes or until the buck is hanging on the meatpole. Most of the case-hardened trophy hunters I know never stop talking, thinking, dreaming, reading, looking, breathing, and plotting *big antlers*. I know of no other game animal which can so possess and consume an otherwise rational and civilized human being!

The title of this chapter suggested not only the answer to *where* to kill a trophy buck, but also *when* to do it. The when part will not require many words. The best time to go deer hunting is when you can go, when the season is open. I spend literally every minute available to me in the field during the open season and in Texas that usually averages more than twenty days each year. It isn't enough, but it's the best I can do and still manage to make a living. One of the most successful hunters I've ever known was a retired gentleman who disappeared into his deer camp about a week before opening day each year and never went home until the season closed, about seven weeks later. If his family wanted to wish him a good Thanksgiving, a Merry Christmas, or a Happy New Year, they knew where they could find him. Selfish? Sure, but that's what the really big bucks can do to a man, and he harvested more than his share, over the years. And he truly loved the deer, more than almost any other man I've known; they seemed to be the hingepin of his whole life.

If the season in your state is open during the rut, or any part of it, that is the best time, by a mile, to be in the woods. There is no contest; you will never have better odds on a trophy whitetail than when his mind is preoccupied with sex. I have devoted the next entire chapter to that all-important subject.

Although most big racks seem to come from Canada or the midwest these days, this record-book rack (unscored, but obviously above the 170-point minimum) was taken in Old Mexico. *(Photo courtesy of Robert Rogers)*

8 The All-Important Rut

I am constantly amazed at the number of fairly experienced hunters who really do not understand the biological mechanics of whitetail reproduction, men who don't know the difference between a rub and a scrape. Without such basic knowledge, a hunter's chances of catching up with a trophy buck range somewhere between none . . . and none *whatsoever!*

I have described the annual antler-growing-and-shedding cycle of the whitetail, controlled as it is by levels of the male sex hormone. Once his antlers are clean and polished in early autumn, the buck is capable of breeding. At about the same time, he begins to feel a restlessness and a sudden resentment toward the other bucks in whose company he has spent the summer. As the season progresses, he becomes downright belligerent, and settles any small differences of opinion as to his proper place in the dominance rankings with his gleaming new weapons. Note that these fights have nothing to do with any particular doe; they're purely for the purpose of establishing status for the exhausting days which are to come.

Finally, the dominant bucks stake out breeding territories, usually much smaller than their own normal residential territories (which are not defended among the bucks). These breeding territories are marked around their boundaries with secretions from several glands, including the preorbital and forehead glands, and probably saliva and the secretion of the interdigital glands as well. This secretion is deposited on the foliage and stems of various bushes, many of which are also thrashed soundly by the proprietor of the territory with his antlers.

Rubbing is actually a form of scent-marking, using the glandular skin of the forehead. The tree will be scarred, severely damaged, or possibly even killed—depending on the buck's mood—but the physical damage is always less important than scent deposition. *(Photo by Mike Biggs)*

These so-called "breeding rubs" are entirely different in appearance from those made a couple of months earlier in the process of polishing the antlers. Breeding rubs are much more savage, with the bushes or saplings severely damaged and sometimes killed. Branches are broken and tossed away, and every part of the shrub scarred. I have seen small trees, as large as 4 inches or more in diameter, actually killed by girdling when a buck selected them for rubbing targets. The ground at the base of one of these rubs is usually torn and pawed, and sometimes the buck kneels and gores the soil, leaving the marks of his antler tines and knees. Of course, a breeding rub will also be much fresher during hunting season than the antler-cleaning rubs.

The buck does not necessarily stake out his entire breeding territory with rubs, but he often hooks or strikes random small bushes in passing, without pausing to really work them over seriously. A breeding territory can sometimes be identified merely by several, or even dozens of, minor rubs along with a few major ones within a 100-yard radius. Since he'll make one or two new ones each

This is the most spectacular rub I have ever seen—a 6-inch-thick cedar tree actually killed by girdling the bark! Nearby were a fresh scrape, many smaller rubs, and the signs of an epic buck fight.

A good buck makes his scrape, a pawed-out spot in the earth in which he will "rub-urinate" (depositing tarsal-gland secretions), defecate, and even ejaculate. This is his notice to the world that he is a hell of a fellow— and available. *(Photo by Mike Biggs)*

Scrapes are frequently located around isolated shrubs or trees in clearings, near trails, and invariably beneath low-hanging twigs that the buck licks, nibbles, and batters with his antlers, as shown here. *(Photo by Mike Biggs)*

day during the peak of the rutting time, a noticeable variation in freshness will be evident.

Somewhere in his territory, the dominant buck makes one or more *scrapes.* A scrape is a pawed-out spot in the soil, perhaps a couple of feet long by 15 inches wide (sizes vary considerably), almost always located on a trail in a clearing, and invariably located so that twigs and foliage from a shrub or tree overhang it. The maker urinates in his scrape, in such a posture that the urine runs down over his tarsal glands and carries their secretion to the ground. He paws like a mad bull, until the scrape is muddy and smelly, and may even ejaculate in it. In the process, he will mesh his antlers with the aforementioned overhanging branches and twist and batter them, and he also nibbles the leaves and twigtips. No one knows the significance of these actions, but they're never omitted.

Speaking of knowing things, I must confess that when I wrote this book, I knew all there was to know about scrapes. Now, with twenty more hunting seasons under my belt and a lot more gray hairs under my hat, I find that my body of ignorance has grown apace, and that there is a lot about scrapes that puzzles me. I have read all the whitetail experts' explanations of primary scrapes, core scrapes, hub scrapes, satellite scrapes, secondary scrapes, and many more, and they have not enlightened me. The whitetail deer, like most mammals, apparently lives in a world of chemical communication that we feeble-nosed humans cannot begin even to comprehend. I believe that buck rubs, scrapes, licks, and probably much more are all about such communication, but with subtleties beyond any human understanding. Nothing about scrapes or their function in whitetail society is as simple and cut-and-dried as it has been made to sound, by me as well as other writers, lecturers, videographers, seminar-givers, etc. Therefore, everything said about scrapes herein is to be regarded as conditional, based on my own best observations and those of reputable contributors to whitetail literature. What follows immediately is the simplest practical interpretation of what scrapes are and do, from the hunter's viewpoint.

This scrape of his is the dominant buck's sign before all the deer world that he is standing at stud for all comers. He sticks pretty close to the scrape, often refreshing it or making a new one nearby, at all times during the rut when he is not actually occupied with a doe in heat.

A doe in heat, finding an active scrape, deposits her own urinary sign if the buck is not around. When he returns to check the scrape and detects her scent, he takes her tracks, trailing with his nose to the ground exactly like a hound. The tail position shown in this photo is characteristic of a trailing buck. *(Photo by W. A. Maltsberger)*

Now comes the object of all this strenuous activity, a doe in her estrus period. Like the buck, she is incapable of breeding during most of the year, usually coming into her first annual heat in October or November, depending upon the latitude. The sign that she is in heat is the wetting and blackening of her hock glands, just as in the male. When the urge comes over her, *she goes looking for a buck.* It's important to note that it is *not* the other way around; the buck does not go looking for a receptive female. He sets his little sex trap—his scrape—and waits for her to take the bait. The odor of the scrape, which is evident even to the human nose, draws a hot doe like catnip draws a cat. If the proprietor happens not to be in the store when she visits the scrape, she leaves her own urinary calling card and wanders on. The buck, who checks his scrape often during the day or night, detects this invitation and takes up the trail. He trails the doe like a hound, nose to the ground and following every twist and turn of her wanderings. We do not know the exact source of the scent which permits the buck to follow one particular doe through areas with many deer tracks and trails. Whitetails have an interdigital (between-the-toes) gland which secretes a waxy substance and permits a doe to follow her fawn by scent, or vice versa. Perhaps the secretion is distinctive enough between deer to enable a trailing buck to follow a specific doe, or perhaps he detects the odor of his own scrape on her hooves. However he manages it, he is usually successful in locating her even when the trail is hours old.

When he finds her, he may simply walk up to her and copulate with her with no further preliminaries. I've seen this happen, with none of the coy dodging and lustful chasing which are supposed to be a part of the ritual. The chase, however, may be more common; in short, the buck chases the doe until she catches him. Every hunter has probably seen this activity, although few have witnessed actual mating. One reason for this is the fact that copulation is very brief, rarely lasting more than twenty seconds.

If a doe does not conceive during her estrus period, she will cycle out of heat about twenty-five hours after she first becomes receptive to a buck. Conception ends the estrus period within a few hours. A buck may remain with a receptive doe for the entire period and service her repeatedly, but the odds are that he will never be away from his active scrape even as much as one full day at a time,

This buck has trailed the doe that left her scent in his scrape to where she is feeding with her female fawn (above). In the lower picture, the ritual chase is on. At this point, a nearby hunter may hear the buck making a series of remarkably piglike grunting sounds. *(Photos by W. A. Maltsberger)*

This buck, carried away by endocrinological overload in the rut, is actually mounting a plastic doe decoy! See notes on decoying whitetails in Chapter 14. *(Photo by Mike Biggs)*

a point of considerable importance to a hunter who would like to know where a given buck is likely to be.

If the doe doesn't conceive within twenty-four to twenty-six hours of entering her heat and cycles out of estrus, she will cycle back into heat 26 to 32 days later. If not bred then, she will have one more estrus about a month later, and that will be her last one for the season whether she conceives or not. Since not all does in an area are on exactly the same cycle, this suggests that rutting activity may be observed over a four-month period. This is true, but the peak period of rutting in any herd usually covers about two weeks or less, with another week leading up to the peak and one more tapering off, resulting in evident rutting over no more than a one-month period.

A very few female fawns which happened to be born unusually early in the spring may have an estrus period very late in the winter, the first of their lives, and these young does can create a brief, violent spurt of rutting activity among the bucks in a well-balanced herd about one month or so after the normal rut seems to have ended. These does will be so few, and competition for them among the males will be so intense, that it may seem to an observer that the "rut" was very late, but this is a false impression.

In herds with a bad sex ratio, the available bucks may not be able to get around to all the does as soon as they become receptive, and there will be little competition. Under these circumstances, many younger bucks will have their opportunities to mate and the dominance order breaks down completely, permitting inferior sires who would not be allowed to pass on their characteristics in a balanced herd to breed. A single buck is capable of servicing as many as thirty does during the entire breeding season. A doe, by the way, may also accept the attentions of two or more bucks during her estrus.

Now let's go back and review this process from the point of view of the hunter. A dominant buck stakes out a breeding territory and makes a scrape (sometimes several) to which the receptive does are attracted. The buck guards his territory jealously, and will not permit another breeding male to enter it. A hot doe seeks out the scrape and either encounters the proprietor or leaves her sign and he trails her. These points are important: a territorialized (dominant) buck does not roam at random in search of does; they come to him.

However, once on the trail of a hot doe, he will follow her anywhere, even into the breeding territory of another dominant buck.

I believe that all my observations over thirty-five years of watching and hunting whitetails point to a theory which is exactly opposite of most hunters' ideas about breeding fights between bucks. It is that *whitetails rarely, or never, fight over does*, although it often appears that a nearby doe may be the object of a battle. Instead, I believe that these fights are *territorial*, and occur only when one dominant buck is led into the breeding territory of another dominant buck, usually by a seductive female. Especially for the hunter who prefers to rattle antlers, the difference is crucial.

In fairness, I know a few whitetail experts whose opinions I profoundly respect who disagree with all this. One is a Texan named Al Brothers, a professional wildlife biologist and successful ranch manager who wrote, with fellow biologist Murphy Ray, a book entitled *Producing Quality Whitetails*. This book has become the bible of Texas hunters and landowners who care about quality hunting, and it has broad applications in many other states. It is revolutionary in a way, and deserves far broader circulation than it has received. In it, Brothers reports having seen more than one buck use the same scrape, which knocks my theory into a cocked hat! And, believe me, I've known Al Brothers for years, and if he says he saw it, it happened.

However, he does not say whether, in his opinion, each of the bucks involved was a dominant male. It seems to me possible that another buck might become excited about a scrape if he discovered it in the owner's absence, especially if a hot doe had visited it in the meantime, and freshened it. In personal conversation, Brothers has told me that he has seen more than one buck at a scrape at the same time, and there was an obvious pecking order followed as the animals used the scrape.

I must add that Brothers's property has an abnormally high ratio of bucks to does (due to expert management of the harvest), in which there are actually *more* breeding bucks than females. Since the typical ratio even in a protected herd seldom rises above one buck for every two and a half does, it may be that rutting behavior is somewhat distorted where the ratio is as high as one and a half bucks for every one doe.

In the first edition of *Hunting Trophy Deer*, I commented that I had never seen anything like this. Well, now I have, more than once, and Al Brothers, as usual, was correct. I cannot fit such an observation into my theory of breeding territoriality, but every buck fight I've seen (with one possible exception) appeared to be associated with territory rather than with the favors of any specific doe. Often, no doe was anywhere near the combatants. Furthermore, I've often seen from two to as many as five bucks following the same hot doe at the same time, without a fight developing, and theorize that this situation can be explained by the fact that the swinging group happened not to be within the breeding territory of any one of the males.

I have seen a big buck offer threat displays to lesser bucks in the presence of a doe in estrus, but the latter always yielded without actually locking horns. Perhaps the controversy merely means that we have not yet learned to look inside a wild animal's mind and to sort out his various motivations and reactions. Perhaps one buck reacts somewhat differently from his fellows, or bucks in one herd do things one way while a different population, in another part of the range or another state, do the same things a little differently. I know that every time I begin to think that I have whitetails all figured out, one of them does something to make a complete fool of me!

The timing of the rut varies quite a bit in different parts of the whitetail range, and even in different regions of the same state. What we call "the rut," incidentally, should be defined as that period during which the greatest number of does within a herd are in or near estrus. As outlined, all the bucks are in breeding condition continuously from the time they peel the velvet from their antlers until they shed them.

Several factors seem to control the rut's onset, including the length of daylight periods, physical condition, and weather. Latitude has some effect, with the more northerly herds rutting earlier as a rule, but there are exceptions to this. Quite possibly, the rut's timing within a specific population has simply become traditional, if we can use that word about animal behavior, meaning that a herd ruts at a given time mostly because their ancestors did it then. The timing of the rut also varies slightly from year to year, although I doubt that the variation is as great as local hunters may believe. In the region in which I do most of my deer hunting, we can count on the

Notice the prominence of this breeding buck's tarsal glands, a sure sign that the peak of the rut is upon him. Notice also the black streaking from the glands down to his rear hooves, caused by his urination over them in his scrape. The swollen neck and prominent scrotum are additional signs of his breeding condition. *(Photo by Walter Elling)*

mating season being in full swing by December 15 every year, although the highly visible parts of the activity may not be noticed until a week or so later. Local landowners and hunters often comment that the rut didn't begin until New Year's Day, but every research program by Texas biologists, carried out in January, has revealed nearly 100 percent of the does with fetuses about one month old.

The importance of the timing of the rut has to do with its coincidence with the local open hunting season. If the season fails to take in at least a part of the rut's peak, hunters' odds on a trophygrade buck are seriously reduced. The reason is that this two- or three-week period is the one and only time of the year in which the big, dominant males are likely to be just a trifle less cautious. They are much more active during this period, at all hours of the day and night, and much more liable to show themselves away from impenetrable cover during legal hunting hours. If a really mature, trophy whitetail is ever in his whole life going to do something *dumb*, it's most likely to be when he has his mind on a receptive female.

And the brutal truth is that no matter how skilled the hunter, the majority of all really big bucks are taken because they made a mistake, and not because they couldn't cope with the hunter's cunning. In fact, the highest art of the whitetail hunter is simply placing himself in a position to take advantage of a big buck's mistake when and if it occurs. You can write that down and say I said it. The concept will be expanded upon in subsequent chapters.

Since the outset of the rut must dictate a fairly radical revision in the hunter's tactics, we must be able to determine when it happens, and there are many signs. Obviously, if bucks are seen scraping, rubbing, trailing, or chasing does, or in close company with a single doe, there can be no doubt. But in many herds, it's not all that easy to lay eyes on a buck, much less watch his actions, and in such areas the does can give us some clues. If most of the does seen are still followed by their fawns of the year, chances are they are not yet close to estrus, although these family units sometimes reassemble after the mother has conceived and cycled out of heat. The tufts of long hair which delineate the tarsal glands on the insides of the does' hocks appear pure white until the rut nears, at which time they turn from brown to almost black. After conception, or between estrus periods, this tarry appearance slowly bleaches out, leaving only a brownish tinge.

If sightings of actual deer of either sex are not definitive, rubs are the best indications of a rut in progress. An abundance of fresh, vicious rubs is a sure sign, and sometimes the incidence of rubs seems to double or triple almost overnight when the rut kicks off in earnest. Rubs are not difficult to see, but you have to look specifically for them; if you're looking for deer, you'll notice few of the rubs which are in sight. Certain areas and certain species of shrubs are more attractive to bucks aching to make a rub, and it pays to learn about them so that, when you find yourself in a promising area, you can shift your visual gears and be alert to fresh rubs. Almost everywhere in the whitetail range, the bucks will choose saplings and bushes with resinous sap above all other available kinds. On my east Texas ranch, the forest is mostly of hardwoods, post oaks and hickories, with a very, very few loblolly pine trees. The bucks in the area like the young pines around these few big trees so well that they invariably kill every pine sapling before it reaches a trunk diameter of 2 inches. The parent trees themselves would not exist if they hadn't grown there before the restocked whitetail herd became large and old enough to have plenty of breeding bucks. Pines, hemlocks, cedars, and other conifers are favorite rubbing targets everywhere they may be available. Rubs are quite often concentrated along game paths and around the margins of semi-brushy clearings, where young trees are pioneering the open land. Whenever I find myself in such an area where specimens of favored rubbing species exist, I take time out from my hunting to look specifically for rubs, and I've killed several good bucks because I did so.

Finally, people whose business takes them into the woods—farmers, foresters, game wardens, and such—can usually be of help in knowing when or whether the rut has begun locally. Even if they aren't hunters, their reports of seeing bucks in company with does or actually in pursuit of them are all you have to hear. Perhaps the best indicator of when the rut will kick off in your neck of the woods is when it began last year and the years before that. Variations do occur, but in most seasons the mating time falls within a fairly restricted period. In the absence of fresh intelligence to the contrary, as above, knowledge of the history of the local rut is your best guide in planning hunting time.

"The rut" is much more conspicuous in some seasons and areas than in others. I've seen what I call a "slow rut" in regions with a very high buck ratio when the does' coming into heat seemed to be spaced out rather than concentrated within a few weeks. When this happens, a doe enters her estrus, almost immediately acquires masculine companionship, conceives, and passes out of heat within a few hours. The result is that the hunter may see none of the frenetic, helter-skelter breeding activity that we think of as a rut, although the biological mechanics are all taken care of. I theorize that weather conditions may bring this slow rut about, but it's only speculation.

However it occurs, the rut is indeed all-important, especially to the trophy hunter. In normal years, it is the single most significant couple of weeks in the entire fifty-two, and trophy planning must take it into consideration, at least in those states where the hunting season overlaps the rut.

In case you believe that I may have overemphasized the rut's importance, let me tell you a story. Years ago, a friend and I arrived late at night at the headquarters of a vast ranch on Texas's Mexican border for a four-day hunt. The ranch was famed for light hunting pressure and enormous whitetail bucks, and we were privileged to have about 25,000 acres of prime trophy habitat to ourselves, as

I consider these the finest photographs ever secured of a pair of really big bucks in battle. In the first picture, each has begun to lunge forward. The fight then becomes a pushing match, rather than a fencing duel, with the stronger, heavier buck the winner most of the time even if he has slightly smaller antlers. *(Photos by Taft Morrow, Maltsberger Ranch, Cotulla, Texas)*

invited guests. The manager, an old friend who, unlike many rural residents, is not only an avid hunter but an excellent judge of trophy heads, greeted us with the information that hunting, even in this hunters' paradise, had been very poor through the first half of the six-week season.

"We just aren't seeing any bucks," he told us, "and especially no big ones. Even though I've been watching some real mossy-horns all summer and know right where they stay, I can't find them now. You'd almost think every buck on the place bigger than a forkhorn had crawled into a hole. The radio says there's a norther coming and it may help; if not, you boys have certainly got your work cut out for you. I wish you luck!"

Before midnight, a roaring cold front blustered through that country, dropping temperatures more than 30 degrees before morning. It was still blowing at sunrise, but the skies had cleared and the temperature was unusually low for this subtropical country.

Before one p.m. that afternoon, Don Ruthven and I had seen no fewer than thirty-one whitetail bucks (not counting spikes) on this ranch where bucks had been almost impossible to lay eyes on since the season opened! Every single one of these deer was either trailing a doe or in actual, all-out pursuit of one. That weather front had turned on the visible rut as though a switch had been thrown. The next morning I collected the finest whitetail buck of my career till then, and we saw, but could not kill, one of the three or four bucks I've ever seen in the wild which I'm certain would have made the Boone and Crockett records. There were bucks everywhere we looked, many of them heavy-antlered brutes in the prime of their maturity, acting like sex-obsessed schoolboys, scampering about in the open in broad daylight as though every ounce of caution had been forgotten.

That is the most dramatic example in all my hunting life of the difference the onset of the rut can make. It's true that this ranch was lightly hunted and held a large herd of whitetails with a good sex ratio and normal age-class distribution among the bucks. You may never see such a spectacle, and I may never see it again, but it's still worth a little thoughtful consideration by hunters who never really attached much importance to "the rut."

9 When and Weather

That weather conditions can be all-powerful in a trophy hunter's luck is admirably illustrated by that last anecdote in the previous chapter, but there seems to be quite a bit of controversy about exactly how. Modern man spends most of his life in central-heated, air-conditioned, insulated buildings and vehicles, and has the technology to keep an astronaut comfortably dressed in outer space. To many people, weather is whatever a grinning TV weather gal says it is. To a deer, weather is reality, often bitter, which literally threatens his life at times and always controls his life to a degree we humans have thankfully forgotten. That's a useful thought to file away in the back of your hunter's mind and remember when plotting strategies, particularly as a part of deciding when and how to hunt.

To begin with, I'm more convinced with every passing season of watching deer in the field that they like any kind of weather we humans like, and for the same reasons. And that weather which we find depressing and uncomfortable has exactly the same effect on whitetail and muley spirits. They may behave differently, in order to stay alive, but their reactions are basically the same as ours. To illustrate, think back over the last few years, remembering those bright, still, crisp days which are all too rare during the hunting season, the days when it was a joy to be afield. I suspect that you will recall that those were some of your most productive hunting days, at least in terms of deer sightings and signs of movement, even if you didn't collect a buck. By contrast, I recall 1976, the dreariest, wettest, coldest deer season within my memory in Texas. Day after day after day we fought deep, sloppy mud, sopping-wet boots and clothes, continual downpours, and misty, gray days when visibility was better suited to duck hunting than to deer hunting. Rifle stocks warped and changed zero, scopes fogged, and barrels rusted. Four-wheel-drive hunting cars were constantly bogged to the frame, and many hunters were unable to get close to their leased hunting grounds until the last week of the season. Taxidermists' records are a good and largely overlooked source of data on such matters, and those of the 1976 season told the story; most taxidermists received fewer than half the usual number of heads for mounting. Even though I hunted hard and well, in excellent country, rain or shine, I saw very few deer and even fewer bucks. In terrain where we expect to see about fifteen deer and three or four bucks per hunter each hunting day, we sometimes went for weeks without spotting antlers. The deer didn't like the weather any better than we did, and they simply lay low.

I've shot a few good bucks in chilly, damp, misty weather, but in looking back over my hunting notes (which include temperature, cloud cover, wind conditions, etc.) I find that my recollection is not incorrect that by far the majority of the bucks I'm proud of have fallen on bright, sunny days. I recently performed an informal survey among hunting friends of mine and discovered that they remember the same thing: with few exceptions, most of their bucks and their best bucks have fallen on clear days (see page 106 for more information.)

I hypothesize that careful, scientific observations would probably reveal that whitetail movement is inversely proportional to the percentage of the sky covered with clouds. I know this is not the accepted hunter's theory, but I haven't shot some of the old bucks I have by accepting orthodox thinking.

There is, of course, some scientific basis for this idea, in that clear skies usually—not always—accompany a high barometer . . . which brings me to the next unorthodox theory.

I believe that most wild creatures are sensitive to barometric matters in ways that we humans have long since lost, assuming we ever had them. Briefly, I know that whitetails tend to move more when the barometer is moving, in either direction, than when it is steady, and that they do not like to move at all when it is *low* and steady. They are apparently aware of impending weather fronts long before we can sense a change in the making, so much so that careful

Hunting in heavy fog is futile, but a light, early-morning fog can be very productive. If the fog promises to burn off, it's wise to be in the field when it does.

observation of the deer can actually help in making firsthand weather predictions.

Throughout my boyhood I hunted whitetails on the flat, live-oak-studded coastal prairies of Texas, on a 3,500-acre ranch which was mostly open woods except for a dense yaupon thicket which bounded a creek through the middle of the pasture. This thicket was about the only real protection the deer had from inclement weather, and we would observe them making a beeline toward the thicket before we got a cold, wet, windy front, and leaving it well before the weather cleared behind the front. They were, by the way, much more reliable than the weather forecasters of that day, back in the 1940s.

Regardless of weather factors, whitetails tend to be crepuscular (active at twilight) or nocturnal. Heavy hunting pressure magnifies this tendency.

Deer also understand that their movements will be hampered during such bitter weather, and they tend to feed voraciously on the day before frontal passage, while the barometer is dropping steadily. Then they'll hole up until the weather clears. If the front stalls and the rainy spell is prolonged, it pays to be in the woods when the first ray of the sun breaks through at the end of the period; chances are that every animal on four feet will be instantly out and about (including domestic livestock) within minutes.

Incidentally, hunters in my part of the world place great store in domestic livestock as indicators of what deer are doing, saying that if the cattle are lying down in the fields, the whitetails will be doing the same, and that when one species gets up, stretches, and begins to feed, so will the other. The correlation is not perfect, in my experience, but it's good enough (perhaps 75 percent accurate) to base hunting tactics for the day on most of the time.

Not much whitetail habitat is arid in nature, but some parts of the Texas, New Mexico, and great plains and western states deer country is, and there's a rule that I find as good as gold for these areas: whenever a shower falls after a prolonged period of dry

Deer sense barometric trends before meteorologists can and tend to move most freely on a rising or falling barometer, less freely on a steady-high glass, and least on a steady-low one. They frequently forage heavily just before a weather front passes, then lie low until the skies clear behind the front. *(Photo by Mike Biggs)*

weather, everything wearing deer hair will be on the move as soon as the rain ceases, for at least a couple of hours, regardless of other weather factors.

I know hunters who are so convinced that wind puts deer down and keeps them inactive that they'll hardly go out in windy weather. I think this depends upon the prevailing weather in the individual region under discussion. In some areas wind is a routine condition, and still days are the exception. In such country, the deer are accustomed to wind, whether they *like* it or not, and seem to keep pretty much on schedule regardless of wind. In south Texas and some other areas I've hunted, I particularly like to hunt with a strong, fresh, gusty norther blowing, provided the sky has cleared and it's cold. Especially during the rut, such conditions seem to stimulate every buck in the pasture to be about his business. Furthermore, the strong wind makes still-hunting productive by covering the hunter's sounds and partly camouflaging his more obvious movements amid the whipping shrubbery and underbrush and the waving grasses.

The kind of wind whitetails *don't* like is the wind from an unusual direction (for that season), the gusty, variable, treacherous breezes which signal unsettled weather. It may be that in regions where wintertime winds are not a regular thing (if there are any such regions) the deer may be made nervous by a strong wind, but I welcome them if I'm in big-buck country. Dead-calm evenings are exciting and very often productive of deer sightings, especially if cold and clear, but I haven't shot many trophy-grade bucks on such occasions.

During the interval since this book was new, I have carried out a systematic, computerized study of the responses of whitetails to multiple weather parameters, based on more than nine thousand individual sightings over sixteen hunting seasons. Some of the computer's findings have been complete surprises (example: I'd have bet that deer move best under clear skies, but the database says they don't give a damn about cloud cover), whereas others have jibed with my impressions from years of observation. All these records have been accumulated during open season (November, December, January) on one ranch, near Laredo, Texas, on the Mexican border. It may be assumed that the adaptable whitetail's responses may vary somewhat in different latitudes and climates, but differences are likely to be in degree rather than in kind. For quick reference, my study will be identified throughout this book as the Los Cuernos database.

With regard to wind, the sensitive database reveals that Los Cuernos deer pay no attention to wind direction and little to wind velocity alone . . . as long as velocity remains at or below the twenty-to-twenty-five-miles-per-hour range. Gusts above that velocity tend to inhibit whitetail activity seriously.

Temperature is one point on which I agree with the orthodox thinking, which is the colder, the better. Deer do tend to move about more when it's really cold, apparently to generate body heat just as we do. If, however, the bitter cold goes along with a strong wind and precipitation, they may hole up in gullies and draws which offer

Cold, crisp, bright weather is always good deer-hunting weather, but I disagree with the theory that wind hampers the whitetail hunter. I prefer a steady, even gusty, wind to near-calm conditions when the wind direction is usually treacherous. *(Photo by W. A. Maltsberger)*

protection from the elements. In general, I like to hunt the low country in such weather, and switch to the ridges and slopes when the weather conditions improve.

I have noted, however, a few occasions when the weather was abnormally cold for the latitude but there seemed to be almost no whitetail activity, even though all other factors seemed right. I have no explanation for such observations, other than the fact that every rule concerning whitetail deer has its exceptions, and I wonder whether any of my fellow hunters in the northern states have seen the same thing among deer herds accustomed to persistent subzero temperatures. I have hunted in New Hampshire, but do not recall noting this phenomenon.

On the other hand, whitetails in southern states may move very freely on very warm days under stable weather conditions. Again, where the deer are accustomed to it, heat seems not to inhibit activity. In fact, the single biggest buck which has fallen to my gun in fifty-five years of hunting was slain while I was wearing a short-sleeved shirt and sweating a bit.

The Los Cuernos database informs us that although it's true that deer like cool weather better than hot, it isn't all that simple. It isn't merely a case of the colder, the better. Whitetail activity does not show a graduated response to the thermometer—with more movement in the forties than in the fifties, even more in the thirties, etc. There seems to be a rather hard cutoff temperature, above which deer movement is sharply restricted, and below which other factors entirely control the volume of movement. In south Texas, that cut-off point is around seventy degrees Fahrenheit, but south Texas has a relatively hot, dry climate. In other areas—where it may never get as warm as seventy degrees during deer season—it seems logical that similar observations would show the same pattern, but with a lower cutoff point. On your hunting grounds, the deer may tend to lie down when the temperature hits fifty degrees or maybe even forty, instead of seventy.

My database has also postulated another, less defined activity cutoff point on the low end of the temperature spectrum. On the Tex-Mex border, deer commonly refuse to move at all in abnormally low temperatures—which, down there, is between ten and twenty degrees. Even on low-twenties mornings with calm winds, we frequently see little movement until later in the day, after the sun has warmed the air a little.

Although not strictly a climatic factor, the moon must be regarded as important to the deer hunter. I've seen scientific correlations which tended to show that the phase of the moon has nothing to do with whitetail activity if all other things are the same. Which convinces me that either deer haven't seen the same charts or all other things are never the same. I will go to my grave unshakably convinced that exactly the opposite is true, and that moon phase is critical to a hunter's plans. There are two schools of thought on the moon. The first is that deer tend to be active whenever the moon is up, even when this occurs during the daytime, and to lie down when it sets, either day or night. I've never been able to satisfy myself that this is true.

The other theory is that whitetails are wont to utilize the light shed by a bright moon for nocturnal feeding which reduces their level of activity during the hunting hours next day. This I believe with all my heart and a sheaf of notes made over the years from my own observations. Dark nights, whether from a new moon or from one which sets early in the evening or rises just before dawn, make the best hunting days, and the more hours of light from a half-moon or bigger during a given night, the less whitetail activity is likely next day. A heavy cloud cover which makes the night dark even when the moon is full seems to be just as good for hunting next day as a clear night with no moon at all. Particularly under heavy hunting pressure, deer tend to become more and more nocturnal, but cannot forage as effectively. An almanac which lists phases of the moon and the hours of rising and setting can be, therefore, a valuable tool in planning the season's hunts.

Any discussion of the importance of the moon inevitably brings up questions about the Solunar Tables (charts published in book form, in *Field & Stream* magazine, and in many local newspapers), which purport to list major and minor activity periods for wildlife. Originated by outdoors writer John Alden Knight, the tables have an impressive following among experienced hunters and fishermen, and are said to be used by birdwatchers, scuba divers, and others interested in predicting wildlife movements. I've kept fairly careful notes on what the Solunar Tables say versus my observations

relative to whitetail deer for about four years, and I can only say
that the jury is still out. There are some striking correlations, and
some equally striking failures (my biggest trophy whitetail appeared
during an "off" period on the tables). Yet I keep thinking—perhaps
hoping—that I do see at least a little useful information for the deer
hunter there. It would be nice to have such a tool; we need all the
help we can get against trophy bucks. But it appears that, at best,
the Solunar Tables can give us a useful clue only when whitetail patterns are not otherwise disrupted by weather, the rut, heavy hunting
pressure, or something else not considered in the formula from
which the tables are computed. They do seem to work better in the
summer (on whitetails) than during hunting season, better on song-
birds and squirrels in my back yard than on deer, and better on fish
than on anything.

The Los Cuernos database clearly shows more sightings—of
bucks and does—on mornings after moon-dark nights when other
influences are about equal. Moon data is collected under only three
headings: *full, half,* and *dark.* The moon is thus rated *half* for half
of the month—one week waxing, one waning—and the database
reveals that some 85 percent of all the antlered bucks seen showed
up on days after the moon was *dark* or *half*—but those days represent only about 60 percent of the days on which we hunted.

Although the database is not set up to record such things, the
computer between my ears tells me that on days following bright,
moonlit nights, whitetail activity tends to be shifted to later in the
morning, and to peak during the midday hours of eleven to one.

Obviously, a careful consideration of all weather elements—
cloud cover, temperature, wind, moon, humidity, precipitation, and
barometer—will help any hunter plot his day's efforts, not only as to
when he concentrates his hunting but where and how. Big bucks
seem to react to all these matters in about the same way that all
other deer do, and, with few exceptions, mule deer are similar to
whitetails in their reactions. The choice of hunting in heavy cover
in the low spots as against in the upland areas, or hunting from a
tree stand or overlook as opposed to still-hunting, antler-rattling, or
whatever, cannot be intelligently made without taking note of all
weather elements. I strongly suggest that every hunter have at least
an accurate thermometer and barometer in his camp, and that he

maintain some kind of notes of every day's hunting, listing all pertinent weather data and deer sightings, along with where the deer were and what they were doing. It doesn't have to be a very elaborate journal, and over the years certain correlations which may be distinctive to the weather or the deer in his particular region will surely begin to emerge, revealing patterns the understanding of which will be of immense value to the trophy hunter and which cannot be gotten out of this or any other book on whitetails. They will, of course, be of equal value to the meat hunter, as well.

As time passes, any serious hunter begins to find himself automatically and unconsciously aware of the sum total of weather conditions at any moment while he's afield, and cranking these matters into his course of action on a minute-by-minute basis. When he does, he will have perhaps regained a tiny portion of the environmental awareness that his ancestors lost somewhere during the millennia, and it will make him a better hunter.

Playing with the Los Cuernos database has highlighted for me the potential error in planning a hunt solely on the basis of any single weather parameter. Predicting whitetail movement by looking at a thermometer or weather vane is likely to be futile. Many of these weather factors are tightly interconnected. Certain wind directions and velocities, for example, tend to be associated with certain barometric movements and/or sky conditions, and trying to pin down to which factor the deer are responding is a fool's errand; they're actually responding to the overall set of conditions. It makes more sense to think in such terms as, "Whitetails move more freely on a rising than a falling barometer when all else is equal." When all else—including such important influences as recent hunting pressure and the progress of the rut—is not equal, caution in assigning reasons for deer reactions is strongly recommended. Even with a tool like the database, I can fool myself by asking the wrong questions. Weather is an important part, but by no means all, of the equation.

10 Reading Sign

Once I had the pleasure of spending a couple of weeks in the jungles of southern Tamaulipas, Mexico, hunting jaguar with an Indian named Jesus. Jesus was a *tigrero*, a professional jaguar hunter who was called in by ranchers when a jaguar began to make a nuisance of himself by killing livestock, especially colts. I've known some of the best of the hunting guides and African native trackers, but Jesus impressed me more than any of these by his ability to read sign. Not just tracks, but all kinds of sign. He could read the jungle, as we walked through it, more easily than you can read the billboards along the freeway. He knew not only which animals had passed this way, but why, what sex, what their business was, and whether they were successful. He knew these things not only about the mammals but about the birds and reptiles and some of the insects. He did not frowningly *study* the sign; he simply read it as you scan a newspaper.

The jaguar is one of the continent's most difficult trophy animals to collect without dogs, and Jesus never used dogs, yet he had killed as many *tigres*, I believe, as any human in North America, and perhaps more. Once, when my hostess in camp on the Rio Soto La Marina complained to Jesus that a whitetail deer was raiding her vegetable garden, he went and studied the sign, and then rigged up a sharpened stick in such a way that the buck—for it was a buck— would impale himself when he jumped over the fence. He got the animal on the first night! How long do you think it would take you to kill a whitetail without a weapon and with no dogs, pits, or snares, much less to get one specific animal, and a buck at that?

Jesus thought nothing of it. The sign had told him what the buck would do, and the rest was easy. I'm keeping an eye on Jesus just in case these science-fiction machines which can transfer the total contents of one man's mind to another should ever become reality; I'd love to be able to apply his sign-reading ability and knowledge of wild animals to my never-ending search for an even bigger whitetail or mule deer buck.

Until such machines are readily available and the bugs are worked out of them, however, you and I will have to do the best we can to read deer sign with eyes more trained to traffic lights than to the subtleties of the forest. We may never equal Jesus, but we may be surprised at how much we can learn about the ways of deer with a concerted application of such senses as we do have.

The first necessity is to stop believing that such talents as Jesus's are superhuman and beyond any hope of our attainment. The things he saw were there in plain sight for me to see as well, but I didn't know what to look for or the meaning of what I saw.

The things we need to see in deer habitat are not invisible; they're merely things we haven't trained ourselves to look for.

The best of all possible "sign" is a glimpse of the buck himself, but the canny hunter can learn to read tracks, browse marks, scrapes, droppings, and rubs to gain an overall picture of the deer herd in a certain locality. *(Photo by Jerry Smith)*

Seeing sign is one thing, and interpreting it correctly is something else entirely. Here I examine a rub which, by its height and the size of the tree, was probably made by a very big buck.

Check a buck scrape for fresh urine spots and tracks, from which the size of the buck may be deduced.

Obviously, we must know where to look for sign, and that's not as simple as it may sound. For example, you look for deer tracks on the ground, don't you? Right, but if you spend all your time in the woods with your eyes glued to the earth, you aren't going to see very much of the *makers* of all those tracks. Tracks, except in snow, are mostly to be seen in certain areas, along game trails, near water, and in places where ground-cover vegetation doesn't conceal or distort them. Learn to keep your eyes roving, not looking for tracks so much as for places where tracks may be seen if they're there. Then stop and examine such places intensively, see what there is to be seen, and let your eyes move on. Furthermore, in many parts of my hunting grounds I really don't care very much about tracks, whereas in other spots, where my experience and instincts tell me there just might be a trophy buck, I'm looking for confirmation of those suspicions. Eventually, a sort of routine develops, in which you sense where you need to look for footprints, where you may be able to find them, and which ones are there. Your brain files away visual images in an orderly fashion without much conscious effort on your part. I can walk along an old trail through heavy brush and at the end of a mile I will know where every large deer crossed, but I won't necessarily remember actually seeing individual hoofprints. I think that's verging on Jesus's mode of operation.

Snow, of course, is different. Not even a complete greenhorn can miss seeing deer tracks, but it takes experience to interpret the signs, to know how long ago those tracks were made, and whether they may have been made by a buck of interest to the hunter. I'm really not much good at it, because I don't have the chance to practice the skill. Of the states in which I've hunted deer—Texas, New Mexico, Colorado, Montana, Arkansas, South Carolina, New Hampshire, Vermont, Georgia, and Louisiana, as well as Old Mexico —snow is a sometime thing during all but the special post-season hunts in the mountain states. I can tell you something about the age of deer tracks in desert sand, moist earth, and even tall grass, but the chances are you could teach me a thing or two about trails in snow, if your country has offered you the chance to learn.

In any medium, however, certain things hold true. Nobody— except possibly Jesus—can reliably tell a buck track from a big doe track . . . until you find yourself looking at a *really* big buck track.

An old doe may leave prints exactly like those of an ordinary buck, but no doe's hooves can match those of an exceptional buck. Not only are his prints longer and much deeper, but they're usually more splayed, with the hoof tips blunt, far from the dainty heart-shaped tracks of the typical doe. His trail, if you can see it, will be wider; that is, there will be more lateral spread between the prints of his right and left feet, and in a light snow or heavy mud, the walking buck will drag the tips of his hooves into each track. However, in deep snow, all deer tracks reveal conspicuous drag marks.

All this assumes that the hunter has progressed to the point that he can tell at a glance the difference between deer tracks and those of sheep, hogs, goats, javelina, and other cloven-footed beasts. If not, buy a book; nobody was born knowing these things and there's no shame to squatting over a patch of mud with *A Field Guide to Animal Tracks*, or asking someone more experienced in that area to explain the fine points of difference.

Besides tracks, common deer sign includes drippings (the familiar oval brown pellets of wintertime change to softer, segmented feces somewhat similar to swine drippings in spring and summer) and urine marks, in snow or sandy land. For obvious reasons, a buck deposits his urine farther forward of the rear hoofprints than does a doe.

Browsing and grazing marks (deer rarely graze on natural forage, but often do on crops) are fairly easy to detect. Neither species of deer has teeth in the upper front portion of the jaws, so leaves have a pinched-off or crushed appearance where deer have fed. Of critical importance to any hunter is learning which foods deer utilize in his region. Although the animals are extremely selective if they have any choice, they subsist on widely different sorts of vegetation in various parts of the range, and a listing here would require the remainder of this chapter to cover the nation. Your state game department will probably be happy to furnish you with a list of favored foods in your area, and learning to recognize these plants is essential to every sophisticated hunter's operations.

We have covered buck rubs and scrapes elsewhere, and, of course, they are among the most important kinds of sign for any hunter. About the only thing I can add here is a technique to determine the freshness of rubs. Obviously, those on which the sap and

This rub, smoking fresh, was obviously made by a breeding buck. Sometimes something about the size of the antlers can be guessed from a rub; note the gouges made by the buck's fighting tines on a stem behind the main rubbing target.

The fact that this rub was old and dried out during hunting season indicates that it was made by a buck cleaning his antlers of velvet long before the onset of the rut. The age of the rub, however, must be judged by the humidity level of the last few days and its exposure to sun.

shredded fibers of the plant bark are completely dried out are old. If doubt exists, take the back of your knife blade and scrape away some bark adjacent to the rubbing damage, in order to compare the color of wood and inner bark. In guessing at the actual age in days of a rub, remember to take into consideration whether humidity has been high or low, and whether the rub is in a shady spot or exposed to the sun. I have often been able to get an idea of tine length on a rub by noting damage to secondary stems of the plant behind the main rubbing target.

For some reason, I have discovered more mule deer beds than whitetail beds, although I've spent far more time in whitetail country. Muleys tend to bed in thin cover on mountain points, where they have a good view and can catch scent on rising thermals, usually on south-facing slopes. In the southwest, I've often found them lying up in thick cedar just below the rimrock (and often just above talus slides). Warm weather seems to make mule deer uncomfortable, and they like to have heavy shade on their beds. It's not uncommon to spot them actually lying on snowbanks in such places, in which case abandoned beds are quite conspicuous.

Whitetails, with their cozy home ranges, tend to bed within the same general area for fairly long periods of time. They almost never lie in exactly the same bed twice, however, so don't count on that in executing a stalk; that mistake has cost me a couple of good shots. Shade seems not to be as important to a whitetail as to his big-eared western cousin, but concealment most definitely is near the top of his list, and it's rare to locate a bedded whitetail buck from any distance. He, too, favors sunny southern slopes if the cover is there. A bed of either species is merely an oval-shaped spot, smaller than you might think, in which the grasses and leaves are pressed flat. Almost all hoofed animals, when rising, urinate at once if not startled out of the bed.

Whitetails are extremely sensitive to disturbances on their bed-grounds and quick to abandon them more or less permanently (or at least for the duration of a hunting season) if surprised there. Where I can identify regular bedding areas, my practice is to stay strictly away from them during and just before the open season. I may set up ambushes on the animals' routes to and from the bed-grounds, or try to draw a buck out of them with the rattling horns, but I treat the "bedrooms" themselves as though they were sown with land mines!

Following a heavily used trail or runway from a foraging area, especially uphill or, in level terrain, toward heavy cover, is a good way to stumble into bed-grounds. An alert tracker can avoid this by watching the trail, which will branch and rebranch until it fades away to nothing as it enters the bedding area.

As important as scouting for sign is before the hunt, it's even more so in a case where a shot has been fired and the buck is not on the ground where expected. When this happens, hang your cap on a bush at the point where you thought he would be or where you think he was when fired at, and return immediately to the position from which you fired. From that spot (sometimes identifiable by the ejected brass cartridge case), check again to make sure you took the right line, and try to pick out a landmark near the buck's position when the bullet arrived. Go back to that spot and look for deep, slashing tracks or freshly disturbed leaves where he whirled to run. Having located his exact position to the best of your ability, get down on your knees if necessary and look for deer hair. It will always be there, although it may be hard to see, if the bullet touched him. A wound may show no blood, but it isn't possible for a bullet to even scratch a buck without cutting some hair.

It may be in a tuft, or it may be scattered. It may be brownish-gray or it may be white (giving some idea of where on his body the wound may be), but it will invariably be there if there was a wound.

The presence of blood, naturally, makes it unnecessary to look for hair. A high-velocity expanding bullet which exits often makes a fan-shaped fine spray of blood on the ground beyond where the deer was standing, and it's easy to overlook in the excitement of the moment. I assume that most readers of this book will not need to be told that bright-pink, frothy blood indicates a lung hit (and a dead deer pretty close by), brownish or greenish matter mixed with the blood a gut shot, and dark-crimson blood a muscle wound. Splinters of bone on the ground nearby invariably indicate a broken leg, a truly sad discovery.

Unless you're pretty confident of a heart or lung wound from the evidence, the best thing to do at this point (I've finally decided) is to sit down and fidget for fifteen minutes by the watch before taking the trail. I'm aware that, in crowded woods, this procedure may give another hunter a chance to tag your deer, but failing to do it will cost you even more wounded deer in the long run. Besides, trophy hunters rarely find themselves hunting in crowded woods.

After those agonizing fifteen minutes have passed, take the trail very, very slowly, one step at a time. Be ready with the rifle and never take a step without searching every nook and cranny of the woods with your eyes. Then stop, locate the next track or blood spot, look up, and take your next step. At this point, the buck probably has not gone far (we're assuming his wound isn't immediately fatal) but he will be extremely alert. Your best chance to finish the affair now is to spot him before he moves out again, and to kill him the instant you locate him. Jump him now and you will have a long, discouraging, and probably unsuccessful chase, resulting in loss of the deer.

If he doesn't stop, or if you do jump him, the best bet is to get help, if available, or a trailing dog, if legal. If neither is possible, you'll just have to settle down and trail him an inch at a time. Try to guess where the wound is in his body, from blood sign, the tracks, or blood on grasses or brush at body height from the ground. This may help you deduce his escape pattern. For example, if he's running on only three legs and you've found bone, you may theorize that he'll tend to go downhill into heavy cover. Muleys won't follow this rule, but I once predicted where a whitetail buck which had been wounded and lost on my ranch would go and, two weeks later, found his carcass within 30 yards of the spot I'd named. There was no crystal-ball work in this prediction; I knew the contours of the country intimately, and I knew the species.

Often, a very lightly wounded deer—even one with a wound which is not seriously disabling, much less fatal—will stop and lie down within less than 100 yards, if he isn't pushed. If, for example, a shot is tried at dusk and the deer is hit but manages to make it away from the scene, it's well to leave him overnight, and take the trail only after good shooting light next morning. If I had done this, I would probably not have lost one of the only two bucks I've ever failed to bring in which was hit. He may also have been the closest to a Boone and Crockett record at which I've had a chance, which only triples the tragedy. Knowing what I do now about trailing cripples, I'm confident I could have at least had another good shot at him next morning. As it was, I pushed him, jumped him in heavy brush twice, watched the blood trail dwindle to nothing, and never saw him again. He was hit high in the left front leg. There is a risk, of course, that this tactic of leaving a buck overnight will result in his loss to coyotes, or even to another hunter, but pushing a wounded whitetail which can travel more than 300 or 400 yards results in his loss about 90 percent of the time unless an experienced dog is available. This will even be true in snow except in the case of wounds to major arteries or veins, which will not close up and end the blood trail.

It's easy to lose a deer in heavy cover, even though he may be dead within 40 or 50 yards. With his last ounce of strength he'll dive or crawl into the thickest brush he can find. A blood trail may not really begin until a wounded buck has traveled farther than that, and you'll have to do the trailing the hard way. I've seen African trackers at work who were infallible on wounded game on any kind of ground, blood or no blood, even when the animal was in a large herd of his own kind. But I have yet to see anyone in North America who could perform such feats of trailing.

There are a few tricks which help, however. One is to carry a wad of toilet paper in your pocket for marking a trail. Tie a strip to a bush over every blood spot or positively identified track or sign of the wounded buck. This often reveals a "line" which helps the hunter guess the direction his quarry took, and it permits him to go back and start again at the last sign whenever he loses the trail. If he has to go get help from his hunting buddies, the markers will help them take up the trail at the freshest point without loss of time.

If help is available, have a buddy do the trailing while you follow him a few yards to one side. Let him look for tracks and you look only for the deer. Be very quiet, communicating with hand signals if necessary, and there's a good chance you'll have a shot as the wounded buck attempts to sneak away from the man doing the trailing.

By the way, for reasons unknown to me, women are often more successful blood-trailers than men. My wife, who is an enthusiastic hunter in her own right, has demonstrated this talent several times, leaving no doubt that she can unravel a difficult blood trail better than I can, despite my far greater experience. Whether this is because the color perception of women is better than, or different from, mens', or whether they are simply more patient and meticulous, I do not know. But the female edge is not simply an unusual talent of my wife's; this phenomenon has been observed often and is recognized by many veteran hunters of my acquaintance.

As a final effort with a trail hopelessly confused or lost, mark the last sign with paper and walk slowly in expanding circles. You may spot another drop of blood, or you might even stumble over the deer. Watch particularly for the white belly of a buck lying on his side, dead.

I once spent about two hours on my hands and knees, trying to trail a buck I was sure was dead across rocky ground. Although my bullet had drilled the rear lobes of both lungs at only 40 yards, there was insufficient blood sign to follow. Finally, the widening-circles technique located him, but not by my noticing his belly; he had died on his feet and fallen into a thicket of mesquite stems which actually held him in an upright position. When I first spotted him, I thought for an instant that it was a live deer with his head down. This was a big twelve-pointer which probably hadn't lived forty-five seconds after the bullet struck him, but I almost lost him.

It should go without saying that any hunter who fires at a deer *must* satisfy himself that he missed or make every effort humanly possible to recover the animal. I've seen at least a half-dozen fine bucks which fell dead within 25 yards or less of the spot where the bullet hit them but which were lost because the hunter assumed a miss, failed to locate the exact spot to look for sign, or carelessly overlooked the evidence of a hit. Trailing a cripple is a sad and depressing task, but it simply must be done. No man who even pretends to claim the honorable title of "sportsman" will run the slightest risk of leaving a wounded deer in the woods, and, harsh as it may sound, I believe no sportsman has the right to fire at a deer until he has mastered at least the fundamentals of reading sign and trailing.

It takes too long to grow a fine whitetail buck and they're too rare to waste by incompetent shooting (about which there will be more, later) or incompetent woodsmanship. And, for that matter, the burden of responsibility to recover all game fired at is just as great in the case of a spike or a doe.

11 The Mystique of Still-Hunting

An entire book easily the size of this one could be written about that most fascinating and least understood hunting technique called still-hunting. Such a book would logically begin with a definition, but the easiest way to get the idea across is to describe what still-hunting is not. First, it is *not* stalking; an animal to be stalked is located, usually from a considerable distance, after which a route of approach to his position is figured out and executed, taking advantage of terrain and wind. Note that a stalk is predicated on the hope that the game will remain more or less stationary for the time required to complete the stalk, and that usually other animals are not much of a factor except possibly at the very end of the stalk. I once killed a great Stone ram in British Columbia which we located from several miles away on another mountain. That stalk took almost four hours but the habits of mountain sheep are such that we had at least a 50-50 chance that the ram would still be there when we arrived.

Many hunters believe that stalking a whitetail deer is impossible. It's only *nearly* impossible. It can occasionally be done, however, and now and then stalking will get you a buck which can't be had any other way. The first problem is that whitetails can seldom be spotted from a great distance, and the second is that, unless bedded, they rarely stay put long enough to execute a long stalk. I once did spot three bucks bedded across a wide, open meadow and managed to circle the clearing in the woods and approach within less than 50 yards. None was worth shooting, but I could easily have killed any of them. That stalk required only about thirty minutes, but it's still the longest successful stalk I've made on whitetails.

On the move in good whitetail habitat, practicing the most demanding, exhausting, and exciting of all deer-hunting techniques: still-hunting. Camouflage—if legal—is important.

Most of the others have been on deer seen within about 400 yards, where a direct approach could be made in broken brush until the last few steps. And many more have been total failures.

Muleys are much more susceptible to stalking than whitetails, in much the same way that other mountain game is stalked. They can often be seen from a considerable distance and permit a carefully laid-out approach within rifle range. The fact that mule deer are much more often seen in their beds also gives the stalker more time to operate.

But back to still-hunting. It is not stalking, and neither is it stand-hunting, despite the similarity of names. Stand-hunting is, as we shall shortly see, sitting in one place and watching for a buck to move within range. The place may be in a tree, or a tower stand, or on a stump, or in a ground blind, or just against a convenient tree trunk, but it is a specific, stationary location. Stand-hunting is the most successful of all whitetail-hunting techniques and very often good for trophy bucks, but it isn't still-hunting.

Still-hunting *is* a sort of blend of stalking and stand-hunting. It has been described (by me) as *random stalking*, stalking the cover rather than a specific animal whose precise location is known. But a good still-hunter spends a very great deal of his time motionless, like a stand-hunter, watching and listening.

Still-hunting is also a high art. Not one hunter in fifty who says he's been still-hunting actually has been; what he's been doing is walking through the woods hoping to see a deer in time to try a snap shot at a waving white flag. That bears about the same relationship to true still-hunting as your fourth-grader's crayon "art" bears to something by Norman Rockwell. Still-hunting is by several miles the most difficult of all common deer-hunting techniques to master, the most demanding of patience, and the most fatiguing. It is not a particularly productive method in terms of deer sightings, but it is very often the best of all possible ways to sight a trophy buck. It is not applicable to all types of terrain and cover, but there are places in which still-hunting is the *only* way to hunt, and many of these are the places inhabited by monster bucks, the ones with the trophy racks.

Perhaps a better way to describe the still-hunter is to say that he moves through the forest like a ghost, invisible and utterly soundless, that he sees everything and is seen by nothing. That's the way it *should* be, but, of course, such stealth is beyond the ability of any human. Nevertheless, that's a good model upon which to base your still-hunting efforts and technique.

For openers, let's look at clothing and equipment. Everything a still-hunter wears or carries must be quiet, which dictates soft-soled boots, soft-finished fabrics, and nothing in the pockets to jingle or rattle. A major source of irritation to me is the fact that so few goose-down-insulated hunting garments have a soft outer shell to reduce scratching, scraping, and crinkling. One solution, in all but the coldest weather, is wearing a down-insulated vest under a buckskin or wool shirt or a jumpsuit. Buckskin, by the way, is a super-practical material for hunting clothes; it is silent and warm, and it dries soft after wetting.

Still-hunting clothes should also be inconspicuous, which brings us to a ticklish subject for me. The wearing of blaze orange, as required by law in many jurisdictions and by common sense in many others, has proved beyond any question to be an invaluable safety precaution. I recommend it without reservation; there is an extremely good chance that it may save your life.

There is also a good chance that it will cost you the buck of a lifetime. The retinas of deer may not be sensitive to blaze orange, and they do not see a blaze-orange vest or jacket in the same way that another hunter sees it, but don't ever let anybody tell you that they can't see it at all! Even in a black-and-white photograph, blaze orange stands out rather conspicuously, because of the almost-fluorescent intensity of the hue. I've proved to my own complete satisfaction that safety garments of blaze orange will attract the attention of whitetails. Obviously, no trophy on the face of the earth is worth the risk of being shot with a high-powered rifle, so the choice is clear in most regions. But wherever visibility garments are not required by law and I'm hunting private property on which I know the whereabouts (and temperaments) of my companions in the woods, I choose to wear camouflage. *Complete* camouflage—head to toe, including face and hands. I've been accused of wearing camouflaged underwear but I refuse to comment upon that accusation. I've camouflaged rifles, binoculars, spotting scopes, cameras, staffs, tripods, and all manner of equipment, and such efforts are always worth the time and trouble. This is one area in which the bowhunters are far ahead of gun hunters in general; camouflage is their uniform, and so it should also be for the still-hunter, where absolutely safe.

We laugh at silent-movie scenes of would-be safecrackers sandpapering their fingertips to increase sensitivity, and stand respectfully silent as a pro golfer cranks up his concentration for a championship birdie putt. Still, I know expert still-hunters who almost go into a trance as they take the first few steps on a morning's hunt. I'm one of them.

Look at it this way. In our crowded, noisy, civilized world, our senses are constantly assaulted from every direction with demands for our attention, not to mention just plain racket. As a result, we have developed a remarkable ability to simply tune out sounds, sights, and smells which are meaningless or annoying, never allowing them to become a part of our consciousness. Try this, if you're reading this in the peace and quiet of your own home: close your eyes and really *listen* to that "peace and quiet." Suddenly, you'll hear things that never got through your mental filters until now—the blower of the central heater or air conditioner, the barking of the neighbor's dog three houses down the street, the muffled rush of traffic on the expressway a few blocks away, the TV behind a closed door in the kids' room, perhaps the hum of a clothes dryer or dishwasher in another part of the house. When you really open your ears to your environment, you'll suddenly discover how effective are those mental filters.

Look, after all, at the lengths to which emergency vehicles must go, with sirens, yelpers, bright paint jobs, and flashing, multicolored lights, just to get us to notice them!

A wild deer in the forest is not incessantly assaulted in all his senses as we are, and has not developed our automatic defenses against distraction. There are no "meaningless" sounds or smells to him; he hears and interprets every one. In fact, his life depends on his susceptibility to distraction; if he becomes too intent on anything—like a doe in heat, for instance—he is immediately vulnerable.

And when a still-hunter enters the forest to deal with such an animal on its own turf, he must learn to open up his receptors, to lower his filters, to switch off his defenses against distraction. For

The jig is up! This buck has become aware of the still-hunter, and the instant that front hoof hits the ground, every other deer within a hundred yards will be aware of him as well.

most city dwellers, this is almost impossible at first. It takes practice, surprisingly enough, *just to be aware* of your surroundings. I often think that those people with the reputation of "instinctive" hunters are mostly people with an unusually high natural awareness of what goes on around them.

Whitetails are seldom seen standing around in the open during hunting season. The still-hunter must develop the knack of focusing on incongruous lines, shadows, and shapes—half concealed behind the first screen of brush.

Many experienced still-hunters agree that it's surprising how often the first part of a buck they notice is his rack.

I have killed several bucks which I heard before seeing them, and one or two which I actually smelled first, but, for the most part, the hunter's most valuable sensory organs are his eyes, and he can train his eyes to be better than they customarily are. By concentrating, he can learn to notice detail which would escape him in his normal environment. Little exercises—like forcing himself to notice the vein patterns in the leaves of his wife's indoor plants, or trying to note every single item in a store window as he walks past it (writing it all down and checking the list against the actual window)—

The ability simply to see deer is critical —and not to be taken for granted— especially in still-hunting. Anyone would spot this buck standing in the open, of course . . . but how many would notice the second one, back in the brush? *(Photo by W. A. Maltsberger)*

really do sharpen up the eye for *observing* the world around us. Most of all, the hunter's eye can work in conjunction with his brain, which can tell it where to look and what to look for.

Years ago, on a safari in Mozambique, Africa, my professional hunter was most impressed—and occasionally annoyed—at the ability my companion, Jack Carter, and I had to spot animals in the bush. We often saw game before the professional hunter did, and now and then before the native trackers who were with us did. Finally, he asked us how we did it, especially as it was the first safari for both of us, in strange country, and we sometimes didn't know what sort of animal we were looking at. The answer was so simple that I don't think he ever really grasped it; we were both case-hardened, old-time whitetail hunters with years of experience in two tricks. We didn't look for *whole* animals, but merely objects which somehow didn't fit the patterns of the brush, and we constantly searched into the *edges* of the cover with our eyes, never expecting to see a whole animal standing in the clear.

Every deer-hunting book or article ever published has emphasized these two things, but I still know hunters who look only for a whole deer and find it difficult or impossible to see a fragment of a deer tucked away in the bushes. This is an art the still-hunter *must* develop, else he's better off on a stand. In thinking back, I seem to recall that certain portions of a whitetail's anatomy have caught my eye more than others, and these are the paired white stripes which outline the tail in its normal position, the hock angle of the hind leg, the eyes and/or nose, and the antlers. It's surprising how many times the first thing I saw on a buck I eventually killed was his rack, until I consider how much time whitetails spend in brush just about head-high to them, and how a polished antler can flash and gleam in the sun. The antlers are regularly the part that I notice first on bedded bucks. Color is also important, especially the white on a deer's muzzle, ears, throat, and rump, and so is shape. A lot of stumps and logs look a lot like a deer's body, but the body of a real deer never looks exactly like a log. It's not uncommon to see a formation of tree branches which gives me a thrill in its resemblance to antlers, but I never saw a real rack that even for a split second suggested a tree limb.

The fact is that a flesh-and-blood buck, especially one in the trophy category, will damn seldom be observed standing boldly in the open, away from confusing undergrowth, and if you're going to see him at all it will have to be by picking out pieces and parts of him and mentally fitting him together like a jigsaw puzzle.

One way to do it is to train your eyes to look *into* and through the brush instead of at the outside perimeters of it. Always assume that the deer will be motionless; any movement will catch your eye instantly and you don't have to consciously look for it. A pair of good binoculars is invaluable (yes, even for still-hunting in heavy cover), precisely for the reason that with them you can focus out the first screen of brush and look back into the cover. Until you try this, you won't understand how striking is the effect; very often you'll spot a blob a few feet inside the edge of the brush which may or may not be a deer, but which a slight twist of the focusing knob on your binoculars will resolve into a full-fledged, real-life buck, sharply seen in all his outlines. A scope sight on your rifle will not yield this effect, in addition to which raising the rifle makes too much movement and is quite tiring. I have my binoculars up and down two or three times each minute while still-hunting, and would just about as soon go hunting without a rifle as without binoculars.

Still-hunting, as mentioned, is a technique specialized to certain types of terrain and cover. It doesn't work at all in open country where the hunter is unable to take the same advantage of brush that his quarry does, but must expose his moving figure to unseen eyes in many directions. And it works very poorly in the other extreme: dense brush where there's no possible hope of seeing a deer more than a few yards away and long after the deer has studied you intently enough to recite your age, hat size, and the caliber of your rifle!

Even in heavy timber, still-hunting is impractical if the mature forest has no understory of brush, as is the case in many aspen groves in muley country and in pine monoculture areas in the South.

Ideal still-hunting country is broken cover, with alternating patches of thin brush and smallish, irregular clearings. A little gentle roll to the landscape hurts nothing, either. In such terrain, the hunter can slip along, keeping himself mostly within the edges of the cover, and can open up two or three new vistas of 50 to 100 yards with each dozen strides he makes.

In planning a morning's or a day's still-hunting, some advance knowledge of the route is invaluable, which is why I like to walk over the country a few times before the hunting season opens. I file away in my mind the watercourses, thickets, game trails, areas of heaviest deer sign, and possible routes. I note the direction of the sun relative to the area, how both the northwest wind and the wind which prevails between fronts will lie across the country, how I can get into the area without disturbing it, and approximate times

required to cover certain distances. I rarely still-hunt at random; if
I'm in a specific area, it's because I at least suspect the presence of
a likely buck thereabouts and I plan the hunt to give me every possible advantage in approaching what I consider the likeliest pockets
of cover.

Every hunter recognizes the importance of the wind, but I'm
surprised at how few attach much importance to the sun's direction.
And I was struck dumb with astonishment at the advice I once read
in a deer-hunting book by a well-known outdoors writer to the effect
that the still-hunter should always proceed in an easterly direction
in the morning, wind permitting, and a westerly direction in the

afternoon. The theory was that this
tactic allowed him to skyline deer
more readily!

My theory is that a deer would
have to be gagged and bound to be
seen at all by such a hunter, who
would spend all day blinded from
trying to peer directly into the rising
or setting sun!

In fact, a low sun at your back
is one of the most overwhelming
advantages you can ever contrive
against the razor-sharp eyes of a
whitetail. The best whitetail buck I
had ever taken until 1973 lost his
life just because I had this advantage.
I had still-hunted within about 50
yards of his bed, just as the sun rose
above the horizon squarely behind
me. He heard the faint crunch of
gravel underfoot, and stood up, literally squinting into the sun at my
form towering out of the waist-high

I contend that the sun over a still-hunter's shoulder
is the greatest single advantage he can gain. Not
only can he see the deer better, but they're partially
blinded in looking toward him.

brush. I could see him as though a tremendous searchlight had been focused on him from over my shoulder, and I could take my time, evaluate his rack carefully, raise my rifle, and make the neck shot cleanly. If the situation had been reversed, so that I was looking into the sun and he could see *me* as in a searchlight, he would have been gone before I could have shifted the rifle's muzzle 6 inches. This buck had only to take one step in any direction to disappear.

The advantage of a sun behind the hunter works both ways. The deer cannot see the hunter as well, and the hunter can pick out deer in the brush which he would have little chance of noticing otherwise. The white patches on a whitetail deer, especially the ear linings and throat patch, which are in more or less constant motion, stand out in the brush like a rat pill in a sugar bowl to a hunter with the sun behind him. If I have to take my choice between the low sun and the wind, I'll take the sun every time and settle for a crosswind or even a quartering breeze with pleasure.

I took this exceptional buck while still-hunting with the low morning sun directly behind me.

One reason is that I know exactly what the sun will do, whereas the wind is unreliable, at best. Even in flat country, it's nearly impossible to predict where eddies of scent will wind up, and in hilly terrain it *is* impossible. The wind can do strange things with a hunter's scent, but it can only do them in one place at a time, leaving me the rest of a 200-degree semicircle to do my hunting. Shifty, variable breezes are maddening to a still-hunter, but don't let them intimidate you. I've killed a number of bucks which *seemed* to be straight downwind from me but never showed any symptom of smelling a human. Conversely, I've had bucks spook from my scent when I was certain I had the wind solidly on my side. The two best winds for still-hunting are a steady, strongish northerly breeze and no wind at all, in that order, but neither of them can compare to the low, bright sun as an ally in this type of hunting.

As to still-hunting technique, the all-important mandate is to go *slowly*. This is the most difficult thing to learn in still-hunting, and it's what makes this pastime so tiring. Depending upon the cover, a few hundred yards in an entire morning may be too fast! Very commonly, I've still-hunted from sunup until noon, and then turned and walked back to my car, striding out at a normal pace, in less than fifteen minutes. Most people discover that such hunting demands an unexpected reserve of self-discipline and patience. You have to keep telling yourself that just a dozen impatient steps can cost you the buck that you've planned for during a whole year. I find that it helps me slow down if I actively imagine just that buck, constantly standing just behind the next patch of cover. I picture him in my mind's eye, seeing just how he'll be turned, imagining his astonishment at seeing me, and picturing how easy the shot will be if I can just do everything right for a few more minutes.

And the buck—or at least *a* buck—really *is* standing there, just as I pictured him, just often enough to keep me going!

A good rule is as follows: never take a single step until you have visually examined every possible cranny in the cover which is visible from your position. Then take one step, or ten, smoothly and quietly, to secure a fresh vista, and stop and stand motionless while you probe the cover again with your eyes. In some areas, this rule will allow you to move fairly fast, perhaps a half-mile per hour, while in others your progress may not be at one-fifth that rate. Time

Still-hunting is the art of being inconspicuous in the woods. This hunter shows how *not* to top a ridge.

must be of no importance, a difficult thing for modern man to believe, because it's of no importance to the deer. How much ground you cover is nothing, provided you cover it correctly, which is to say that you see literally everything there is to see.

Every hunter can learn a lot from the deer he hunts as to how to handle himself in the woods. Keep yourself inside the edges of the brush, as a buck does. When you must cross an opening a few yards wide, do it smoothly and swiftly, after satisfying yourself that you're alone. When you stop, always choose at least a wisp of cover into which your motionless figure will merge as you stand motionless, looking. Never skylight yourself, and remember your silhouette; if you're in deep shadow with a bright meadow behind you, you'll be more conspicuous than if you were standing in the center of the meadow in full sunlight.

If all this sounds like an awful lot of trouble, be assured that it certainly is, and that this is why there are so very, very few skilled still-hunters on the face of the earth.

The expert still-hunter eases over a ridge behind some concealment and pauses to study the surroundings thoroughly before exposing himself further.

Never forget your silhouette; even in full camouflage and in shadows, you can stand out against a bright background. On the other hand, so can a big buck, so keep an eye out for his silhouette.

But there are additional rewards to this game, other than the fact that it is sometimes the only way to penetrate an old buck's domain that offers any hope of a shot. One is that an expert still-hunter sees the woods world functioning normally, unaware of the human presence. I've had the pleasure of catching all kinds of wild animals going about their daily business. I've seen foxes and bobcats hunting within a few yards of me, and coyotes make their kills. I've gotten close enough to javelinas and other species almost to kick them if I chose. Rare birds delight my eyes. Above all, when a hunter masters the disciplines of still-hunting he senses the rhythms of the real world and becomes a part of them. The intensity of concentration required for this kind of hunting can produce a sort of psychedelic "high" of total awareness of the natural world around one. For many, it's an almost mystical experience, from which coming back to camp is a definite "crash."

But, mystique aside, still-hunting is the deadliest of all big-buck hunting methods, a *sine qua non* of the trophy hunter, and an adventure all unto itself.

12 Stand-Hunting and Miscellaneous Methods

If still-hunting is the epitome of the hunter's arts, then stand-hunting is the peak of his wisdom. Hunting from a stand is the going-away best of all methods of seeing whitetail deer, and I know many serious trophy hunters who have never killed a buck in any other way. The reason for this outstanding success is twofold: first, whitetails are inclined to follow similar patterns of movement from day to day if not disturbed, and second, the hunter is motionless while the deer is moving. Since whitetails' eyes are incredibly keen for motion, and those of the typical hunter not so hot for anything *except* motion, this situation shifts the odds considerably in the hunter's favor.

Some of my companions have the habit of sitting in a stand for the first couple of hours each day and for the last hour before dusk, and still-hunting through midday. The idea is to be sitting still in a good place when the deer are most likely to be afoot, and moving through promising cover when they're bedded down. It sounds like a good idea, but it doesn't work very well. To begin with, whitetails' periods of movement are not that predictable, and a well-chosen stand is just as likely to produce at noontime as early or late. This is especially true during the rut. Then, the chances of even the most expert still-hunter getting a shot at a bedded buck are just barely this side of my chance of becoming the Emperor of the United States.

Which is another way of saying that *either* the still-hunter or the stand-hunter enjoys his best odds when the deer are active, and that the choice of techniques may not logically be based upon the time of day. Stand-hunting is best in open country where still-hunting cannot be practiced, and in areas known to be frequented by the deer for any of a number of reasons, including favored forage, water, or access to or from bedding and feeding areas.

Although a different ballgame from still-hunting, stand-hunting is by no means devoid of skills. Perhaps the most important of these is selecting the stand location, which requires considerable scouting for sign, and considerable understanding of what is found, not to mention sun and wind directions. There are several things covered by the word "stand." In areas where they're legal, tree platforms are probably the most common sort of stand. These may be anything from a board in a crotch to very elaborate roofed and carpeted structures lacking only elevators and flush toilets for convenience. In regions like my beloved south Texas, where trees stout enough to support even a primitive platform are few and far between, the same function is served by tower stands. Again, these may be nothing but a chair on a tripod, on up to regular little houses with sliding glass windows. Either kind of stand elevates the hunter's eyes high enough to cover a good deal of country which couldn't be seen from the ground, and, in theory, places him above the normal line of vision of the animals he hunts. His scent may also pass over the heads of downwind deer, but there are so many ifs and buts to *that* idea that it's better saved for a paragraph of its own.

If the deer are fairly close to the stand, the extra height *may* prevent them from seeing the hunter, but I've had does stand at the very base of a tree and stare fixedly up at me while I earnestly tried to resemble a hoot owl. At longer ranges, they'll spot movement in an elevated stand just as quickly, perhaps even more quickly, than the same actions on the ground. Best to settle for the improved visibility from a high seat and keep still, unless the stand is enclosed.

There are problems unique to a tree or tower stand. One is that the simplest forms are downright dangerous, especially well-aged tree stands. I have a close friend who fell from a tower stand and broke his shoulder and back, and I know of a few deaths resulting from a rotten board or branch suddenly giving way. There are also a few cases of a dropped rifle striking the ground on its butt and firing straight up, with regrettable consequences. Always make certain the structure is sound, well guyed (if a tower), and easy of access, and that the rifle is unloaded while ascending or descending.

Stand-hunting—from tree-stands, tripods, or elevated box blinds—is by far the most popular and productive of all hunting methods because the hunter waits, silent and motionless, allowing deer to come to him.

Another problem is wind, not only because it may almost freeze a hunter in his elevated perch, but because the movements of a tree, waving in a gusty wind, offer a fascinating extra dimension of challenge in long-range shooting, to put it mildly. Despite these various drawbacks, however, elevated stands are just the ticket in many areas and good ones are well worth the trouble and expense to set in place.

Which should be done, I must add, many months in advance of the hunting season, to permit the local whitetails to become accustomed to their presence. Remember my little story about the fawn and the salt block? Well, a hulking new structure of unseasoned wood in his bailiwick turns an old buck off about as effectively as a new runway for jetliners would, at least until he has a chance to decide that it presents no threat. Old bucks arrive at such decisions with great deliberation.

The same applies to ground blinds, in general. They can be constructed of natural materials which blend into the local landscape, and should be, but deer—especially adult male deer—will inevitably give them a wide berth for a while. A ground blind may enable the hunter to move about inside it a bit without alarming nearby deer, but it does nothing to conceal his scent, and this must be considered in selecting a suitable location.

Certain deer "stands" are really nothing more than well-located stumps, logs, rocks, or tree trunks which offer a hunter a fairly comfortable place to sit, overlooking a trail or attractive area which deer are known to "use." Over the years, such places become well recognized and even formalized with names among the local hunting fraternity, and will very consistently produce shots at bucks.

The comfort of such places is important, simply because a man can sit motionless a lot longer if he's comfortable than he can if he's cramped, cold, twisted, jabbed, or poked, and motionlessness is the key to hunting this kind of stand. They are usually located so as to have a prime, but fairly restricted, view, and the shot, if any, will be short. That means that the deer and the hunter will be close enough together that the hunter's only hope, if any, of being unobserved is to become a part of the log or stump. For about the first twenty years of my hunting career, I practiced stand-hunting exclusively, and all our stands were nothing more than a tree trunk against which to lean while watching a preferred crossing. In those days, I developed some specialized techniques for stand-hunting which worked, but which I find no longer so workable as my joints begin to creak and my muscles to cramp more quickly. The techniques are still good, but I'm not, as I travel through what I prefer to call "late middle age."

I could always handle a rifle pretty swiftly, and shot well on moving targets, under pressure. So I developed the habit of poking my way back into some of the densest thickets I could find, locating tiny clearings along well-used game trails, and taking a stand on the downwind side. Very commonly, I could see no more than 20 yards in any direction. I'd sit with my back against a tree, with my right leg flat on the ground, flexed so that my heel was against my bottom. My left knee would be propped up slightly, with the rifle resting on it, my hand on the pistol grip. I accepted the fact that any buck I saw would be virtually in my lap, and that the slightest movement on my part would send him flying. Every shot would be running at close range. I discovered that, from the position described above, I could roll up to a free-swinging kneeling position in a split second and kill a buck even if he ran back to my right.

It was tense and exciting hunting. I learned to sit literally like a statue, moving nothing except my eyeballs for hours at a time. It was more or less accidental at the time that the places I picked were exactly the right kinds of spots for the biggest bucks in that area. During those years I never failed to kill every buck I shot at, some as close as 7 yards—just 21 feet—using an old Savage Model 99 .300 Savage with a big rear peep sight.

I can't do it any more, but it's a good technique, and I learned a lot about deer, their reactions, and their reflexes. I learned that I often heard them coming, and once heard an animal behind me. I didn't dare turn until I was ready to shoot, and I couldn't tell whether it was a buck or a doe. Then I heard him thrashing a bush, and whirled like a snake uncoiling. The rifle was on him almost before he threw up his head, and the bullet took him through the lungs before he took the first step. He was a nice eight-pointer, big for that region.

I placed great store on eye contact, in those days, and I still do, although I don't hunt that close to my deer very often. If a doe came pussyfooting down the trail and spotted my immovable figure, she

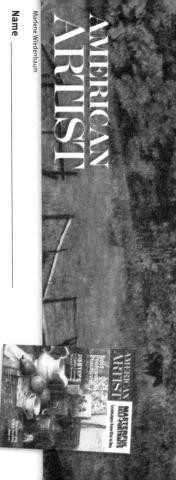

AMERICAN ARTIST

Marlene Wiedenbaum

Name _____

Address _____

City _____ **State** _____ **Zip** _____

E-mail _____

To contact you about your subscription, events, special offers and free projects.

Canadian orders add $10 per year. International add $15 per year.
Payment in U.S. funds only. Payment must accompany international orders.

☐ **2 years** (22 issues)
only **$52·95** ◀ **BEST DEAL**

☐ **1 year** (11 issues)
only **$29·95**

UA010

might fidget around a good deal, but often would pass on without snorting and disturbing the countryside, as long as I never made direct eye contact with her. The instant our eyes met, however, she'd react as though I'd tossed a firecracker under her nose! I do believe that animals can sometimes "feel" a predator's eyes upon them, and, furthermore, that *I* can feel such things now and then. Some of the best hunters I know agree that they have that sensation of being watched occasionally, and that a careful search usually reveals some sort of large animal watching them. Perhaps this feeling means that the hunter really is beginning to open up all his sensors to the wild world around him. In any case, it isn't hard to test: just try staring fixedly at a doe at fairly close range some day, making certain she has no visual, aural, or scent clue to your presence, and watch her become increasingly nervous and alert for what appears to be no good reason.

There are a few other tricks to stand-hunting which are worth mentioning. One concerns the approach to the standing place. I try to approach upwind, of course, but it may not be possible. If not, I'll walk straight *downwind* to the stand, preferably across the middle of the most open area visible from where I intend to sit. In this way, I'll have my chance at a buck before he reaches either my trail or my scent stream, provided the wind is steady.

Since I wrote the first edition of this book, I've learned a lot about whitetails, and perhaps the most significant single lesson centers on stand burnout. This refers to the rapid decline of productivity of a stand that's overhunted. You may be confident that, if you hunt the same stand on any part of three consecutive days, most whitetails living in the vicinity and along your route to and from the stand will recognize that location as dangerous. This will be true even when you aren't aware of spooking deer from the stand or of being noticed by them. The treacherous thing about burnout is that it may be camouflaged by the fact that you continue to see about as many deer from the stand as when it was first hunted. If you're alert, however, you'll eventually note that the quality of sightings, if I may employ that word, has subtly declined in any of several ways. The most common ways are that you see fewer and fewer bucks from it, and that the deer you do sight tend to be just out of range. Another giveaway is that the deer seem to spend a lot of time watching the stand, even when it's unlikely they could have detected you in it.

What has happened is that the deer have "patterned" you. They've identified the stand site as a possible peril, and they commonly confirm their suspicions by scent by moving in close to the stand, from downwind, after dark. Once burned out, it takes many months, perhaps years, to rehabilitate a stand location so that deer again feel at ease near it.

Several tactics help avoid stand burnout, but none are sure-fire. One is to erect portable stand equipment long before hunting season, to give the herd time to get over their nervousness about something new. Another is to have enough stands in place around the area that it is not necessary to hunt a given spot more often than once every three or four days. A third is to leave no stands in the woods, carrying equipment in and out and setting up at different trees or sites every day. Still another is to use no equipment whatever, hunting on the ground from a different spot on each visit.

I'm well aware of the drawbacks to each of these tactics, and recognize that different regions and situations can suggest still others. But overhunting a stand of any kind—tree, tripod, ground blind, whatever—is practically a guarantee against success there. A knowing hunter has no choice but to find a way to counteract stand burnout; the penalty for failure to do so is . . . failure!

The total absence of wind is very regularly more of a problem than even a variable breeze, especially for a hunter in an elevated stand. Before sunup on a cold morning, his scent will sink to the ground beneath him and form an invisible pool of odor which may be about 10 yards in diameter. The slightest breath of air, then, will cause this concentrated scent pool to slide away, usually in a south-westerly direction just as the sun cracks the horizon. Once the sun is well up and the earth begins to warm under its rays, all scent rises and the problem disappears until after sunset, when the flow may reverse once more. In sloping country, always recall that your scent tends to sink and roll downhill in the absence of wind before sunup and after sundown. This phenomenon cost me a shot at a good bull elk one evening in New Mexico, and may have cost me more white-tails than I know. If there's a breeze, at least you can keep your scent away from an animal on a trail downhill from you; if the air is still, you can't, nor can you predict at what point in his progress along the trail he'll detect it.

The whole principle of stand-hunting, of course, is the assumption that the deer will be on the move for one reason or another. In crowded woods, the hunters who consider themselves still-hunting are reason enough, and he who can read the sign well enough to spot regular crossings and escape trails can reap the harvest. As previously mentioned, however, one will only rarely encounter a real trophy buck in such country. In trophy-deer areas, stand-hunting is still valuable, although selection of stand locations must be based on different factors. Without a mob of other hunters milling around to drive the whitetails hither and thither, one has to understand what makes whitetails move normally, when'll they move, and by what routes. During the rut, a stand downwind from an active scrape is the best of all possible bets, and, lacking a scrape, a string of fresh rubs will serve. At this time of year, any place where does are seen in good numbers is a potential stand site, on the theory that one of them must eventually come into heat, pick up a buck, and lead him past the stand.

One thing to be kept in mind, when the hours grow long near noon, is that almost every cloven-hooved animal on earth seems to share the habit of rising from its bed sometime during the midday hours for a stretch and a few minutes of feeding. After fifteen to thirty minutes, it lies back down (seldom in the same bed) and remains there until time for normal activity rolls around. Deer are no exceptions.

A question I am often asked is whether it's worth hunting a stand if a deer has been shot there within the last twelve hours or so. The answer depends on whether the special buck you had in mind was the one killed; if not, the presence of a pile of guts will have no effect whatever. I've watched deer amble by, sniff the pile, and browse on.

Oddly, many of the people who ask this question never inquire about a much more pertinent matter. Stand-hunters who answer the calls of nature from or near their stands are stacking the odds against themselves. Whitetails, at least, seem to be frightened at the odor of human urine. I know of no better way, in fact, to block a trail or crossing than to urinate in it. No buck will pass that point for a good many hours. It's a trick I've used now and again to prevent a certain buck from using a favorite path of his, such as a fence-crossing on a boundary fence. For what it's worth, human feces seem not to alarm whitetail as nearly as much as urine.

For the record, I have recently read reports by alleged deer-hunting authorities that say that human urine is no more frightening to whitetails as, say, that of cattle or sheep. Maybe so, but I'll continue to stick by every word of the preceding paragraph, and to order my own hunting accordingly. You're free, of course, to choose to conduct yourself in the field otherwise . . . but don't throw the piss bottle away yet!

A stand may take strange shapes. A friend of mine who hunts the big bucks of south Texas in heavy brush with bulldozed lanes or *senderos* crisscrossing it likes to locate a regular crossing used by a desirable buck. He knows that the bucks rarely pause when crossing these *senderos;* they usually stop in the edge of the brush, look both ways, and then hop across too quickly to raise a rifle. So Al drags a log out in the middle of the *sendero* 50 yards or so downwind from the crossing and lies down on his belly behind it, laying his rifle across the log in shooting position. He says that a buck will almost always stop for a moment to stare at this new element in his surroundings—and a moment is all Al needs to center the crosshairs and press the trigger! As in this case, and as in most other kinds of hunting, a stand is always more likely to produce if positioned with one *specific* buck in mind.

There are several other legitimate methods of hunting whitetail deer, to which I intend to give rather scant notice. This will infuriate hunters who favor these methods, but I have my reasons. The ruling one is simply that I do not regard these techniques as very suitable for *trophy* hunting, however productive they may be for meat hunters. Or they're so specialized or regional that either I don't know enough to write about them intelligently, or they're of little use to the majority of the readers of this book.

One of these may be called "trailing," and I've done a little of this. It involves picking up the fresh track of a good buck in snow and following it until the buck is discovered. The foremost proponent of this method of hunting literally runs on the track, for miles and days, if necessary, until he gets his shot. It goes without saying that a hunter needs the physique and physical conditioning of an Olympic athlete to be successful, and he also needs deep woods with

Stand-hunters observe many facets of deer behavior, including these two modes of crossing a fence. When a big-antlered buck is being pushed, he often jumps (he's capable of clearing at least 7 feet vertically), but when he's moving at leisure, he's likely to crawl

few other hunters. The theory is that the buck soon realizes that he's being followed, but that he will eventually become more curious about this hunter who is following him so doggedly than frightened of him. He may also become tired, and sooner or later presents the opportunity for a shot. I have not the slightest doubt that trailing in this fashion works (for a very few hunters) or that it occasionally produces a trophy buck. I do seriously doubt that it will ever become a widely popular method of hunting.

Gang driving is already a popular hunting technique, but, from my somewhat limited observations, it simply cannot be expected to deliver real trophy bucks before the guns. Again, different groups of hunters have different ideas about what a "trophy" is, so perhaps I

under, a movement so quick and smooth it may appear that he simply walked through the wires. *(Photos by W. A. Maltsberger)*

shouldn't say that. I've taken part in quite a few drives, as both a driver and a stander, and I know that the method can be exciting and productive when executed under the direction of a knowledge-able hunt master. But I've never seen (or heard of, from first-person sources) a five and a half year old buck being taken in a drive, especially a noisy drive. I've circled the driven area after a drive was completed and observed the tracks of big bucks slipping away through the drivers time and again. Remember the experiments in Michigan and South Dakota with the radio-tagged buck with the orange ear streamers? Consider trying to catch animals like that in even the best-organized drive, and perhaps you'll see why I tend to discount this method for the real wallhanger bucks.

There is one kind of drive, however, that I regard as reasonably promising for big bucks, but it requires exactly the right situation. That situation is when a very limited patch of good cover is surrounded by large areas of open country. Examples are brush-choked draws or watercourses winding through open terrain, or small but dense motts of hardwoods and brush in otherwise unforested country. Big bucks are likely to hang out in these and many similar situations, because it's difficult to approach or to penetrate these strongholds without the bucks' knowledge. Where such cover exists and a good buck is known to inhabit the area, a two- or three-man drive may very well be successful. One man drifts down through the cover, as slowly and carefully as though he were still-hunting alone, while his companions cover the open terrain around the cover. The keys are that the cover itself be too small, or at least too narrow, to allow the buck to double back past the driver, and that the countryside roundabout be open enough so that the buck cannot slip away unseen.

If you think this sounds like a cinch, you don't know the abilities and nerve of big whitetails. I have actually watched a good buck enter such a place and then executed just such a one-man drive to perfection, never to see the animal again, at least that day. I might have sworn that he couldn't escape except by climbing a tree or by digging a hole . . . and maybe that's what he did! I've circled the area, found no fresh tracks leaving, and then pushed through the cover again. Still no buck. Your guess is as good as mine, but we both know he simply lay down and let me walk past, probably very close.

Still, now and again, this small-cover, one-driver technique will dredge a big one out of his stronghold. It's worth trying.

Another of my favorite drives is called the tandem drive. It takes two veteran hunters who know and trust each other and who know the terrain to be hunted. The two hunters still-hunt upwind through appropriate cover in tandem, far enough apart that the rear man can glimpse his partner occasionally to keep track of him. This spacing will usually be from one to two hundred yards, depending on visibility. The perfect scenario is as follows: a buck, sensing the approach of the lead hunter, moves stealthily to one side out of the man's way and circles in behind him as he passes, running straight into the trailing partner, whom the animal has overlooked in the intensity of his concentration on the leader. In other words, the buck dodges the hunter of whom he is aware, only to expose himself to one of whom he isn't.

It sounds too simple, I know, but it often works like magic, because of the whitetail's instinct to circle for the wind from any potential danger, plus his reluctance to leave his familiar stronghold. The trailing hunter usually gets most (but by no means all) of the chances. His responsibility is to keep track of the man ahead and to discipline himself to refuse all shots except at targets well out of line with his buddy, to one side or the other.

In areas where it's legal, the hound-dog men claim good success on big bucks. If so, there's a certain element of luck involved for the obvious reason that no hunter can possibly have time to evaluate a trophy rack before shooting, when he has only seconds to snap-shoot at a fleeting brown form in the thickets. Furthermore, I'm not aware of any state where hound hunting is legal which regularly produces genuine trophy-grade whitetails. The dogs are simply not compatible with trophy hunting in the pure sense, which is not to say they aren't a legitimate hunting tool in some areas and for some purposes.

"Rocking the draws" is a technique, however, which can produce trophies, can be used on both whitetails and mule deer, and has application in a much wider geographic area than it is now popular in. The requirement is a semi-open terrain with brushy draws and headers in which the deer tend to hole up at midday, a supply of fist-sized rocks, and a leather sling of the sort used by David to blow Goliath away. The trick works best with one man as a slinger and one or two more strictly as riflemen. The header is approached from above and the slinger begins flinging stones down into the brush. Irregularly shaped missiles which hum wickedly in flight are preferred, and this eerie droning plus the crashing and rolling of the stones in the brush is too much for the nerves of even the toughest old mossy-horn. The trouble with the technique is that almost all shots are at very long range and most of them are running chances, producing little opportunity to accurately size up a head and far too much opportunity for wounding.

This is the major objection to the practice (legal only in Texas, as far as I know) of cruising brushy country in a Jeep or truck with a special seat mounted high enough to see over the brush. Obviously, the method is useless in timber, but it will produce a lot of deer

A specialized method of hunting either whitetails or mule deer is slinging rocks into brushy draws around midday, with a rifleman who's good on long running shots standing by.

A close-up of the technique of slinging, using the same kind of sling David used on Goliath. Once in a rare while, a Goliath of a buck can be slain with the help of a sling.

Cruising and looking for deer from a high seat mounted on a vehicle is legal on private property in Texas, but very rarely produces a good shot at a big buck. The adaptable whitetails have this tactic all figured out.

sightings in appropriate terrain. The old bucks, of course, know all about those strange, moving towers, and, again, one almost never seems to get a standing shot at a good head within reasonable range. Nor do I consider the whole idea sporting, even though legal (there *is* a difference!). I mention it here only as an introduction to something I once saw a buck do. I was sitting in a tower stand atop a ridge, from which I could see about half the county. I had spotted what seemed to be quite a good whitetail about half a mile distant, and was studying him through a 40x spotting scope when I saw him stop browsing and look alertly in one direction. Taking my eye from the scope, I immediately noticed a pickup truck driving slowly along a ranch road which passed very near the buck's position. Returning to the eyepiece lens, I watched the animal stand listening to the oncoming vehicle (which he couldn't see) for a minute or so, and then turn and walk deliberately around behind a clump of dense brush. There he lay down and seemed, from my angle, to stretch his head and neck out along the ground. The truck bounced along, passing no more than 50 yards from where the buck lay and jumping three does and a smaller buck which had been feeding near him. The driver of the truck stopped abruptly and put binoculars on the fleeing deer, then cruised on. When the truck was out of hearing, the big buck rose to his feet and continued his browsing as though nothing had happened!

Now, gents, I actually witnessed that performance with my own eyes, aided by the 40x telescope, and it gives a bit of insight into what manner of beast this is that we have set out to collect for our trophy room. I might add that although I couldn't be certain at that distance, it was my impression that this was not even a fully mature buck!

There is one more hunting technique which I cannot resist describing, if only because it has been misdescribed and misunderstood until now. It's the subject of the next chapter.

13 Horn-Rattling

In essence, horn-rattling (as it's universally called in Texas, where we do know the difference between horns and antlers) is nothing more than the simulation of the sounds of a fight between two whitetail bucks, to attract bucks within gunshot range.

"Rattling" is neither a myth nor a tall Texas tale. It works in Texas, and it will work if conditions are right (which is a big "if") anywhere whitetails roam. My respected friend Mr. Bob Ramsey, one of the world's most knowledgeable horn-rattlers, has correspondence in his files from hunters who have rattled up whitetails in New Hampshire, Pennsylvania, Georgia, Florida, Michigan, Iowa, Louisiana, Arkansas, and three Canadian provinces. The technique is original to Texas and widely practiced, yet there are parts of Texas where all you'll get for your trouble is bruised fingers.

About those special conditions. First, the local deer herd must be in or near the peak of the rut if the rattling antlers are to produce. The week or so prior to the rutting peak is by far the most productive time for aggressive rattling. Where a hunting season fails to overlap the rut, rattling is of no use to a hunter. Second, there must be a fairly good balance to the herd, with a decent buck ratio. Where five to ten (or more) does exist for each breeding buck, rattling may work, but too rarely to rely on as a regular hunting method. In much of America's deer country, exactly this condition does occur, including some parts of Texas.

Third, for *consistent* results, a horn-rattler must know what he's about. Not that there's any magic secret to the sounds made with the rattling antlers; different experts produce very different sequences of sounds, but all will rattle up whitetails. If there's a secret, it's in knowing when and where to rattle, rather than how to rattle.

There is also the matter of knowing where *not* to rattle, and heavily hunted public land is one of those places. Expert rattling, on public land, may be tantamount to suicide! Imagine the state of mind of the average public-land hunter, stumbling around in the woods looking for deer, when he hears the sounds of two bucks fighting furiously. As he approaches the scene of the supposed battle, he sees a movement in the bushes, and he *knows* it has to be a buck. Guess what happens next.

I've rattled up bucks, ranchers, does, other hunters, coyotes, wetbacks, more bucks, game wardens, and several other assorted species of wildlife. *Don't* try it on public hunting lands during the open season; readers with the good taste to buy books like this one are far too scarce as it is, and I don't want to lose any.

Some veteran rattlers believe that bucks come to the sound of the horns because they believe the fight to be over a receptive doe, and they hope to make off with her before the combatants notice. I think this gives the deer too much credit for reasoning ability. I further think that battles between bucks during the rut are over territory, rather than individual females. Although I have seen bucks of every size from nubbins upward respond to the sounds of the rattles, those which came in most furiously were the biggest bucks (territorialized, dominant, breeding males), and they usually responded close to an identifiable breeding territory. In any case, I

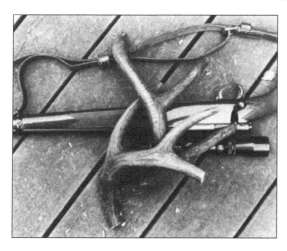

The notches filed on this pair of rattling horns (now retired because of brittleness) show that twenty-eight bucks have been shot while responding to their sounds. Almost all had ten points or more.

This is what a big whitetail looks like as he charges the sound of the antlers. If his tail is at half mast, as shown, he's completely fooled; if it's down, he's still suspicious and great care must be taken with subsequent sounds.

know of nothing in deer hunting which comes closer to being a lead-pipe cinch than rattling the antlers downwind from a fresh scrape.

We see two different kinds of responses, the "chargers" and the "sneakers." The chargers are the bucks which literally charge the sound of the horns, eyes blazing, nostrils flared, hair standing on end, ears drooping and laid back (a characteristic threat gesture). They may come from any direction, occasionally including downwind, and they come at a dead run, swatting and slashing with their antlers at inoffensive small shrubs which get in their way. It's quite a sight, and one which can produce quite a variety of reactions in a first-time hunter, from frozen astonishment through various degrees of hysteria. The chargers sometimes wind up within a few feet of the hunter, and there's an almost irresistible impulse to shoot *in self-defense*!

The chargers are always exciting, but very few bucks put on such an exhibition when coming to the rattling horns. Most appear walking briskly or actually stalking the sounds, circling and testing the wind, reluctant to expose themselves until they have the situation sized up. Really big bucks may respond in either way, and no one knows why the differences. Perhaps the proximity to a scrape, the skill of the rattler, the stage of the rut, the number of times the buck has been fooled with the horns, or just the mood of the moment makes the difference between a charger and a sneaker. Whatever it is, the hunter must set himself up for the sneaker in every case; the charger will be easy if one happens to show up.

The ideal rattling spot, therefore, is one near an active scrape or at least in an area known to be inhabited by a dominant buck, with good concealment for the hunter, and good visibility in all directions, especially downwind. Again, I like to have my scent blowing across the center of a large opening, if it must blow anywhere at all, so that a buck circling for my scent will show himself to me before he catches the scent stream. However, rattling is largely futile on really windy days. Cold, dead-calm, bright weather is perfect, and a little breeze is acceptable, but a strong wind cancels out rattling as a viable technique.

The most common error made by inexperienced horn-rattlers is timidity. The trick is to make a *lot* of noise, but the right kind of noise. According to my lights (equally successful rattlers are sure to disagree), the right sequence of noise is roughly as follows. I try to locate my position next to some dry brush and, if the locality is gravelly, so much the better. I begin by clashing the two sawed-off antlers together as loudly as possible, and then mesh the tines and shake them, pushing them together very hard, to produce a somewhat disjointed sequence of rubbing, clattering sounds. After perhaps thirty seconds of this, I rip them apart and immediately use them to thrash the dry brush and pound on the ground to simulate thumping hooves and antlers against the shrubbery. I often rattle standing up, in which case I stomp furiously with my own feet and bash the limbs of whatever tree I'm using for camouflage. All this is done as loudly as I can make it; the more I can sound like a pair of bull moose having at each other, the better I like it.

Some horn-rattlers choose small antlers, saying they don't intimidate bucks. The author prefers big ones, saying he can rattle big horns quietly if needed but he can't make little ones sound big—and too much noise when rattling antlers is a contradiction in terms!

An important part of the rattling sequence involves crashing and rubbing bushes and thumping the earth to simulate *all* the sounds of a real buck fight. Sometimes a buck will respond without the rattler ever clashing the rattling horns together.

I then lay the rattles aside and get my hands on my rifle. It's very common to have a buck on top of you even before you complete this whole sequence of racket. If nothing shows up, however, within ten to fifteen minutes, I go to work again. (Ramsey advocates waiting at least half an hour before continuing.) This time, I omit the initial loud clash, merely meshing the tines and tickling them lightly for a few seconds, hoping to pull a buck which hasn't shown himself out of the brush. If he fails to appear after a minute or two, I thrust one rattle into the dry bush and shake, twist, and scrape it violently, then go back to the ground-thumping and gravel-raking. Of the hundreds of bucks I've drawn to the rattling horns, I think most of them have appeared during or just after this second sequence, and I stay on hair-trigger alert to drop the horns and grab the gun.

Another five to ten minutes later, I may repeat the performance, with or without the first clash, and with plenty of brush-busting. I will not leave a well-chosen rattling stand for at least thirty minutes, or for fifteen minutes after the last buck appears. Yes, it's quite common to attract more than one buck to the same stand. My lifetime record is eight at one place in about two hours, and I returned to the same place the next morning and rattled up four, of which three were strangers and the fourth was shot by my companion. I have a witness to the eight-buck performance, and photographs of every one of the deer.

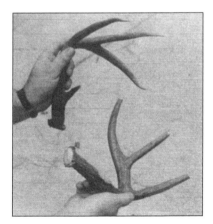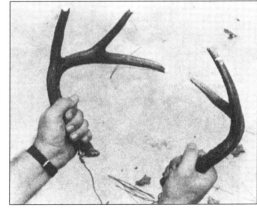

The process of converting a set of antlers to rattles is shown at left by a comparison between an unmodified antler at top and its mate, bottom, which has had the eyeguard removed, the tines tipped, and a thonghole drilled. The basic grip used by most veteran horn-rattlers is illustrated at right.

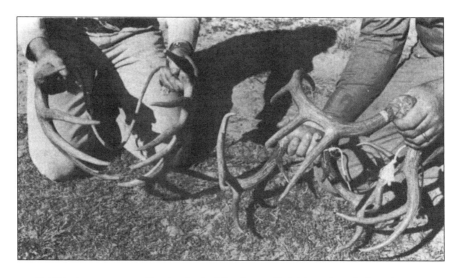

At left is shown a conventional pair of rattling horns. At right, a set made from the complete racks of two different bucks, used by knifemaker Doyal Nolen with good results. (Photo by George Martin)

Bucks which come to the sounds of the antlers often behave in peculiar ways, even though they may not "charge." They may stand around and watch you do things that no sane whitetail would let you get away with. Once I rattled up a nice eleven-pointer for my wife, but she couldn't see him through a fogged riflescope. He stood there, at about 100 yards, and watched us switch rifles, after which she killed him in his tracks. We were in camouflage, but had no concealment at all from the buck's angle, and he must have stood motionless and stared at us for two or three whole minutes. Another time, a male companion and I rattled a while, rejected the three bucks which showed up, and decided to move on. We both stood up to relieve ourselves, in the middle of which process we glanced over our shoulders to see a fine, wide eleven-pointer staring at us from about 90 yards. We were fully skylined and talking in normal tones, yet he stood there long enough for my friend to kneel, grab his rifle, size up the head, and drop him with a single bullet. At such times, it appears that a buck, especially a big buck, is so programmed to see two bucks fighting by the sounds he heard from a distance that he simply doesn't believe his eyes.

This doesn't mean that a hunter can take liberties when rattling. Careful selection of concealed positions and silent, motionless scanning will get more bucks than standing atop a pickup-truck cab and clashing the antlers (although I've seen deer respond to that tactic, too).

On the whole, I find horn-rattling the single most thrilling and satisfying of all whitetail hunting methods, and probably the one technique most productive of bigger bucks, on the average, than any other . . . when it works. But, like any other hunting method, horn-rattling doesn't always work. There's no magic to it (contrary to some accounts), and some days you do and some days you don't score with rattling. Sometimes, even in good rattling country, I seem to hit a slump when I can't rattle up a jackrabbit for days on end, rut or no rut. I believe such slumps account for the all-too-common hunter who has tried it and thinks it's a bunch of Texas bull.

Or, he *knows* it works in his non-Texan neck of the woods and prefers that competing hunters *not* know it! Think it over.

Next question: does horn-rattling work on mule deer? Answer: I don't know for certain, but I don't believe it does. I can't do it, and I know many Texas rattling pros who can't do it. I've seen big muley bucks fighting, with other bucks paying no attention whatever to them. On the other hand, I know one or two people who claim to have killed mule bucks over the horns, and I do not think these men are lying. All I can say is that the preponderance of evidence, in my mind, suggests that rattling in mule deer habitat is a waste of valuable hunting time.

If so, why should this be? I think it's because the muleys are not territorial. Muleys occasionally fight over does, but not over breeding bailiwicks. Muleys do not respond to horn-rattling. Whitetails do come to the horns, and are known to be territorial animals. It seems to support my theory that whitetails' battles are over territory and not over specific female deer.

I have emphasized that horn-rattling works only around the peak of the rut, but it's also true that the horns are useful to a hunter at other times and for purposes other than attracting the bucks to the gun. One misty morning in late November, I climbed into a high tower stand before daylight and watched for a shootable buck until nearly ten a.m. I saw only a few does and yearlings. Although I knew positively that the rut was not in progress in that area, I clapped the rattling horns together a time or two before departing—and was amazed to see no fewer than four antlered bucks

Some rattled-up bucks do come in really close! If you think this isn't exciting—especially when he comes at a dead run—you're not a hunter! *(Photo by Mike Biggs)*

get up out of their beds within 200 yards of my stand. None was an acceptable trophy, and I watched two of them lie back down while the other pair drifted away. Those deer weren't about to actually approach the sound of the horns, but it got them on their feet for a few minutes and gave me a look at them.

On another occasion, a friend and I were walking down a road inside the boundary fence of our property when we saw a doe emerge from the brush 150 yards ahead of us and jump the fence. Suspecting what was about to happen, I snatched the rattling horns from my shoulder and when the buck stepped out I crashed them together. He froze, staring at us, for just long enough that my companion could knock him down. If I hadn't stopped him with the horns, that buck would have been over the fence (into country where we couldn't legally shoot him) and after his lady friend before my buddy could have brought the rifle to bear. I could recite literally dozens of instances when the rattling horns have helped, even when the buck had no intention of actually coming to the sounds.

For example, it's axiomatic among rattlers that you can't rattle a buck away from a hot doe (only partly true; if you get close enough without his sensing you, you can often make him come 50 yards or so, at the gallop), but a clash of the antlers may make him at least take a few steps away from her side and expose himself to see where the racket is coming from. In other words, even when you can't pull a buck in close, you can sometimes set him up for a long shot.

Horn rattling mixes quite well with other hunting techniques, especially still-hunting. In fact, when the moon of madness is upon the rutting whitetails, my favorite manner of passing a day afield is "walking and rattling," still-hunting for a half-mile or more at a stretch, then picking a promising spot to rattle the horns, then moving on. Rattling may be most productive early in the morning and late in the evening (most real buck fights seem to be at night), but it will definitely produce at any time of day. One veteran of my acquaintance claims he actually prefers to do his rattling between noon and two p.m., and he has a row of whitetail trophies on his den wall that might make your eyes bug out.

One important tip to the would-be rattler concerns the situation in which a buck shows up which he doesn't wish to kill. Watch this animal very carefully, because he'll sense the arrival of another buck long before you can, and will point him as reliably as a good bird dog points quail. Now and then, if two evenly matched deer happen to meet in front of a horn-rattling hunter, he'll be able to see them tie into each other. It's worth seeing, and it will make him a more convincing rattler in the future for having heard the sounds of a real buck fight at close range. He'll know that whitetails' battles are more shoving contests than fencing duels, and that the combatants usually spend more energy demonstrating their ferocity to each other by savaging innocent bushes than in head-to-head battle.

All this can occur before a hunter who rattles from a tree stand or tower, although I prefer to do my rattling on the ground. I can't really put on the total performance in a stand, including the ground-thumping and brush-thrashing, but I certainly have rattled bucks up to a stand. If the rut's going good, it may be worth trying.

When this book was first published, so-called "grunt calls" had not been invented. I'd occasionally heard deer grunting in the woods since boyhood, and in the 1940s knew one expert who claimed to call up bucks by imitating such sounds with his mouth, but this idea has become widely accepted only during the last decade. Even then, I was slow to climb aboard the buck-grunt bandwagon, and so omitted the concept from the original manuscript.

For a long time after manufacturers started showering me with grunt calls, I was skeptical. I knew some bucks (especially young ones) would respond now and then, but I'd also seen many (especially mature ones) utterly ignore such calls and a few even flee from them, and I couldn't visualize a way in which a grunt call might be of use to a serious trophy hunter. But that was then, and this is now. I still tend to regard grunting as a refinement, rather than a vital skill, but there are times and places in which it's useful, and nowadays I usually have a call stuck in my hunting-shirt pocket.

Because grunt calling is excellent window dressing with a horn-rattling performance, I've chosen this spot to stick it in, but there are a number of things to keep in mind. One is that both sexes grunt at all times of the year, and another is that grunting can convey many different kinds of messages between deer. A third is that if whitetails actually did a lot of grunting, a hunter would hear a lot more of it in the woods than we do. The only place I've ever heard what I'd describe as a chorus of grunting was in a large clearing in

Michigan at dusk, with about eighty whitetails in sight. The air was perfectly still, and the sound was an eerie, almost continuous subliminal rumble coming from all directions.

Deer grunt mostly to identify themselves and reassure other deer. Does call their fawns to nurse with a very soft grunt, and thus a grunt, almost the first sound a young deer hears, has only the pleasantest associations. Most whitetail grunting simply identifies its maker as a deer and locates it. Often, when a deer may have caught a movement or a slight noise of mine but isn't yet sure that I'm a danger, I can cause it to relax visibly by letting it hear a single, short, very soft grunt. A sequence of eight or ten somewhat more emphatic grunts within four or five minutes, repeated not more often than about once an hour, sometimes entices either young bucks or does to approach my stand. I don't know exactly what I'm saying to the animals with such grunts, but they appear to be confident and relaxed.

The one kind of whitetail grunting that almost every hunter has heard is that of a rutting buck trailing a doe. This is a series of harsher, more aggressive grunts spaced irregularly, ten to twenty seconds apart and continued for several minutes. Individual grunts are short but sharp and I like to vary their sound by cupping my hand over the tube and directing the call in different directions, to imitate a trailing buck grunting as he trots through the woods.

The tending grunt, made by a buck when with a doe in estrus, sounds the same as the trailing grunt, but is rendered at extended intervals without any set sequence.

There is also a slightly prolonged grunt that changes pitch, almost like a very brief growl, that I use only in connection with horn rattling, immediately before the initial antler clash. Whether this actually improves my rattling returns, I cannot say, but it sounds better to me.

There is one other important use of a grunt call, and it is to make a whitetail buck stop and look, perhaps giving a hunter time to size up a rack or to draw a bead. In Alberta, one cold, still morning, I actually made a buck that was with a hot doe stop and look back, at about three hundred yards. This alone makes a grunter a worthwhile thing to have in your pocket while in the field.

Most of the grunt calls made today—and every call manufacturer makes at least one—imitate a whitetail grunt adequately. It is not a complex, inflected noise and not nearly as expressive as, say, a duck or turkey call. The one feature in which I find many grunters lacking, however, is that they cannot be blown softly enough. Most deer grunts are very low-intensity sounds, and by the time enough air is flowing through many calls to get the reed vibrating, the resulting grunt will be too loud. And, like all wild-game calling, the cardinal sin in grunting up whitetails is overdoing it. Less is better.

There's still a lot for us to learn about grunt calling. Expert European hunters can practically converse with roe deer in their own complicated language of age- and sex-specific squeaks, bleats, and whistles. Whitetail lingo does not seem to be that complex . . . but then, what do we know? A few years ago—after maybe fifty centuries of contact between humans and whitetails—we humans hadn't figured out that the few, scattered deer grunts we heard had any meaning at all.

There are a thousand stories in Texas about weird rattling experiences, and most of them are probably true. One is about the fellow who was clearing weed seeds and grasses from the radiator of his bulldozer and was almost run down by a buck which mistook the rattling of his stick against the bars of the grille for a battle. Another tale is about the hunter who shot a buck whose antlers clattered against the stony ground as he kicked his last—and drew a much bigger buck out of the brush. One version of how the whole idea began has it that a fellow near Cotulla, Texas, was driving a wooden-wheeled wagon along a ranch road during the rut. The spokes in his wagon wheels were dry and shrunken, and rattled as he drove along—and you can figure out the rest. There are yarns about hunters producing rut-maddened bucks by banging a knife handle on a gunstock, or merely by breaking off a brittle branch. I myself inadvertently left my rattling horns at home during a hunting trip and rattled up four whitetails in one day with a pair of bleached, dried-out shed antlers from the previous year which I picked up in the woods.

Whether you buy any of these tales, don't make the mistake of believing that horn-rattling is a fraud. Far from it, it's one of the most productive and exciting of all gimmicks for a trophy buck, in the right places and at the right times. If you don't believe that, you may be cheating yourself of some superlative experiences.

14 Unorthodox Tricks

The big buck had the drop on me. I was crouched at the intersection of two *senderos* (straight seismograph roads through the brush), rattling the horns. I was just reaching for the horns for another session of banging and thrashing when I saw him. He was standing in the brush across the road, with those great dark eyes locked onto me like a fighter plane's target radar. I was kneeling, in full camouflage, with my rifle across my knees, and I figured I'd get it just about halfway to my shoulder before he disappeared. Instead of trying to outdraw him, so to speak, I began to raise my right hand slowly toward the bill of my cap, keeping hand and arm in front of me. It seemed to take an hour, but I forced myself to make the movement slow and smooth. When I got to the cap bill I took it firmly between thumb and forefinger, counted to three, and flicked the cap sailing to one side. At the same time my left hand was swinging the little Sako Mannlicher, and that buck's eyes were still riveted on my cap, spinning away into the brush, when the bullet struck him!

You think you'll have little use for that oddball trick? OK, there's no extra charge for it in this book—nor for the similarly oddball gimmicks which follow. Most of them have set up a buck for me at least once in my years, and if he's the buck of a lifetime, once is enough.

On another occasion I was still-hunting across a central Texas pasture in which a nice whitetail buck was known to live, along with about a million damned sheep. In the course of the morning, a young doe got me pinned down and was just about to blow the whistle, literally, on my hunt. She'd seen me move, but really hadn't figured me out, although she was growing perceptibly more nervous

with each passing second. One whistling snort from her dainty nostrils and I could pack up and head for the nearest hot cup of coffee. Behind me, suddenly, I heard a merino ewe call softly to her lamb, and it gave me a wacky idea. I took a deep breath and issued my first and best imitation of a sheep's bleat, knowing I had nothing to lose. If the little doe exploded, I was no worse off than if I did nothing; she was about to explode anyway.

Her reaction was almost magical; instantly, she relaxed and began to browse. Within a few minutes she was out of sight and I went

Whitetails reveal certain built-in escape behaviors that a knowledgeable and imaginative hunter can use against them. *(Photo by Mike Biggs)*

on with my hunting. I didn't kill the buck that morning, but I learned something, and it is that there's more than one way to camouflage one-self. The doe had seen me; at least, she'd seen *something* which she couldn't identify. In desperation, I fed one of her other senses false information. She was accustomed to sheep everywhere in the pasture, she saw an unfamiliar but unidentifiable shape in the brush, she heard a sheep bleat—ergo, she went her way. She may have thought it was a strange-sounding sheep, which I'll admit it surely was, but nothing in the combination pushed the "hunter alert" button in her brain.

Since that day, I have always carried a deep-toned predator call (a Burnham Brothers D-4, to be specific) in my right shirt pocket while hunting, and have used it several times to reassure deer that I was something besides a human being.

You say you don't have any sheep in your deer woods? OK, but maybe you'd better practice hog noises, a horse whinnying, or other such sounds. You probably can't convince a deer that you're a squirrel, but I've seen the day I'd try anything, including gnawing hickory nuts!

That sense of desperation, of nothing to lose, has caused me to try a lot of things which made me glad nobody else was around to watch. Some of them worked, and more of them didn't, but the good ones are worth passing along. Most are based on a sort of backhanded logic.

For example, every hunter knows the situation in which the woods are hopelessly noisy for any kind of still-hunting. Ankle-deep dry leaves and crusted snow are the usual problems, and now and then clinking, tinkling rocks baffle the most expert hunter. Now, we can't walk quietly, so what do we do? Obviously, sit in a stand, and let the deer do the rustling and crunching. So I started out one afternoon to walk a mile or so through tinder-dry, deep leaves to reach a certain tree through the deepest, crunchiest drifts of oak leaves I could find, but I kept my eyes roaming the edges of the brush and the rifle at low port arms, ready to swing. Sure enough, I walked right up on two does, standing half-hidden behind some yaupon. I kept walking, watching them from the corner of my eyes, until I was 50 yards past them. Then, without breaking stride, I turned and lifted the rifle. The crosshairs came to rest on a shoulder for more than long enough for me to whisper "Bang!" before they dashed away.

Two or three years later, under very similar conditions, I did the same thing to a buck, except that this time I spun and shot him just as his muscles bunched to whirl. This was not a giant trophy buck, and I'm not so sure that such an animal would be so docile. On the other hand, he might be even more confident because of his built-in tendency to hide instead of run. One of these days, my "loud-hunting" technique (as opposed to still-hunting) just may get a shot on a noisy day that no amount of pussyfooting could possibly produce.

Where the woods are impossibly dry and noisy, a deer in cover that thinks it hasn't been noticed may allow a man to get within range if the man abandons stealth completely, approaches obliquely, and seems to ignore the animal. *(Photo by Mike Biggs)*

Really, about the only difference between this method and what most of the clowns wandering around in the woods these days do in the name of "still-hunting" is that I know how to see deer in the brush, and how to shoot quickly. The trick, of course, is to see the deer before he runs, and to alter my noisy course so as to pass well clear of him, convincing him that he hasn't been noticed. The slightest hesitation in my walking, however, will send him on his way in a flash.

One of the wildest things I ever did in the woods was to chase a fleeing buck openly and at a dead run. I've often made a short dash to one side or ahead to gain a view of a small clearing in the thickets after jumping a buck without getting a shot off, and have occasionally had another glimpse. And I have, just as often, moved stealthily ahead on his trail . . . and never laid eyes on him again. What possessed me to break into a mad run one evening when I jumped a buck and a doe quite by surprise, I will never know. What I do know is that, as whitetails commonly do, this one dashed about 40 yards through the brush and stopped to look back just before

Deer often wait for corroboration from another of their senses for a danger warning. If the hunter can feed a buck's ears or nose false information, he may be able to get away with actually allowing the animal to see him. *(Photo by W. A. Maltsberger)*

stepping into the next thicket across a small clearing. About the time he turned to gaze, I popped out into the clearing and he stood for a few seconds in what appeared to be open-mouthed astonishment. No, I didn't shoot him—his rack was below standards—but I believe I could have. Maybe he was just a dumb buck. Maybe he was reluctant to leave the doe, a much more likely theory. Maybe he was simply taken offguard because I did the unexpected and, for the first time in his life, his programmed escape mechanism failed. Who knows? All I can say is that if he'd had bigger antlers, I'd have collected him in a way that none of my hunting friends would ever have believed.

And maybe, if he *had* had bigger antlers, and the age and wisdom to go with them, he would never have fallen for such nonsense.

The subject of deer-attracting scents comes up regularly around my campfires, and I must state that I have never really become convinced of their value. I've tried most of the advertised brands, using them just as recommended, and the kindest review I can give them is that they do not frighten deer away. Neither do they seem to hold any strange power over the whitetails, in my part of the world at least. Whether they're compounded to smell like apples or sex, it may be that their greatest contribution is masking the human scent enough to provide a bit of olfactory camouflage. I'm forced to add, however, that one respected deer-hunting buddy of mine reports that Mennen Skin Bracer simply drives does wild; he has no data on bucks' reaction to this particular shaving lotion.

On the subject of scent-masking, there's a good deal to be said for it, and several ways to go about it. The most effective I've discovered is pure, natural skunk musk. Not the synthetic products, but the real thing, right out of the skunk. The only source I know of is Burnham Brothers Sporting Goods, Mason, Texas, and the price is probably around $25 per ounce by now. It's sold in half-ounce vials, and, believe me, a half-ounce of genuine skunk smellum goes a long, long way. My manner of using this stuff is as follows: dip about an inch of the end of a pipe cleaner in the musk, and twist the other end around your hatband or cap button, letting the pipe cleaner stick out, away from contact with your hat. If the pipe cleaner is kept in an old toothbrush container between uses, it will probably last all season with undiminished ferocity, and your wife may let you in the house at the end of the hunting trip. If *you* can stand it, you'll find that it confounds the nostrils of a whitetail rather effectively, and is especially useful while rattling or stand-hunting.

Another friend of mine, when he can, excises the tarsal glands from a rutting buck killed by somebody else in camp and carries them on a string around his neck. As I do, he wears a one-piece, camouflaged coverall over his regular garments while hunting, and he stuffs the coveralls into a plastic sack with the reeking glands between weekend trips. We continually flack him about the day when he's going to be assaulted by a rutting buck, but I must concede that he's one of the most successful big-buck hunters I know.

Throughout my hunting life, I've found myself thinking of does—which were not legal game in Texas until I'd voted in my first presidential election—as decoys. When I could get a couple of does feeding on acorns or oats in front of my stand, I automatically became more alert, knowing that they were by far the best buck lure going.

I was right about that, of course, but another new development in deer hunting in the last few years has been the appearance on the market of artificial deer decoys. I have experimented extensively with a few of these for several seasons, and am undecided about the proper point in this revision of *Hunting Trophy Deer* at which to insert them.

A hunter who's willing to try something new and who has an intimate knowledge of whitetail habits (especially rutting habits) can sometimes collect a head that conventional techniques would never deliver. *(Photo by W. A. Maltsberger)*

Perhaps this chapter on tricks and gimmicks is as good as any, although I do not mean to disparage deer decoys as mere gimmicks. They definitely have an effect on the behavior of both bucks and does, but I still regard decoying as very specialized, invaluable in certain narrow circumstances but not a primary hunting technique.

When first deployed in whitetail habitat, a decoy will always elicit some sort of reaction from deer . . . but the nature of that reaction is unpredictable. It can range from flight to an outright physical assault on the decoy. Most commonly, the reaction is intense curiosity. If any of the deer in your woods exhibit total indifference to your initial decoying effort, it's a sure sign that somebody else beat you to it. Deer quickly learn to ignore the fake deer among them. This leads to the first rule of decoying: don't overdo it, and never leave a decoy in place in the woods in your absence. I try not even to use a decoy in the same spot twice more often than every other season.

Next, I use only female decoys, and only during or near the rut's peak. All the decoy models I've seen are excellent, but the one I prefer is the Feather-Flex bedded deer. It weighs less than a pound, is easily transported and quickly deployed, and can be presented as either a doe or small buck. This is a natural application for the various urine-based "hot-doe" buck lures, by the way, but a squirt of juice on the decoy's rear end will not mask a nearby hunter's scent. Always position the decoy upwind. An absolute rule: never set up the decoy so that it appears to be looking at your blind or location; nervous whitetails routinely look where they see other deer looking.

I reserve decoys for specific spots and purposes, such as trying to bring a buck into a position where I can see, evaluate, and perhaps shoot him. This is not the same as using the decoy as the primary attraction to bring a buck in from a distance. In fact, setting up where the decoy can be seen from a distance may be suicidal; deer decoys have been shot from long range with high-powered rifles while bowhunters were concealed quite close to them.

A typical decoying situation occurred a few seasons back when I was concentrating on a certain tremendous fourteen-point buck. The deer was seen several times crossing a private ranch road at its intersection with a small draw where trees and shrubs squeezed in to narrow the right-of-way. Prevailing wind directions and lack of ambush cover made it an awkward spot to hunt, especially since the clear width of the primitive road at the draw was only about two deer lengths.

I deployed Jezebel, the hussy doe decoy, on the shoulder of the road on the near side of the crossing, and slathered her fanny with doe pee. All I wanted her to do was to buy me a little time. If she could entice the big buck into taking a few steps toward her, that would be icing on the cake, but I hoped he would at least stop and stare at her for a minute, instead of flitting across the road so quickly I couldn't lift a rifle. This buck's head was so big that evaluation would be superfluous; all I needed was a few extra seconds to make a clean, certain shot.

Jezebel did her customary professional job . . . but not on the buck I came for. She stopped two magnificent bucks—one ten- and one twelve-pointer—cold and held them there for several minutes, in the meantime keeping their eyes so riveted on her that the twelve-pointer walked within a few yards of where I sat, camouflaged in the brush, with never a glance in my direction. I could have killed him a dozen times . . . and I wonder to this day why I didn't! But the guest of honor didn't show up—and who shoots a twelve-pointer when a fourteen-pointer is expected by at any minute?

Decoying is great fun, and every serious trophy hunter should understand the technique, but I believe it's best used very sparingly and discreetly, at times and places where nothing else will do the job. Then it may make the difference between success and failure.

Although some of the gimmicks described in this chapter (and some which I'm too embarrassed to include) may sound humorous and of extremely limited utility, there may be something to be learned from them as a whole. It is that the really good hunters are always thinking creatively, never doing things by rote, never taking things about deer for granted. They observe the deer and try to interpret what they observe, not from the conventional, orthodox point of view but with a new twist. And they stay loose, sometimes operate on spur-of-the-moment theories, try new tactics. Many of their stunts are merely hilarious failures, but now and then they stumble onto something that makes a real difference. After all, how silly did the first guy feel who sat down with a pair of old shed antlers and started beating them together in the woods? Probably one hell of a lot sillier than did a fellow named Henderson Coquat in 1949 in Webb County, Texas, when he rattled up and shot a buck which still ranks No. 95 out of the more than 1,200 typical whitetail heads listed in the Boone and Crockett records!

Call them oddball, weirdo tricks if you wish, but never sell short the hunter's one great advantage over his quarry, which is the power of *imagination*.

15 Choosing a Weapon

Having alienated the hound hunters and drivers in an earlier chapter, I'm now about to infuriate the archers, muzzleloaders, and pistoleros by pointing out that these weapons are unsuitable for serious trophy hunting. But before the letter bombs begin arriving, let me hasten to point out that I often hunt with a muzzleloading rifle or a handgun, and could be described as an enthusiast of such armaments. Furthermore, I have the deepest respect for serious bowmen and, indeed, feel a profound empathy with their approach to the sport and the skills they must develop. They're *hunters*, and that's vital in the pursuit of trophy whitetails.

I'm aware, also, that bowhunters have collected some magnificent heads, trophies which not only placed in the archers' own Pope and Young record book, but scored well up in the Boone and Crockett listings (which make no distinction between weapons systems, as long as they're legal). Some of the bowmen's whitetails are deer I'd cheerfully run barefooted through a prickly-pear cactus patch to get a shot at!

Nevertheless, the archery tackle, charcoal burners, and belt guns all share one fatal limitation for trophy hunting, and that is range. Few handguns and fewer handgunners are capable of quick, precise fire at more than 100 yards (no offense; I've served on the board of directors and selection committee for the Outstanding Handgunner of the Year Award for years). The same is true of muzzleloading rifles, especially with round balls, and, of course, the archers are thinking in terms of perhaps 40 yards. Within their ranges, all these weapons are lethal, in the hands of skilled hunters, but those ranges are necessarily limited. As I have been at some

pains to point out in earlier chapters, a mature whitetail buck is so
formidable an adversary, by his very nature, that a hunter needs no
additional handicaps. What he needs, instead, is the most efficient
tool which fits into the legal and ethical schemes of sportsmanship.
A chance at a really superb trophy buck comes very seldom, sometimes only once in a lifetime. It's often a difficult shot, through
brush, at a bad angle, and/or running, and usually must be quick.
The hunter who has invested several years of planning, study, and
scouting and executed his hunt with the skill and woodsmanship
required even to lay eyes on a real trophy buck is unwise, in my
opinion, to rely upon a primitive weapon.

The obvious exception arises during one of the special primi-
tive-weapons hunting seasons now common in good deer states.
These early-season hunts are attractive for several reasons, the best
being that the woods are much less crowded and a genuine hunter
has a better chance to operate. They also extend the duration of the
total annual season for the man willing to master one of the so-
called primitive arms. Since these are the only weapons legal during
this time, they're obviously the weapons of choice, and if a trophy is
to be hunted, he must be hunted with the bow or black powder. Of
course, the rut seldom, if ever, coincides with a special preseason
hunt, and this vastly reduces the odds on an elder, trophy-class
buck.

There is always the guy who is determined to use only the bow
or a frontstuffer, regardless, simply because he enjoys the extra challenge of such weapons, and he may now and then get a really big
buck all figured out and go after him, successfully. I stand in awe of
such determination. The fact that the minimum Boone and Crockett
score for the bowhunters' record book is 135 points (recently raised
from 125), compared to the B&C minimum for a typical whitetail of
170 points, may make the point more convincingly than I can.

To prove that I do not take muzzleloaders lightly, I point out
that with them I've hunted not only deer but Alaskan moose;
Colorado black bear; New Mexico elk; Wyoming pronghorn; and
Texas wild hogs, javelina, and various exotic species. I am not a
"buckskinner"; I hunt with black-powder arms simply because I
love the guns and their historical ambiance and derive a special satisfaction from the effort. I was into muzzleloading rifles before the

first replica hit the market and when many original caplock rifles could be bought in hockshops for less than $50. To me, therefore, a muzzleloading rifle simply looked and felt "right," with a long barrel, full stock, percussion or flint sidelock system, open sights, and set triggers. For many years, I resisted, or ignored, the rise of the in-line guns. Finally, with an invitation to hunt in the big-buck country of Pike County, Illinois, during a brief gun season when only muzzleloaders and shotguns were allowed, I took the plunge. I acquired an ultramodern .50-caliber in-line gun, scoped it, and went hunting. With it, I suffered the only misfire I've ever experienced with a muzzleloader on big game, and lost a fine buck. This was certainly not the fault of the in-line style, and not necessarily the fault of the individual model I carried, but it soured prospects for my becoming an in-line enthusiast.

The in-line guns handle well, shoot with phenomenal accuracy, and are well thought out and safe, and they feel right to one familiar with modern arms. With due diligence in selecting and testing balls and loads, I found my rifle capable of surprising groups out to 150 yards, a distance at which I would not even think of shooting at an unwounded animal with any of my fine traditional guns. I can no longer deny that the muzzleloading rifle, in its evolved in-line pattern, is a proper tool for a serious trophy hunter (although I could quibble with its definition as a "primitive" weapon, especially when scoped).

Although not normally regarded as a primitive weapon, perhaps the shotgun should be. Except for its repeating capability, it suffers from about the same liabilities as a muzzleloading rifle, including the limitation on effective range. It is, however, the only type of weapon permitted for deer in several midwestern and eastern states. None of these states, as far as I know, requires the use of buckshot ammunition, and many specifically prohibit it.

I grew up hunting in an area shared by shotgun hunters who preferred buckshot, although this was in the 1940s and even then we knew better. Year after year, I kept stumbling over dead and dying deer which had been wounded and lost with buckshot pellets. One buck had had his lower jaw shattered by a single pellet and was in the process of starving to death, in agony, when I put him out of his suffering. From that day until this, I have hated buckshot and am not very likely to change my mind, even though I am fully aware

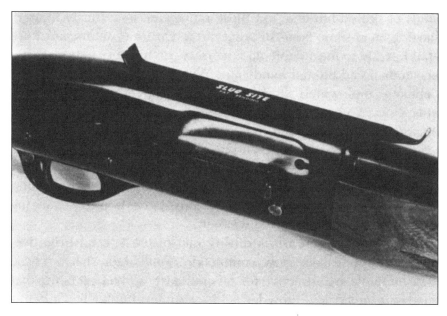

In states requiring the use of a shotgun for deer hunting, only rifled slugs in a gun with sights should be used. Illustrated here is a very inexpensive and effective sight that can be attached and removed without altering the gun. A low-powered scope would be even better.

of the improvements in buckshot ammunition of late. They have been great, but not great enough to make it even marginally sporting for deer. I am particularly impatient with the argument that buckshot is the only feasible armament for the standers on dog drives, because shots are fleeting. If shots are all that fleeting, there can be no possible chance to size up a rack, which eliminates any further discussion for the trophy hunter, and if the shot is close enough to be taken with buckshot, even with luck, it's close enough to be fairly easy with a rifle *in the hands of a practiced hunter!* Further, almost any rifle is more efficient in heavy brush than a buckshot pattern, because of the extremely poor ballistic characteristics of round pellets.

These comments are not to be taken as a condemnation of the shotgun as a venison-getter when properly loaded with rifled slugs. In a good barrel, especially one of the "slug specials" sold by every shotgun manufacturer, and with correctly zeroed-in iron sights or scope, slugs are extremely deadly out to any ranges at which the combination will group five shots within about 8 inches from a rest.

That range will usually be not less than 50 yards, and sometimes close to 100 (occasionally farther) in run-of-the-mill factory barrels. In close cover, that's enough range, and the power is undeniably there. At least in 12 gauge and 16 gauge, the power is there; in the smaller gauges, the slugs just can't weigh enough to deliver adequate energy and penetration.

It is well worth the hunter's trouble and expense, however, to bench-test various brands of slugs in his individual barrel for accuracy. Different brands are quite likely to reveal very wide differences in grouping ability, and the tighter the grouping, the longer effective range the combination of gun and slugs will have. In general, the more open the choke, the better will be slug performance, and most of the slug specials are straight cylinder bore. However, slugs will not damage the choke in any well-made gun, regardless of the constriction; the functional difference is only in accuracy. Some of the high-tech slug ammo developments, in combination with new barrel technology, must be taken seriously as buck-busting combinations, especially the so-called "rifled" barrels (where legal). With special guns, scopes, and loadings, hunters in shotgun-only regions are hardly handicapped in any typical deer habitat.

We come now to rifles, the almost universal weapon of the trophy hunter where lawful. As a full-time firearms writer and editor for half a dozen outdoors magazines, I have the opportunity to test every new model and each new cartridge and I believe strongly in *field* tests, if at all possible. Too many times I have seen range-test conclusions fall apart when the item began to see service in the field. Paper ballistics are nice, but dead deer on the meatpole tell me a great deal more.

It's often said that most whitetails are killed at less than 100 yards, which is probably true. However, this may be as much because the mythical "average" hunter cannot regularly score vital hits beyond that range as it is because so many shots at deer are close-range chances. Heresy, in this land of Daniel Boone and Alvin York? Not at all. Condescension toward my readers? No way! That statement is what is called a perception of reality. Present company is excepted, naturally, but if you'd like to make some money, bet your hunting buddies that they can't stand up on their hind feet with a hunting rifle and keep ten straight shots inside a 12-inch circle at 100 yards. You'll lose a few, but you'll be way ahead on balance. Yet a 12-inch circle just about circumscribes the vital area of a whitetail buck from any angle, and such marksmanship should be the *minimum* acceptable performance for any man who intends to fire at an animal which is capable of bleeding and feeling pain.

My point really is that many shots at whitetails are presented at much greater distances than the solemnly announced 100 yards. In many areas, double that range might be closer to the average, with some feasible opportunities at much longer distances. Even in the thickety midwestern and eastern states the hunter often finds himself looking across abandoned fields, down powerline rights-of-way, and across timbering clearcuts where a deer, if seen, would be far beyond the length of a football field. And it goes almost without saying that perhaps the majority of shots on mule deer are well outside a 100-yard radius. For this reason, I believe the serious trophy hunter is better armed with a modern, relatively flat-shooting cartridge capable of delivering good energies way out yonder than with any of the so-called "classic" whitetail rounds.

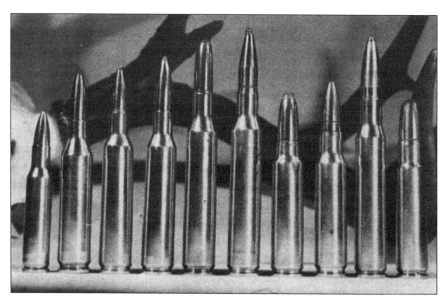

All these cartridges—and many more—are used for deer. I consider the .222 Remington (left) unsporting for any deer hunting and the next three—.243 WCF, 6mm Remington, and .257 Roberts—adequate only in expert hands for big trophy bucks. The rest are suitable, within their range limitations, for such animals: .270 WCF, .280 Remington, .300 Savage, .308 WCF, .30-06, and .35 Remington.

I speak from some experience. I've probably killed more deer with the .35 Remington, .30-30 WCF, and .300 Savage than with all other calibers combined, excluding the .308 WCF. I presently own favorite rifles in all these chamberings. But I have not had one in my hands while afield in trophy-buck country in more than fifteen years. It is my unshakable belief that a hunter should prepare himself for the *most difficult* opportunity which may be presented, rather than for the average chance, and that if the choice must be made between too much power and not enough, the former is the more intelligent and humane choice. If a hunter is carrying a rifle with which he feels confident of his ability to put in a first-round vital hit on a buck at, say, 300 yards, he will obviously find anything closer very easy. But if he totes something with a maximum effective range of, say, 150 yards (which includes most of the classic whitetail rounds) and sees the buck of his dreams at 250, he has only himself to blame. The odds are, too, that he'll show up in camp with a new rifle next season, but it seems to make more sense to get the new rifle *before* you need it.

This does not mean that I recommend some great, howling magnum cartridge, although there are a few magnums on my preferred list. Many nonbelted cartridges will do the job every bit as well, with pleasanter recoil, in more carriable rifles. If you pinned me down, I'd have to say that—for honest-to-gosh *trophy* hunting, remember—I'd want a cartridge driving a bullet not lighter than 130 grains of not smaller than .26 caliber, and would impose a minimum muzzle velocity on such rounds of about 2,800 feet per second. At the other end of the spectrum, I feel no need for anything more potent than a .30 caliber 150-grain bullet traveling at least 2,800 feet per second. To be specific, these criteria would include the 6.5mm Swedish Mauser and 6.5mm Rem. Magnum (both handloaded with 140-grain bullets), .260 Rem., 270 WCF, 7mm-08 Rem., 7x57mm Mauser, .280 Rem., 284 WCF, 7mm Rem. and Weatherby Magnums, .308 WCF, and .30-06 Springfield. Many trophy hunters opt for one of the .300 Magnums, which seem unnecessary to me. Such powerhouse cartridges, however, make sense on the western Canadian prairie grain fields or in the south Texas "brush country." Both Remington and Winchester now offer heavy, long-barreled, super-accurate rifle models—the Sendero and Laredo, respectively—designed for just such venues, and both chamber the big, belted .30s, among other cartridges. Again, I refer only to cartridges for deer hunting, without regard to rounds which you might dream of hauling to Wyoming, Alaska, Africa, or some other big-game country someday.

Pin me down even harder, and I'd say, get a .270, .280, 7x57mm, or .308 WCF.

Yes, yes, I'm aware that I probably left out your favorite, perhaps the .243, 6mm Rem., .250 Savage, .257 Roberts, .25-06, 8mm Mauser, .338 Win. Magnum, or one of the big-cased .35s. Please be advised that I've killed deer with almost all of these, quite a few deer with some of them, and that among them are some particular favorite cartridges of mine. But they have been gradually supplanted by other chamberings as my experience has increased and my orientation toward trophy bucks has become more fixed. Big deer are just that—big. Especially in the rut or when rattled up, all adrenalized, they take some serious killing. The smaller cartridges will do the job some of the time, perhaps even *most* of the time, but not all of the time, which is the minimum acceptable criterion. I wouldn't have to write books for a living if I had the 7mm Remington Magnum concession for hunters who have spent years gaily knocking over Texas Hill Country bucks which probably average about 80 pounds dressed with a .243 and then move to south Texas where the bucks may easily run a full 100 pounds heavier. Every whitetail I've ever socked with one of the 6mm cartridges has gone down at the shot as though someone had dropped a safe on his head, but these rounds—.243, 6mm/.244 Remington, and .240 Weatherby Magnum—have cost me more long, tedious hours of trailing other people's wounded deer than all others combined. On picked shots in the hands of expert hunters, they're magic, but no man can pick his shots on trophy bucks.

Perhaps even more important than choosing the right cartridge is choosing the right bullet. For example, the famous Winchester "Silver-tip" in the 180-grain .30 caliber version is unsurpassed among factory bullets for deep, lethal penetration on heavy game and controlled expansion. For elk and the big bears, I love 'em, but they're much too tough for any whitetails I've ever hunted, and even too much so for mule deer, which average heavier. The 150-grain slugs available in the popular .30s produce much quicker kills.

Best of all, of course, is handloading, if that's your game. When you assemble your own ammo, you have full freedom to choose exactly the right bullet for the job at hand, rather than having to settle for a compromise. You also have access to the superior game-killing abilities of such bullets as the Nosler Partitions, Speer "Grand Slams," Barnes X-Bullets, Trophy Bonded "Bear Claws," Swift "A-Frame," Hornady Interlock, or Hawk.

Probably the most widespread myth in deer hunting is the fable of the "brush-busting bullet." It's supposed to be heavy, blunt-nosed, of large diameter, and with a very moderate velocity. Well, once, in Botswana, Africa, I fired a bullet at a magnificent Cape buffalo bull at fairly short range. The bullet weighed 400 grains (heavy!), was round-nosed, was .41 caliber (large!), and left the muzzle at the very moderate velocity of 2,400 feet per second. It nicked a small mopane sapling and deflected about 6 feet off course during its next 12 yards of travel, striking the bull in the ham instead of the chest. Fortunately, he was already dead from a previous bullet through the heart, but neither of us knew it at the time. Now if that slug couldn't be described as a brush-buster, I can hardly imagine anything which could be fired from the human shoulder which could be! And if it wasn't, neither is a 200-grain .35 Remington slug, a 240-grain .44 Magnum bullet, or even a 12-gauge shotgun slug.

I have run tests on deflection by the hour, and so have most of my gun-scribbling colleagues, and we always come to the same conclusion: there is no such thing as a sporting bullet which is reliable in heavy brush. In most tests, oddly enough, the high-velocity spitzers come through just a trifle better than the bluff-bowed fatties at modest speeds. So you're going against all the odds and evidence when you pick a semi-obsolete cartridge for your trophy hunting, no matter what Uncle Jason told you in your first deer camp. The solution? Use a good modern cartridge and pick a hole in the brush to shoot through. Any other course of action is going to lead to disappointment, and, far worse, a wounded and lost buck.

As to what sort of rifle the chosen cartridge should be chambered in, I'm a good deal more flexible. All of the cartridges on my preferred list above are available in highly functional, accurate, dependable models, most of them in your choice of bolt-action, slide-action, single-shot, or semi-automatic, and, in the case of the

Fine bolt-action sporters available in a wide range of excellent chamberings for deer are (top to bottom) Colt-Sauer, Winchester Model 70, and Ruger M77.

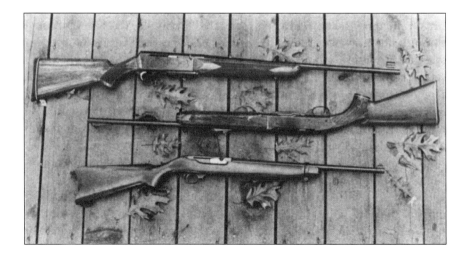

A good selection of semi-automatic rifles is available to the modern hunter. From top, Browning BAR, Remington Model 742, and Ruger .44 Magnum Carbine. Accuracy is good with such rifles, despite reports, but they require more careful maintenance than manually operated repeaters for absolute reliability.

The modern single-shot rifle, as exemplified here by the superb Ruger Number One sporter, is making a strong comeback among sportsmen who know that the first shot is the only good one a hunter usually has.

Lever-action rifles, uniquely American, are always popular for American deer hunting. Top, the classic Winchester Model 94. Bottom, Marlin's Model 1895.

.308, at least, lever-action. My choice is always the bolt-action or one of the good, modern single-shots like the Ruger Number One or the Browning 78, but this choice largely reflects a personal prejudice rather than a hard and sufficient reason. With practice, anyone with enough coordination to be running around loose in the woods with a loaded gun can deliver *aimed* second and third shots with any of them rapidly enough for any practical purpose, but I'm not very concerned about follow-up fire. The first shot at a whitetail or muley is almost certainly the best one you'll have that day, and if you can't hit him with that shot your odds aren't so hot on subsequent efforts. In thinking back, I find that more than 95 percent of all my bucks have been killed or immobilized with the first round, and the rest of them shouldn't have been fired at in the first place.

That's why I do not regard the modern single-shot rifle as a disadvantage in trophy hunting. At its best, indeed, it has the advantage of a longer barrel (for better ballistics) in a rifle which is, overall, extremely light and handy—and "light and handy" *are* very important. For most of my hunting, the following specifications are just about perfect: rifle weight, with scope, not much more than 7½ pounds; overall length not greater than 42 inches, preferably around 40. A man carries a rifle a lot more than he shoots it, and fatigue from an extra pound (unnoticed at the day's beginning) can slow him up just enough to miss a shot at dusk.

Accuracy is an often-abused topic in gun magazines. If your sporter will consistently shoot 100-yard groups of 2 inches or less from sandbags, it's more than good enough and just about as good as you can hope for in an out-of-the-box, untuned, good-quality hunting rifle with factory ammunition, regardless of action style.

Most veteran riflemen-hunters become very sensitive to triggers, and will not have a rifle with a long, heavy, creepy, rough trigger pull. Most bolt-actions these days have triggers which can be adjusted, and if the adjustments can't be made to do the job, any number of custom trigger units are offered to replace the factory assembly. The best of these are Canjar, Timney, and Dayton-Traister, and one or more of them is made for almost every popular bolt-action sporter or military rifle in America. They're worth the money when your trophy buck begins busting brush and your sense of timing on the trigger is crucial to a hit. Contrary to what your old first sergeant told you in basic training, you must know *exactly* when the rifle will fire if you will ever be a good running-game shot, and you must have complete control of that timing.

Unfortunately, custom triggers are available for very few deer-rifle models except bolt-actions, and, at the same time, the levers, pumps, and autoloaders are usually the models which need trigger improvement most.

And if yours is an autoloader, be sure to read the manufacturer's maintenance instructions with care. The self-loaders are a bit more cranky, especially with handloaded ammo, and require special cleaning techniques. Failure to follow these directions will eventually cost you a shot or a trophy; it has happened to several of my friends (all of whom tote bolt guns today). However, when properly

maintained, the semi-autos on the market today are perfectly reliable and considerably more accurate, most of the time, than they
are given credit for by gun writers like me. In some recent tests of
mine, the Remington 742 and Browning BAR, in particular, delivered accuracy about as good as current bolt-action sporters can be
expected to produce, at least with commercial ammunition.

I began my hunting career in 1941, when telescopic sights on
deer rifles were rarities and regarded with suspicion by most experienced hunters. They were too slow, it was said, for whitetails in
thick country, they fogged, they were fragile, and mainly they were
a bit "sissy." Some of these charges were true and some were balder-
dash, but the fact is that the scope has swept the field. I know of not
a single serious trophy hunter who carries a rifle with iron sights.
There must be a reason, and there is: scopes are better!

They are not better however, because they make things look
bigger. Magnification is one of the least important of a glass sight's
virtues. Perhaps the most important—and the reason a scope is one
of the fastest known sights for running game—is the fact that a lens
system places the aiming device (reticle) and the target in the same
optical plane. The hunter's eye is thus not required to try to focus
simultaneously on a back sight, a front sight, and a target. The second major advantage is target *resolution*, which is not the same as
magnification. Through a scope, you see the deer more clearly,
whether he is behind thin brush, in deep shade, or mixed up with
several other deer. Thus you can aim at the animal's vital organs
rather than at the whole deer, half-seen and guessed-at. It makes the
difference between clean kills and botched ones.

The third big plus in riflescopes is the fact that they give you
at least an extra hour of hunting time each day, and it happens to be
the best hour of any day—a half-hour after dawn and another just
before twilight. The large (relative to the human eye) front lens of
the scope gathers in more light than the unaided eye, and makes
shots in bad light as easy as in good light. For the trophy hunter, this
alone is worth the price of the scope, because these are the minutes
when the monster buck is most likely to step into the open.

About the only serious mistakes a deer hunter can make in
selecting a scope are buying a cheap glass, or buying one with too
much magnification. Scopes are one sort of product where you really

Model K3-W • 3-Power

Model K4-W • 4-Power

Model K6-W • 6-Power

Model V4.5-W • 1.5x to 4.5x

Model V7-W • 2.5x to 7x

Model V9-W • 3x to 9x

A good modern scope is of incalculable value, especially for the trophy hunter. These are all Weavers, and all suitable for most kinds of deer hunting, whether for muleys or whitetails.

do get pretty much what you pay for. And if the makers of telescopic sights had never constructed one of more than 4X, no deer hunter would have been handicapped, even for muley. This is not to say that variable scopes with more Xs on the high end aren't useful; on rifles chambered to dual-purpose, varmints-and-deer cartridges, they have very real applications. But I know of no cartridge and no American deer-hunting situation which *require* more than 4X, and none in which I consider anything over 6X to be anything other than a hindrance. Many of my deer rifles carry variables with 1½X to 2X on the low end, and they seem to be set at those magnifications, or not higher than about 3X, most of the time when I'm in the field. Their fields of view are wider at the lower settings, and I know I can hit a target just as reliably at low power as at high power. If you doubt that, take your own variable-scoped rifle to the range and shoot careful groups at 100 yards with the same ammunition with the scope set at its lowest and highest magnifications. Provided you can see the target equally well at both settings, you'll find your low-power groups as small as, or smaller than, those produced at the higher-X adjustments. Surprising, perhaps, but true.

Altogether, I must regard the development of the sporting telescopic sight to its present state of the art to be the single greatest boon to trophy—or any deer—hunters since the invention of the breechloading rifle.

16 How to Shoot a Deer

Superior marksmanship with a rifle (or sighted shotgun, where required by law) is not merely *nice*; it's *necessary*, if one is to call himself a sportsman. To me, purchasing a hunting license and carrying a rifle into the woods does not give anyone the right to fire at a living animal. To earn that right, he is obligated to practice enough to develop skill, enough skill to be morally certain that he can make any reasonable shot presented for a sure, humane kill. There can be no excuse for losing a buck from which blood has been drawn. I've done it twice in 55 years and do not excuse myself for those failures, either. Those memories still haunt me, decades later. In my camp, the failure to find a buck known to be wounded is a distinct stigma, keenly felt by all of us. With more than a dozen hunters, such events do not occur more often than once every four or five years, or perhaps not more often than one out of every hundred deer fired at. And even that one is one too many.

To simply take it for granted that such things are unavoidable is horrible, and if I believed that I would never fire another shot at a living beast. It's true that it does happen to everybody who hunts much, but when it does it should be only because of an unforeseen event such as partial bullet deflection in brush, a sudden gust of wind against the rifle or the stand, or perhaps a sight knocked out of zero. It should never be because the hunter attempted a shot which he wasn't absolutely convinced he could make, under that particular set of circumstances.

We owe it to a superb game animal which furnishes us with days of pleasure and challenge. To shirk the responsibility of

The newly popular metallic-silhouette target-shooting game was designed for hunters and hunting rifles. No slings or special equipment are permitted, and this game is the best possible practice for serious game-shooting.

marksmanship demeans the deer and makes us into what the anti-hunters claim we are: heartless, wanton butchers of wildlife.

That would be the end of the sermon, except for the fact that those same anti-hunting freaks mean to put an end to our wholesome sport, and may do it someday if we continue to give them ammunition. Every dead and unrecovered deer is a potential shot in their locker.

The first step all of us can take to disarm this particular charge of the preservationists is a simple one: we can take care to sight in our weapons carefully, every year. Rifles do mysteriously change zero from time to time, because of warpage in the stock wood or recoil-loosened screws in the sighting system, to mention only a couple of reasons. I usually check-fire my rifles at least once a week during the hunting season, while they're being carried and exposed to weather and hard knocks, and now and again I discover that one has shifted its point of impact for no known reason.

Check all screws for tightness, make certain you're using *exactly* the same ammunition—brand, bullet weight, and bullet style—for zeroing that you'll hunt with, and don't rely on someone else to do the sighting in. Do it on a formal, bull's-eye-type target, from a solid rest, at a known range, and shoot *groups* (at least three shots each), and not single shots. Even when most of your hunting is done at fairly short ranges, adjust the sights to place the bullet holes at least 2 inches above the point of aim at 100 yards. Then check-fire the combination at 200 and 300 yards, if you have those ranges available, noting the rise or drop of the point of impact relative to your hold. In short, learn your trajectory; someday this knowledge will get you a buck you want very badly to possess. Observe how the grouping ability of the rifle or shotgun deteriorates as the range lengthens.

But don't do all your shooting from the solid rest; that's valuable only for removing the human factor as much as possible from the gun/sights/ammo combination. Once satisfied with the capabilities of that combination, put the human factor back in, by shooting at hunting ranges from hunting positions, especially offhand. My business requires me to fire thousands of rounds of centerfire rifle ammunition every year, but I seldom go to the range without firing at least twenty shots at a small bull's-eye at 100 yards, standing. It helps. Your shooting can get rusty without practice just as your golf swing can.

If any rifle club in your area has a metallic-silhouette program going, by all means give it a try. This is the rifle competition for hunters, and most ordinary hunting rifles can be competitive. No special equipment is permitted. It's a tough game, but fun, and the best readily available practice for live game I can think of.

If possible, use your regular deer rifle during the off season as a varminter, busting jackrabbits or woodchucks with it where this is safe. Reloading is also fun, and reduces the costs of such shooting by at least two-thirds. Every shot you can fire with that deer rifle between seasons makes it a little more a part of you, a comfortable old friend, and an extension of your will. Confidence plays an enormous role in good shooting, and it's impossible to fire enough shots at big game in a lifetime to develop that confidence; it must be done on other targets, between big-game seasons.

In the process, you'll find it's pleasant to have the reputation as "the best shot in camp." It's never the "in" thing to be a bum with a rifle, no matter how hard a would-be hunter tries to convince himself to the contrary. Besides, shooting is a delightful and absorbing hobby even if one never fires a bullet at game.

If it simply isn't possible to fire your rifle regularly, because of weather or lack of opportunity, there is one more helpful exercise, called dry-firing. In fact, dry-firing is useful even if you're fortunate enough to be able to shoot live ammunition regularly, and is practiced daily by every champion competition rifleman I know. It's nothing more than picking up the rifle, making *certain* that both chamber and magazine are empty (*every* time!), cocking the arm, aiming carefully at some convenient target, and squeezing the trigger. The target can be a spot on the wall, a leaf on a tree outside the window, anything, as long as it's small enough to require some concentration to hold the sights on until the striker falls. I also have a pet fireplug, visible from my study window at a range of about 150 yards, which gets "killed" a couple of dozen times each day. Dry-snapping at targets on the TV screen teaches one how to get the shot away quickly. However it's done, about fifteen minutes of dry-firing practice in your own home each day will positively do wonders for your shooting skills.

To translate this new-found or newly honed skill into clean kills in the field requires some knowledge of the anatomy of game animals. We hear a great deal about the "shocking power" of high-velocity bullets; there certainly is such an effect, but it never killed a deer, in and of itself, in my experience. What kills is the permanent disruption of vital tissue, and by that is meant *quickly* vital— heart, lungs, major chest arteries, spinal column, and brain. A hit in any of these organs will put a deer down either in his tracks or within 100 yards, usually much less. The first three listed vitals are grouped together in the largest part of the animal's body, providing the largest target for quick, painless kills with the smallest opportunity for error.

We also hear a great deal about undue spoiling of good meat. Well, a bullet through the ribs, just behind the shoulder line on a broadside shot, spoils less edible meat than a bullet anywhere else in the animal's body.

Yet "the experts," whoever they may be, always take the neck shot, right? Wrong! I have yet to meet a *real* expert who always takes

Few hunters have the opportunity to really study deer anatomy. Note the low position of the heart and the inviting opportunity offered by the central lung shot. On a broadside shot, place the bullet about halfway up the depth of the chest in line with the rear of the foreleg for a certain, humane kill. *(Photo by W. A. Maltsberger)*

the neck shot. They may take it when it's all that's presented, or when the shot is close enough and there's leisure enough to be certain. But the neck shot is the most treacherous of all targets taken deliberately, and failed neck shots are one of the leading causes of unrecovered deer. The "kill-clean-or-miss-clean" philosophy sometimes enunciated as justification for the neck shot is a fraud, too, since only the spinal cord itself is quickly fatal in the neck and it's no bigger than the pistol grip of your rifle stock. Damage to the jugular vein, esophagus, or trachea will kill, too, but you won't find the deer.

The heart is also a tricky target, easier to hit than the cervical spine if you know where it lies (which most hunters don't) but also easier to miss while breaking a foreleg. To be sure of the heart, you have to place the bullet through some of the shoulder muscles, which is good-eating venison. My observation has been that, on the average, a whitetail will run a little farther with a heart shot than with a lung shot, although either is a swift, clean kill.

The heart is very low in the chest, centered not more than 3 inches above the line of the brisket or chest between the forelegs. Because hunters gut their kills in some position other than the normal standing posture of a deer, the actual location of the heart among the vital organs is somewhat difficult to visualize. It's even more difficult to figure in any angling shot.

On the straight broadside opportunity, I believe most hunters will be most satisfied if they'll forget the baloney about neck or heart shots. Lay the vertical cross hair up the rear edge of the foreleg and the horizontal one from one-third to one-half of the way up the chest. This puts the bullet in the solid center of the lungs. If the sights waver downward, it gets the heart; upward, and the spine is smashed. A slight miss forward takes the aorta off the top of the heart, and may even get the base of the neck. It's the surest, easiest, quickest, and least meat-wasting of all the shots offered by a deer.

If the opportunity is not a perfect broadside, look for the foreleg on the far side. If the buck is angling slightly away, shoot at the *far* shoulder, not the near shoulder. If he's angling sharply away, you may have to slip the bullet into his flank, behind the last rib, to get to the boiler room. It's hard to make oneself do, and it calls for real penetration ability in a bullet, but it's a very common shot.

Perhaps the best way to visualize the vitals is to imagine a basketball embedded in the largest part of the buck's chest, and to shoot at the center of that sphere for *any* angle.

All of us have had "shoot at the shoulder!" drummed into us since we began hunting, and I think we often do so reflexively without thinking. On any except that rare, perfect broadside shot, shooting at the shoulder is likely to result in a lost cripple. I try to teach kids in my Hunter Safety classes to shoot at the internal organs, not at the external surface features, and it pays off.

On a buck facing straight away, hold fire and hope he'll turn, or, if he's very close, the back of the neck makes a reasonable target. It usually shows a dark line of hair which may help center the bullet. If he's in motion, and too big to pass up, the root of the tail is an absolutely deadly shot. Make it just above the center of the tail, and

Extreme caution is required in shooting at a buck whose body cannot be clearly seen. Trying to guess where the vitals are, especially when only the very mobile head is visible, risks committing the hunter's unforgivable sin: losing a crippled animal. *(Photo by Mike Biggs)*

it will flatten the animal in his tracks (although a finisher will be needed).

Something can be learned by watching the reaction of the buck to the shot. If he bucks and kicks both hind feet straight out behind him before dashing away, it was probably a heart shot. If he humps his back and seems stunned, moving sluggishly, nail him again; the first one was most likely in the liver or guts. Any hit should register with a sagging or staggering, but not invariably. If he goes down and gets back up, the bullet usually delivered some energy somewhere near the spine, but is not necessarily quickly fatal. If the spine is touched forward of the withers, he's instantly dead. If behind the withers, the hindquarters will be paralyzed but the animal will be quite active, trying to drag himself away. He will almost invariably bleat harshly with such a wound. My first one did that (I was twelve years old) and almost ended my hunting career then and there!

I know veteran hunters who will not willingly attempt a run-ning shot at an unwounded buck, and I can't argue with their think-ing: too much chance of wounding. No one can be surgically precise with his bullet placement under such circumstances. Yet a running deer under most conditions is not really very difficult to hit. He looks a lot harder than he really is.

At short range (up to 30 or 40 yards), little or no lead is required if the rifleman keeps his eye glued to the chest, well for-ward, and doesn't blaze away at the whole deer. From 50 to 150 yards, a lead of between 1 and 2 feet is needed, with a fast-swinging rifle, on crossing shots. Beyond that range, any shot is probably not advisable unless the animal is already hit and apparently about to escape. A friend and colleague, former *Field & Stream* Shooting Editor Bob Brister, suggests that the vertical cross hair be held about even with the buck's nose, claiming that this is self-compen-sating for subtle angles. As the deer angles more sharply away, the apparent distance between nose and vital organs decreases, and, of course, less lead is required.

All manner of elaborate tables have been published to demon-strate the exact lead necessary with popular calibers to pile up a running deer. These take into consideration the animal's size and speed, the bullet's ballistic coefficient and time of flight, the phase of the moon, the price of collard greens in Dixie, and sundry other esoterica. As exercises, these tables are interesting, but I have yet to see the man who could memorize them to their many decimal places and then apply them precisely to the problem of a fleeing buck in the field. I think Brister's system makes more practical sense, at least until the hunter has a few running shots under his belt. Then he will have gotten over his intimidation and will know how the sights are supposed to look to him. As in shotgunning, no two people see "lead" in exactly the same way, at least consciously. And, as in shotgunning, the cardinal sin is slowing or stopping the swing as the shot is fired.

I suppose no hunter ever forgets his first running kill. I was still in my teens and I was terrified of the day I'd have to try one. When it happened, on a big ten-point buck, it was so sudden that I didn't think about it. I just started shooting and kept it up until the buck went down. I discovered later that I had at least touched him

The under-the-nose lead is self-compensating, as illustrated in this case with a buck running sharply away from the gun. The required lead is smaller than on a crossing shot (at the same range), and this rule sets up less lead automatically.

A running shot on a crossing deer at about 100 yards calls for a hold on a horizontal line with his chest, just under his nose. As with a shotgun, the rifle must be swinging when the shot is fired.

with all four shots fired, and that two were solidly in the chest. My father, who was hunting a few hundred yards down the way, said that he heard the shots but didn't imagine that I was the shooter, for the simple reason that he didn't believe it humanly possible to fire a lever-action rifle that fast! I'd triggered four rounds while the deer ran about 50 yards, almost one shot for every bound he made. He was stone-dead when I reached him, my first running kill and my first ten-pointer. Since that day, running deer haven't seemed all that difficult to me.

Many hunters have been badly frightened and a few have been injured because, in their excitement, they incautiously approached a downed buck which turned out to be still alive. No matter how certain I am of my shot, I walk up on a deer—or any other animal—quietly, from the rear, and with the rifle ready. I watch the flank for one full minute, for the slightest sign of breathing. If there is none, I touch the eyeball. If there is no quiver in the eyelid at the touch, the thing is finished.

Now is the moment for the inevitable pang of mixed emotions, pride, joy, regret, sympathy, and a strange sort of gratitude toward the deer. The Indians felt it, too, and always thanked the dead animal. The hunters of central Europe have a brief but reverent ritual to honor the animal. There is always, for me, a poignant awareness of a life ended, and there must also be the sense that it was done fairly, honestly, cleanly, with good and sufficient reason, with respect and love.

In my camp, I want no part of a man who cannot understand such feelings, for he is only a killer and no true hunter!

17 Trophy Hunting and Ecology

As suggested in the first chapter, serious trophy hunting has a far smaller impact on the population dynamics of a whitetail herd than any other form of hunting, partly because trophy hunters take only a minute percentage of the total harvest, and partly because the deer they take have already made their genetic contribution to that herd. But there is more to it than that, because trophy hunters prefer to hunt a balanced whitetail herd.

By "balanced," I mean a population which is in good ecological balance with the habitat, at or below the carrying capacity of the range. Just as important, however, is that the herd is also in biological balance, meaning a "normal" ratio between the sexes and a normal age-class distribution. Only such a herd can produce the great trophy bucks we seek. Management for trophy bucks, then, must also be management which benefits the entire population.

By contrast, ordinary hunting somewhat distorts the balance of any herd, because it amounts to what might be called "any-buck hunting," as opposed to "trophy-buck hunting." If meat hunters were willing to harvest any deer, rather than any buck, the distortion would not be so pronounced, but the antlered male is the "status" animal. With a buck and a doe standing side by side, the average hunter will instantly choose the buck, regardless of antler quality. With a big buck and a small one to choose from, the larger animal is almost always chosen, even though he is only a two and a half year old.

The result of all this is that the younger bucks make up the majority of the harvest. In a study done by Pennsylvania's game research biologists, it was found that fully two-thirds of all bucks legally taken by sportsmen are one and a half years old. Another 20 percent are in the two and a half year old age bracket, which means that just less than 90 percent of the bucks harvested in Pennsylvania are two and a half years old or younger. Please note that I did *not* say that hunters killed 90 percent of the available two and a half year old and younger bucks; I said that, of the bucks harvested, that percentage proved to be in those age groups. These figures roughly apply, on a statewide basis, to almost every whitetail population in America, even in Texas, where private ownership of the range might be expected to offer better controls.

In that same Pennsylvania study, only 9 percent of the harvested bucks are three and a half years old, only 2 percent are four and a half, and another 2 percent are five and a half and older. In other words, by the most generous definition, fewer than 4 percent of all bucks taken in that state fall into the trophy age classes. Again, these figures will hold pretty well true in every good whitetail state. Pennsylvania boasts one of the largest whitetail herds in the United States, with about 750,000 animals, and the harvest, according to the latest figures available to me, amounts to about 100,000 deer. That means that the Pennsylvania herd is actually underharvested if we ignore ages and sexes; biologists agree that any thriving whitetail herd can not only stand but will actually benefit from an annual reduction via the gun of about 20 percent, or about 150,000 animals in Pennsylvania. But the *bucks* are not underharvested! The relative scarcity of males in the three and a half year age group and older means only one thing, and that is that the middle-aged deer (two and a half through four and a half) are being taken in such numbers that not even one in ten bucks is allowed to live to full maturity. There are very few real trophy bucks simply because there are almost no bucks attaining sufficient age to replace the inevitable losses among the mature deer, losses due mostly to what is termed "natural mortality," rather than to hunting.

Thus the composition of the herd becomes distorted. There are plenty of deer because even yearling bucks will breed in the absence of competition from their seniors, and because a whitetail buck at any age is promiscuous, servicing from one to two dozen does in a season if they are available. But subtle alterations in the reproductive mechanisms of the herd may be noted. Not only will underaged

Trophy management is biologically sound deer management, and that means a harvest equally divided between the sexes. Here I pose with a "trophy doe," taken with a muzzleloading rifle. Such culling must be done, and the venison is excellent.

bucks breed freely, which is abnormal in a balanced herd, but the lack of competition among the males wipes out nature's survival-of-the-fittest program and allows inferior animals to pass on their genes. Thus, nonselective hunting (nonselective relative to *bucks* at least) rapidly and surely destroys *quality* hunting. Unfortunately, very few deer hunters in the United States have any idea at all of what the term "quality hunting" can mean, never having experienced it. The pictures in this book will no doubt astonish many veteran hunters, who will doubtless assume that these deer were photographed in some kind of a game preserve or in captivity and that they are oversized freaks. They will not believe that such racks can be grown in almost any good whitetail habitat with enlightened management, because they have never seen such a head in the woods. The truth is that almost every live deer whose picture appears in these pages was photographed *in the wild*, on land that is regularly (if sometimes lightly) hunted! There is *nothing* unusual about these bucks *except that they have been allowed to grow up*!

Similar heads could doubtless be seen in your own hunting country, in fair abundance, within as little as three years *if* the herd were allowed to return to a natural balance.

But John Q. Deerhunter won't like the steps which must be taken. For quickest results, the season must be closed on bucks, period. It would harm nothing if only mature bucks were harvested, but not one in one thousand hunters will trouble to learn to judge the age of a whitetail on the hoof. And it would help the program if

He's cute, but he will never grow into a superior buck. This yearling, photographed on excellent range in a good season, may carry a "spike gene," and his removal from the population before he begins to breed is good management if the age-class distribution among the males is normal.

This little fellow is a rarity. Many hunters may refuse to believe the fact that this is an eighteen-month-old buck, but it's true. He already carries ten perfect points and shows unusual spread for his age. Give him four more years and this buck just might be a record-book specimen. *(Photo by Charles Jones)*

the spikes were culled from the herd, in years of good spring and summer forage, but, again, the hunter who sees a spike and an eight-pointer standing side by side cannot resist shooting the bigger animal. So the buck season must be shut down, as a practical matter. This would draw a howl of protest from any state's hunters that you could hear in Timbuktu. It would also be heard in the halls of the state legislature, I can assure you, and the game department would be in political trouble. On top of that, closing the season on males would probably greatly reduce the sale of hunting licenses, undercutting the department's main source of revenues for research, education, and enforcement.

But let's assume that, by some miracle of hunter enlightenment, we could get past that hurdle and back to our management program. The next step is to encourage the harvesting of does, according to professional biologists' recommendations and studies. This would generate added increments of rage from hunters, landowners, and preservationists who cannot seem to understand that at least 50 percent of the does on any range stand there *in lieu*

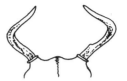

These drawings all represent the first racks of one and a half year old whitetail bucks! On good ranges and in balanced herds, the top three suggest genetically inferior animals, the early culling of which will benefit the herd. Those on the bottom row are promising as future trophies, especially the forkhorn and eight-pointer. *(Reprinted from* Producing Quality Whitetails *by Brothers and Ray)*

  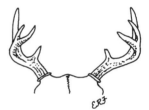

of an antlered buck! Harvesting of females, under scientific regulations, does *not* reduce the total number of deer on a range; it *increases* the number of bucks.

Perhaps you'd better go back and reread that last sentence. It states facts, unchallengeable, verifiable facts which any professional wildlife biologist can support with hard evidence, with the single proviso that the deer herd in question is not already far below the carrying capacity of the range. This can happen in the case of a newly established herd, but not even 10 percent of the nation's whitetail range is understocked. On the contrary, it is overstocked, often disastrously, as proved by the winter dieoffs which occur year after year in most states.

So the process of restoring the trophy-grade bucks to a local deer herd (which is to say, restoring that herd to healthy, normal, vigorous balance) is really fairly simple, biologically, but very difficult politically. First, you reduce the total herd to the carrying capacity of the range, which can only be done by shooting does. Then you allow the bucks to gain the necessary age. If the harvest thereafter is concentrated on the does, spikes, and five and a half year plus males, the equilibrium of the population can be maintained indefinitely, and hunters can find out what *quality* hunting is all about.

This is not some abstract, wild-haired theory. I can show you dozens of ranches in Texas where just such a program has produced just such hunting, and perhaps hundreds more where the management process is in progress, with visible results. Many of the wild bucks illustrated in this book were photographed on these properties.

The whole process must begin with the hunter himself. He is the cutting edge of any game management program, because he alone makes the decisions with his rifle which affect the outcome. He must first accept the idea that old ideas of game management, as epitomized by the antiquated "buck laws," don't work in the current decade. Situations have changed, wildlife research has made great strides, and the future promises even greater and more rapid changes in America's wildlife picture. He must also decide, for himself, that quality hunting is better than mere quantity hunting, and in fact that it represents the last, best hope for our native big-game populations as harvestable resources. The choice may eventually be this: would you prefer to have a chance to kill a really big buck every few seasons, plus a doe or two for the freezer each year, or would you prefer no deer hunting at all? I hope that's a drastic over-statement of the prospects, but the future has a habit of catching up

The emaciated condition of these does is the inevitable result of bucks-only harvest and the overpopulation that inevitably follows.

with us a lot more suddenly than we anticipate, and I fear that just such a choice will be necessary within my own lifetime.

Finally, the hunter must be informed about the population dynamics of the deer so that he can understand the necessity for scientific management practices. This would seem to be the most hopeless of the educational goals. In a hunting society in which people still reject the obvious and desperate need to harvest surplus does, how can we ever convey the not-so-apparent needs for selective buck hunting?

There is an organization in my home state which has set out to accomplish just this, on a voluntary, self-education basis. It's called the Texas Trophy Hunters Association, (P.O. Box 791107, San Antonio, TX 78287-1107). I am a life member, but hold no office in TTHA. In the summer of 1975, the organization had about 800 members, in a state where half a million hunting licenses are sold annually. One year later, Texas Trophy Hunters had *quintupled* the membership, and today it's around 50,000. The organization is dedicated to wildlife conservation, particularly whitetail management. Its principal activity is to educate its membership to the *need* for management *beyond* what the state legislature has done by statute and the Parks and Wildlife Department by regulation, as well as the biological facts of life about deer herds and how they tick as ecological units. The Texas Trophy Hunters Association publishes a slick bimonthly magazine, the *Journal of the Texas Trophy Hunters Association*, which is largely devoted to management techniques and, of course, the results.

Here we have a large and expanding group of avid hunters voluntarily dedicating themselves to modern principles of management, especially trophy management, going beyond the letter of the laws in order to restore balance and ensure quality hunting for the future. And, suddenly, we note landowners (remember, almost all Texas hunting is done on private land, for a fee) joining TTHA, saying that if the people in this organization really believe in the ideas promulgated in the magazine, at chapter meetings, and at the annual statewide conference, they're the kind of hunters these landowners want on their property. All over the southwestern part of the state, at least, we see ranchers, sportsmen, and wildlife biologists cooperating in individual management programs which are bearing fruit. If you think some of the bucks pictured in this book are nice, you ought to read the *Journal* and see what the TTHA members are actually harvesting! The group is still tiny in comparison to the numbers of licensed Texas hunters, but it is an influential group and membership is beginning to become a sort of status symbol hereabouts. If such an idea can work in Texas, perhaps it can be applied with appropriate modifications in other whitetail states, or, for that matter, mule-deer states, as well.

As for personal testimony, I'll add that I've been involved, with a group of friends, in a trophy management program on 10,000 acres of leased land, and I know that hunters themselves can make the difference. I've seen it happen with my own eyes.

The question arises as to how such programs can be administered on public hunting lands, which are where most of the deer are killed in most states. It's all very well to talk about such things in Texas, where the landowner can exert a degree of control over the harvest, but how does it work in Pennsylvania or Michigan or similar states? Well, it can't work at all without the support of the hunting fraternity, and will not happen until the competent professional wildlife managers in the various state game departments receive the solid cooperation of at least an identifiable segment of the hunting citizens. If there is a demand for quality hunting, however, I can imagine no reason why certain areas cannot be set aside for quality management. Many states (Colorado and Wyoming are good examples) are divided up into wildlife management units, and regulations vary from unit to unit according to the needs of the game populations in each area. Why could not just one or two units in, say, Pennsylvania be designated "quality whitetail areas" and managed accordingly? This would mean that permits for both does and bucks would have to be issued, perhaps on a drawing system if the demand became heavy, in order to control not merely the total harvest but the nature of the harvest, at least by sex.

Management can also be practiced by private hunting clubs, which control fairly large tracts of land in many states. In either case, it might very well come to pass that a few such demonstration projects in a given state could show the hunters what can be accomplished, and what they're missing, and bring about a sort of revolution in hunters' standards, even in public-land states.

I do not mean to claim that trophy hunting is the total answer to all of the most pressing problems in American wildlife management. I do wish to re-emphasize that trophy hunting and the game-management practices which go along with it must become a part of the wave of the future. Trophy hunting is, by definition, selective, discriminating harvesting of the resource, and is in complete consonance with the concept of stewardship of our wildlife heritage. Unless the conditions which permit trophy hunting exist, that heritage can hardly continue to exist, and unless what I call trophy hunting has popular support, those conditions cannot be established and maintained. The alternative is what we have in many states today, a pathetic parody of real hunting, a frenzied chasing of a swollen and grotesquely unbalanced herd by more and more people through a steadily deteriorating habitat.

I will hear no more condemnations of "trophy hunting" by bleeding-heart preservationists *or* by guilt-stricken "hunters," neither of whom even know the meaning of the words!

A double tragedy: not only was this buck wounded and lost by careless or incompetent hunters, but the teeth in the skull proved him to be a yearling with his first rack, a genetically superior animal whose contribution to the local population is now lost forever.

18 Management Principles and Problems

The most bitter controversy in all deer hunting today revolves around bucks with unbranched antlers, which we usually call "spike bucks" or "spikes." During my boyhood, spike antlers were considered merely a mark of youth, and their bearers were protected by law. Later, research directed by biologist Donnie Harmel at the Texas Parks & Wildlife Department's Kerr Wildlife Management Area (WMA) was deemed proof by many, myself included, that "spike-ism" is a genetic defect. The work seemed to show that bucks growing spikes in their first year are inferior to those producing branched antlers for a first rack, and that, although the spikes would not remain spikes all the bucks' lives, they could not be expected to develop outstanding trophy heads.

The question of nutrition was carefully considered in the Kerr WMA studies, and it was discovered that a first-year spike was unlikely ever to catch up with his branched-antlered contemporaries, even on more nutritious rations. Three and one half year old ex-forkhorns, in fact, outperformed equal-aged former spikes even when the latter were fed double the protein.

The Kerr WMA deer herd is pedigreed, meaning that the bloodlines of both males and females are recorded for many generations. Efforts to prove the existence of a "spike gene" that can be carried by both bucks and does, and that degrades the prospects for fine antlers in that herd, involved confining does with bucks that were spikes in their first season and then crossing their offspring back to their fathers and tracking the antler-growing performance of the males produced thus. The results seemed to confirm the "spike gene" theory.

Gradually, news of these results spread. In Texas, at least, legal protection for spikes was abandoned, and many trophy-conscious hunters more or less declared war on spikes. I was one of those, except that I moderated my suppression of spikes on my own property with a consideration of forage abundance and quality during the year, especially during the critical antler-growing months of March through May. In dry years, with a failure of the annual spring forb crop, I gave spikes the benefit of the doubt, understanding that a long-yearling buck might be a spike for nutritional as well as for genetic reasons.

In the meantime, research by well-known and respected biologists at Auburn and other southern universities has been developed that seems to contradict absolutely the theory of the inferiority of spike bucks. Dr. Larry Marchinton at Auburn reports having grown genuine trophies, and even record-class bucks, from first-year spikes. Many real experts (biologists, not writers) have chosen sides in the controversy, and the battle lines are drawn. I've read the reports on both sides, and, frankly, they appear to this layman to be irreconcilable. I cannot tell you which interpretation of the data is right and which is wrong, or whether they're both wrong. I can report my own observations from the field, as well as a few notes on the polarized "sides" in the controversy.

First, the question is not as simple as it seems: it isn't a matter of just nutrition or just genetics. Birthdays have a bearing. If a buck fawn was conceived (and thus born) early, and he was blessed with good genetics and good forage, both for himself and for his mother while she was carrying and nursing him, it is entirely possible (although rare) for him to show tiny spikes at less than one year of age. The spikes are usually less than two inches long but they are true, hardened antlers and not "buttons" or "nubbins." Obviously, this is a very promising animal that would be mowed down under a "shoot-all-spikes" policy. Similarly, if a male fawn was conceived (and thus born) very late, he could be too young to produce the forked antlers for which he may be genetically programmed in his second year. Especially in a bad forage season, he may sport only spikes at one and a half, when he should have at least forks. Shooting him may also be a mistake, although no way exists to be sure. Since a whitetail breeding season spans about four months, I

These two bucks, raised in captivity from yearlings on the same quality forage, are the same age—three and a half years old. The only difference is genetics; the miserable little forkhorn was a spike in his first season, while the bigger buck carried forked antlers or better. This experiment, involving several bucks of both classes at Texas's Kerr Wildlife Management Area, has shown that males carrying forked horns or better in their first season grow an average of about twice as much antler material in later years as those which started out as spikes. Which of these bucks would you prefer to hunt next season? It may depend upon what you shoot *this* season! *(Photos by Stan Slaten)*

suspect that such differing dates of conception explain some of the apparent discrepancies between the Alabama and Texas research results.

Furthermore, the age and health of the mother doe before conception and during and after pregnancy may affect the ultimate trophy status of her male offspring much more than we know. Finally, the whitetail deer is said to be the most genetically variable of large game animals, which means that even a professional biologist with a Ph.D. must exercise a good deal of caution when using words like "never" or "always" about whitetail genetics.

The closest thing to a bottom line I can give you is as follows: my present ranch, on the Tex-Mex border in south Texas, has been under my management for seventeen years as this is written. The ranch comprises more than eighteen hundred acres of unimproved, prime whitetail habitat in the heart of Texas's legendary big-antler region, and is neither high-fenced nor artificially fed in any way. For the first eight or nine years, I cracked down hard on the spikes, at least in any year with average or better forage conditions in spring and summer. Since, I have laid off the spikes, except for obvious defectives or old spikes (two and a half years or older). Harvest and other management parameters remain unchanged.

Overall trophy quality of the antlers in this herd, as subjectively evaluated by me, has been unaffected by whichever spike policy was in force. The bottom line, on this open range without supplementary feeding, is simply that neither shooting spikes nor sparing them has made any difference. We have about the same number of big bucks—of the same degree of bigness—and the same average numbers of spikes from season to season all along.

However, whether spikes are genetically defective or not becomes academic in herds in which overharvesting of bucks is so severe that yearlings make up a large percentage of the total male population. In such herds, even the spikes must be carried over. Where this process goes far enough, I suppose the day might come when a spike buck might be considered a trophy! There are a few such areas, even now.

Since so much depends upon the age distribution of the harvested bucks in any trophy-management program, it's natural to ask how the hunter can judge the age of a whitetail on the hoof. To be truthful, it really isn't possible to do so with precision—but it really isn't necessary, either. It's only important that the hunter attempt to divide the bucks he sees into three broad age categories: (1) eighteen months and younger, (2) five and a half years and older, and (3) everything in between. If he shoots nothing in the "everything in between" category (except for obvious freaks), he will never be a detriment to the management program. The reason is that such hunting always permits a replacement supply of bucks entering the mature class to replace losses to hunting and natural mortality among the five and a half year old and older males. Naturally, this assumes the herd has a supply of two and a half to four and a half year old bucks to begin with, not always a safe assumption these days.

The best way to learn to judge the age of a buck in the woods is to learn to age dead bucks by the tooth-wear method and to compare body conformation with known ages. Unfortunately, mature bucks are sufficiently rare that most hunters don't see enough of them to develop an eye for age. Furthermore, judging age requires that the hunter get a good look at the deer, preferably in good light or at close range, and the presence of a big set of antlers draws a hunter's eyes like magnets; it demands discipline to even glance at the *body* of a deer, where most of the clues to age are found.

Nevertheless, it's a knack which can be developed with practice. Eventually, the hunter finds that he simply has an opinion, arrived at unconsciously, as to whether the buck is young, middle-aged, or fully mature.

A yearling buck has a body like a doe, slender, graceful, and rounded (especially the rump). He also has what I call a "baby face," with a slightly *concave* line from brow to nose when seen in profile. The muscular development of his neck and shoulders is just beginning, and he has a "ewe-necked" appearance.

A fully mature buck's body compares with a yearling's just as a grown man's compares to that of a boy in his early teens. The mature buck has a chunky, squarish look to him, with heavily muscled shoulders and hams. His body appears much deeper, so that he may seem to have a somewhat short-legged appearance. Even out of the rut, his neck muscles are thick and heavy. In profile, his face usually shows a distinct "Roman nose," a slightly *convex* line from brow

Good management of a whitetail herd requires good data on the population (size, density, age and sex ratios, fawn survival, etc.), which can be acquired by any of several standard census techniques. Also essential are year-to-year harvest records, including sex, age, body weight, and antler dimensions—number of points, basal circumference, and inside spread, at least. Many managers also record gross B and C scores. *(Photo by Mike Biggs)*

to nostrils. If he is very old, he may also reveal a good deal of graying or white hair around his face, especially on his brow. His gait changes significantly as he grows heavier, from the dainty floating of a doe to a sort of gallop.

Antlers are poor indices to age, but they can reveal certain things. The gnarled angularity, often with random points and much palmation, of a really old buck's rack has been mentioned. The one measurement of a buck's antlers which does seem to show a regular, linear relationship to his age from year to year is the circumference of the basal "burr," but this varies from individual to individual. A very heavy-based rack, however, can hardly be from an immature animal.

To sum it up, a mature buck simply looks and moves like a powerful, prime male, and experienced hunters can often identify a very distant or partially seen animal as a mature buck even without seeing any antlers at all. Perhaps the pictures in this book and those in other publications will help the hunter who really wishes to be able to judge the age of the bucks he sees in the field to learn. The important thing is to *try*.

Because of the sparse canopy of brush in south Texas, helicopters have been used as a fast, relatively inexpensive (on a per-acre basis) tool to gain hard information on the population, sex ratio, age distribution, and fawn survival (or recruitment) rates. The helicopter is useless in more heavily wooded terrain, and, even in south Texas, recent research has cast some doubt on the accuracy of helicopter counts except as trend data. Since good population data is essential for intelligent management, one of the many other censusing methods is needed. These include walking cruise lines, track counts, droppings counts, and intensive driving of selected small areas, with correlations made between one or more of these methods. Population density and sex ratios, at least, can be deduced with a fairly high degree of statistical reliability, and these are the essential figures for any management program.

Predation (other than by hunters) is something which worries hunters and some landowners a great deal more than it does professional game managers. Predators on deer (both species) include feral or free-ranging domestic dogs, coyotes, bobcats, cougars, wolves (in a few favored localities), and lynxes. Of these, only the dogs are dangerously destructive, and then mostly among yarded deer in the deep winter of some northern states. Coyotes, bobcats, and lynxes certainly take a few fawns and even some adult deer, but it seems obvious that if coyotes, for example, could seriously hurt the deer herds, they would have wiped them out sometime during the 10,000,000 or so years that the two species have coexisted. Yet deer are far more numerous today than ever before, taking the continent as a whole. Where coyotes enjoy an excessive build-up of numbers on a temporary basis, they may do some visible damage among the deer, but all species, including coyotes, have internal population-dispersal mechanisms built into their populations which quickly reduce these concentrations. Predator control, however, may be necessary to protect newly established herds of deer in order to accelerate the population increase desired. Otherwise, such controls are largely a waste of time and money, and may affect the deer herd itself negatively.

If you make overlays for the map of Texas, one to cover the areas where the trophy bucks are most common and the other to cover those where coyotes are most common, you'll discover a remarkable

A whitetail doe killed by a mountain lion. The attempt to cover the remains is a sure sign of a cat. *(Photo by Walter Elling)*

Mountain lions are major predators on both species of deer, often subsisting principally on them, but lions are far too few to constitute any sort of population control on deer. *(Photo by Harley Shaw)*

Coyotes are a common predator on whitetails, but there is good evidence that the prairie wolves benefit the herd. The deer have thrived and grown strong despite about 10,000,000 years of sharing the habitat with coyotes.

coincidence between the two overlays. This may or may not suggest a valid cause-and-effect conclusion, but it is undeniably true.

"Carrying capacity" is a term which must be considered in the overall light. The carrying capacity of a range is measured not only in terms of deer units but in terms of animal units, the latter to include cattle, sheep, goats, swine, javelina, exotic game (common in Texas), and other animals which may be competitive at least to some extent with the deer. Some of these interrelationships are quite complex. There is evidence, recently brought to light, that whitetail deer and cattle may complement each other if the cow herd is pastured on a rotating basis. When the cattle have reduced the range grasses they prefer, and have been rotated out of a pasture, the deer move in in numbers to utilize certain forbs which spring up. This, in turn, relieves the grassroots of forb competition for regrowth.

About 80 percent of a whitetail's diet in good habitat is browse, while most of a cow's intake is by grazing. Nevertheless, when the grass is gone in midwinter, cattle will browse in competition with the deer. Whitetails are much more selective in their feeding than any domestic animal, and severe competition can exist even on ranges where there appears to be plenty of greenery to the untrained eye, and no browse lines. Goats are probably the most severe domestic competition for deer, and hogs can be at times, particularly for mast. Management must take all these factors into consideration.

Management for big bucks must also consider the fact that there is a great deal of difference between a range which will merely keep a population of deer alive and one which will permit maximum development of superior specimens. Although whitetails utilize a great variety of plants, they instinctively recognize certain species with premium nutritional content. If the number of deer on a given range is too great, they will broaden their intake to include anything which can support their metabolism and will appear to remain in reasonably good bodily condition. However, where the herd is kept down to the *real* carrying capacity, each individual deer will get a greater share of the premium forage plants, with the result that the average body weight and antler development of the animals present will be measurably greater. In other words, a given range is capable of producing a fixed tonnage of deer bone and flesh. Whether this tonnage is to be distributed among fewer, larger animals or a greater number of smaller, perhaps stunted animals is the decision the manager must make. For quality hunting, the choice would seem to be pretty clear.

The matter of supplementary feeding now and again arises. If nutrition is so important to whitetail quality, why not see to it that they get the necessary supplementation of protein, minerals, and other nutrition? It might work, but, of course, in a wild herd, such a program would be prohibitively expensive. To be effective, it would have to be carried out on a year-round basis. Hay is of no value to whitetails, and grains such as corn or maize provide high energy but do not offer the nutritional balance such a program would have as its goal. Most areas provide sufficient protein and minerals for the whitetails' needs, *if* only the herd can be kept within the carrying capacity of the range.

How about some more numbers to play with? Biologists set a 20 percent harvest as a reasonable one in any mature herd. They also assess a 40 percent fawn survival figure as "normal." What follows is a table which, if thoughtfully studied, will reveal more about the mechanics of a deer herd than this or any other book ever published except the one from which it is reprinted (with permission), *Producing Quality Whitetails* by Brothers and Ray.

TABLE 1

Buck/doe ratio	1:1	1:2	1:3	1:5
Initial population	300/300	200/400	150/450	100/500
*20% harvest	60/60	40/80	30/90	20/100
Adult carryover	240/240	160/320	120/350	80/400
40% fawn survival	120	160	180	200
Sex of fawns				
(1:1 bucks to does)	60/60	80/80	90/90	100/100
Following year's				
adult population	300/300	240/400	210/440	180/500
Number of adult deer				
exceeding carrying				
capacity next year	0	40	50	80

*   20% represents an average harvest, *equally divided between the sexes.*

The table assumes a tract of land with carrying capacity for 600 adult deer, and that the herd is to be maintained at that population if possible.

Brothers and Ray, being professionally trained wildlife biologists, regard the necessity for dividing the harvest equally between the sexes as so obvious that it needs no further explanation. Now let's take a close look at these numbers. Note how important is a balanced sex ratio. Where it is 1:1, removing one-fifth of all the deer on this tract each season with the gun leaves the population stable, exactly the same year after year. Where it is distorted to one buck for five does (many ranges are much worse than this!), a 20 percent *balanced* harvest still leaves 80 more whitetails on the range than it can provide nourishment for. Those 80 compound the problem the next year, and so on, until the herd is completely out of hand and a major (and unnecessary) dieoff from natural causes becomes inevitable. So much for the anti-hunters' "protect them all" war cry!

Perhaps most important of all from the hunter's point of view is that this table illustrates so graphically the futility of trying to increase the resource by protecting the females. Observe that in a herd in which there are *five times* as many does as bucks there are only 180 bucks on the second year, as opposed to 300 in the herd in which the sex ratio is even. A bit of deep thought makes it obvious that this must be. We know the carrying capacity of the range imposes a positive upper limit on the total deer population; therefore, once that capacity has been filled with deer, all females over half the herd are occupying space and utilizing browse which a buck might use in a more balanced herd. Since about 99 percent of all hunters regard the buck as the desirable unit in the herd, every doe over the number required to produce adequate replacements for the population is surplus, and actually preventing the presence of one more buck on that tract. The facts and the logic are inescapable, as is the conclusion: since whitetail fawns are born in 1:1 sex ratio, they must be harvested in the same ratio if natural balance is to be maintained.

But, since there is always great resistance to the idea of harvesting does as a management tool, let's examine Table 2, which shows the effect of a bucks-only harvest on that same hypothetical tract of whitetail range, with all other conditions the same as in Table 1.

TABLE 2				
Buck/doe ratio	1:1	1:2	1:3	1:5
Initial population	300/300	200/400	150/450	100/500
*20% harvest	120	120	120	120
Adult carryover	180/300	80/400	30/450	0/500+
40% fawn survival	120	160	180	200
Sex of fawns (1:1 bucks to does)	60/60	80/80	90/90	100/100
Following year's adult population	240/360	160/480	120/540	100/600
Number of adult deer exceeding carrying capacity next year	0	40	60	100

* Assumes *only bucks* harvested
+ Obviously, 120 bucks cannot be taken from a herd with only 100 bucks to begin with, so a 20% bucks-only harvest is impossible in a herd with such a sex ratio. For the sake of carrying the figures on down this column, however, we will assume that all the does were bred before the last buck was shot.

On the 1:1 ratio, notice that we now have 60 fewer bucks than under a both-sexes harvest (Table 1) and that the average age of the bucks remaining is drastically reduced. In the right-hand column, under the 1:5 ratio, every single buck in the herd the year after such a harvest (and thereafter) must be a yearling! No trophies can *ever* exist in such circumstances. Furthermore, the sex ratio deteriorates disastrously under this kind of "management," and the rate of deterioration accelerates rapidly as the years roll by. This is exactly the situation which develops where a state's deer herd is managed for maximum quantity rather than quality, and readily explains why 90 percent of the kill in many states is of bucks two and a half years old and younger. Yet all this can happen before our eyes in what appears to be a large and thriving deer herd.

If you and your hunting companions have been wondering, for the past few years, why you can see so many deer in the woods and so few antlered bucks, now you know!

19 Mule Deer

We have seen that management of a deer herd for trophy-antler production happens also to be management of that herd for a healthy, normal, well-balanced population, and this is as true of mule deer as of whitetails. It's true, in fact, of every known species of horned or antlered game on this continent, simply because it is management tailored along the lines of nature's own methods. Her methods of correcting imbalances in a herd, however, are much less humane and more devastating than the hunter's rifle.

The classic example occurred in Arizona's Kaibab Plateau during the first twenty years of this century. The Kaibab held a herd of about 3,000 muleys which were renowned for their trophy quality. By government decree, the area was made a game preserve with no hunting allowed. Even this would have been ecologically satisfactory, although wasteful of a resource which cannot be stockpiled, if an intensive campaign to eliminate the natural predators on the Kaibab deer herd had not been mounted. Mountain lions, bobcats, coyotes, and wolves were all but exterminated in the area. Within a little more than twelve years, the 3,000-deer herd had become a 100,000-deer herd, and the Kaibab Plateau, which had been described as a botanist's paradise, became a wasteland as the deer nibbled away the last vestiges of vegetation which might keep them alive a day or two longer. And then they began to lie down and die, of starvation and diseases to which well-nourished animals are immune. They died by the tens of thousands, most of them in a single year. Some conservationists' estimates place the dieoff at nine out of every ten deer, and that formerly lush and productive range has never fully recovered, even now, more than a half-century later.

Yet the wildlife preservationists (as distinct from conservationists) continue to agitate for a similar "management" policy for all of America's big-game species.

May the saints protect the poor animals from such kindnesses!

Muleys are inherently more difficult to develop good statistical data on because of their wandering. Not being confined by habit to the same modest home range inhabited by whitetails, they make identification of individuals from year to year, or even from season to season, sketchy. Well-defined populations are also harder to keep track of. On the other hand, mule deer in some regions may be easier to census than whitetails in some of their thickest strongholds, and biologists in the western states have a very good handle on the numbers they need for professional management decisions. Unfortunately, the biologist only proposes, while the politician disposes, and the well-founded recommendations of the professional wildlife scientists are often ignored in the setting of seasons and regulations, especially in certain states.

The results are evident to any hunter who has hunted one of the mountain states over a period of years. Areas which were two- or even three-buck regions twenty-five years ago are now one-deer, either sex, and bucks are scarce. This is not, as you may hear in some quarters, the fault of the nonresident hunters. It is the fault of politicians (some of them wearing game-department uniforms) who establish harvest regulations based more on the revenue projections for next year's budget and on the demands of equally ignorant resident hunters than on the biological realities of the resource. Most of these departments more or less subsist on the nonresident hunter, but obviously would much prefer that he send his money and stay home.

There is no getting around it; every state game department in the United States has all the legal and moral foundation necessary to manage game resources scientifically for the ultimate benefit of the game, the citizens, and the range. They also have the know-how, the sincere desire, and the dedication to do just that. If they do not do it, it is simply because you and I—the hunters they serve—will not let them.

The above is by no means intended to be a blanket condemnation of all the mule deer states' management policies, and probably applies only to a minority of those states. I will not name them. This is not a copout; the situation, especially regarding mule deer, is an extremely dynamic one and changes can be wrought very rapidly. Over the life I hope this book will have, it's probable that, through administrative changes, some of the "bad management" states will have become "good management" states, and maybe there will have been a few vice-versas. Besides, no one who spends any time in the hunting field needs me to point out where the existing policies are working and where they aren't. If you're seeing a high proportion of bucks and good trophies, the area is well managed. Are you?

Trophy mule deer racks come from a very widespread region, including fourteen states, three Canadian provinces, and Mexico. Colorado boasts a disproportionate number of the Boone and Crockett record heads in both categories (typical and nontypical), with more than half of the top hundred typical records and fifteen of the top hundred nontypicals, including both the new No. 1 and the No. 3 typical heads. By striking contrast, Alberta has few muleys in the record book, but one happens to be the No. 1 nontypical trophy ever measured! In general, Colorado's overall production of really big heads has declined drastically in recent years, but the Numero Uno was taken in that state very recently. I am not familiar with the circumstances of that kill, but I would speculate that the huge rack was taken on private property on which the harvest has been well managed by accident or design. If I were headed for Colorado with a trophy muley in mind, that's exactly the sort of area I'd be looking for, these days. The same comment applies, by and large, to most of the major mule-deer states.

Utah, Arizona, and New Mexico follow Colorado in top-hundred record production, with more than twenty "book" heads each. Idaho has eighteen and Wyoming sixteen heads, within the select top-hundred typical and nontypical groups. Nevada, Oregon, Washington, and Saskatchewan have each placed a few heads in these groups, and Alberta, British Columbia, Nebraska, and Kansas are represented by one each. California has a head in the book but not in the top hundred, and so does the Mexican state of Sonora.

As with whitetails, it's obvious that it isn't impossible to come upon a record-class muley in almost any part of his far-flung range. There is one exception to this rule, and it is that you will not see many Boone and Crockett mule deer in those areas inhabited by the

A mammoth nontypical Rocky Mountain mule deer taken in Colorado's west-central region.

subspecies known as the desert mule deer, mostly in southern Arizona and New Mexico, western Texas, and Mexico. These are smaller-bodied and smaller-antlered deer than the big Rocky Mountain animals, and stand little chance in the B&C competitions. Neverthe-less, a hunter can take a trophy desert deer which is every bit as legitimate a trophy, as judged in its own context, as the biggest Rocky Mountain head ever shot. I presume that individuals of the desert subspecies are not recognized by the Boone and Crockett officials as a separate category (as are the Coues whitetail and the Columbian and Sitka blacktail) because identification from external characteristics is too difficult for the average scorer. A big medium-antlered Rocky Mountain deer would easily make any rea-sonable minimum score established for the desert deer, and only an expert taxonomist could reliably tell which was which.

Trophy mule deer hotspots come and go. When a new area—long unhunted—is opened up, several new record heads are collected during the first two or three years, after which the overall quality

I shot this good muley of the desert subspecies on the Mescalero Apache Reservation near Ruidoso, New Mexico. Except for one possible Sonora, Mexico, head, no desert muley has ever made the record book.

tapers off fairly rapidly, as many of the biggest bucks are harvested and the rest of them educated. Quite often, by the time the general hunting public begins to hear of these fantastic "new" trophy spots, they're on the way down. The Jicarilla Apache reservation in northwestern New Mexico was such a region. For the first few seasons after the Indians opened it up to white-eye sportsmen (for a stiff fee), the reservation probably produced more "book" heads than all the rest of the muley country combined, and certainly many times as many as any other similar-sized hunting grounds on the continent. One party of three hunters from Texas made one of those early hunts and *all three* of them took Boone and Crockett trophies, two typicals and one nontypical! That may stand forever as the most remarkable trophy hunt in history.

The Jicarilla reservation still has some monstrous deer, make no mistake about that, but instead of several record-book heads each season, it now produces perhaps one every few seasons. The odds there are still as good as or better than in most other accessible parts of the range, especially during the post-season special hunt, but they're not what they used to be. In the meantime, new hotspots keep turning up.

A few years ago, some friends of mine and I were collecting some outstanding racks west of Montrose, Colorado, in the Uncompahgre Plateau country, but quality there was declining when I made my last hunt. That territory is so rough, however, that I suspect that a real hunter can still extract a wallhanger buck or two now and then. I have also hunted some good country north of Durango, Colorado, and around the Ute reservation in the southwestern corner of Colorado. Montana's best heads seem to come fairly consistently from the mountainous areas around Bozeman and Sheridan. For fine desert muleys, the Mescalero Apache reservation near Ruidoso, New Mexico, is about the best bet I know, and it's a beautiful country, well managed by the Mescalero Indian tribe.

To repeat, good mule deer bucks will not be found very often, these days, in popular public hunting areas. Where they're to be discovered in public lands at all, it will usually be in country so remote that a major packtrain trip is required to reach it, or in lands to which general public access is difficult or impossible. Throughout the range, however, some spectacular trophies can occasionally be picked up on large private ranches where hunting is controlled carefully, usually on a trespass-fee basis. Such ranches are the best bet for a big muley these days, except perhaps for the first season in a newly opened public area, of which there are fewer and fewer every year.

The same basic principle applies to muleys that we have examined in the case of whitetails, and it is that you must hunt where the bucks have had an opportunity to reach the trophy age of five and a half or better. In previously unhunted country, they may be found almost anywhere, but as soon as the gun pressure is applied, the cunning hunter will be poking far back into the mountains away from any roads, looking for rough, difficult pockets of terrain which have the essentials for mule-deer survival and comfort. It may be even more true of this species than of whitetails that the successful trophy hunter is most likely to be the one willing to work hardest, the one in best physical condition, and the most knowledgeable. The rule still applies: if you look over an area and feel a trifle faint at the very idea of trying to pack a dead deer out of it, it's a promising area. Chances are, every other hunter who looked at it felt the same way, and left it—and its inhabitants—alone.

By a mile, my favorite hunting technique for mule deer is to transport myself to the top of a mountain by daylight, and spend the entire day drifting downhill. If access to the top is only by foot, this means departing camp in the wee hours of the morning. If by horse-back or vehicle, perhaps someone else can accompany me and bring the transportation back down the mountain. This is a delightful manner of hunting, with many advantages. First, it places you above the deer, which is an advantage with all mountain game. Second, it conserves energy, especially for the flatland-born-and-bred nonresi-dent. And third, it's efficient. The hunter can zigzag widely back and forth across the slopes, prying into every likely pocket. Toward midday, he can usually find a high point or shoulder on which to sit and glass a lot of country, watching shady spots for the telltale out-line of a bedded buck. With a good pair of binoculars, he can thus hunt a good many more square miles than he could see on foot in several days, and he can do it without spooking the countryside. If he spots a likely pair of antlers, he can plot a stalk, to take advan-tage of contours and timber and wind, to bring him within range.

One of the best things about this top-to-bottom hunting is that the hunter can get a pretty clear idea of the elevation at which the muley herd is on that mountain on that day, and this is valuable knowledge. With a bit of sidewinding on the mountainside, he may also learn whether the animals are currently clinging to the dark-timbered northern slopes, the aspen groves, the lumbering slashes, the old burns, the lower sagebrush-covered barrens, or whatever. The next few days' hunts can then be planned intelligently, to min-imize wasted time and energy and maximize efforts expended where the deer are at the moment. Such planning will *always* outproduce random roaming, afoot or on horseback, regardless of the size of the local deer population. That should be a restatement of the obvious, but I'm always surprised at the number of hunters, and even local guides and outfitters, to whom it seems meaningless, people to whom "hunting" is a matter of going out and looking for a deer. With muleys, as with trophy whitetails, luck is a sorry substitute for intelligent strategy and skill.

There may be a new breed of mule deer abroad in the land these days. He's a lot like his more sophisticated whitetail cousins in some ways, more nocturnal, a little more thicket-loving, distinctly less inclined to go bouncing off across a wide-open meadow when confronted with danger. He can no longer be depended upon to stop and look back within rifle range, just before he drops over a ridge to safety. He may choose his habitat, as an old whitetail often does, because it's overlooked by hunters, even though it's quite close to human habitation, which means that he may bed in the thickets along the creek behind the barn, and feed in the nearby alfalfa after dark. He may be low when the hunters are combing the timberlines, and high when they assume the snows have brought him low.

And this new breed of muley buck is growing a hell of a set of antlers because he's living long enough to reach maturity. I strongly suspect that these are the animals from which tomorrow's trophy hunters will collect their den decorations, and they'll have to work at it. Can you imagine the challenge offered by a deer with the muley's habitat and some of the whitetail's cunning habits? We may have to develop a new breed of mule deer hunters to cope with him!

20 Field Care of Trophies

When, after all the months and perhaps years of study, planning, practice, and expense, a man finds himself standing over a giant buck, a trophy he has well and truly earned, he still has one last important responsibility to the animal. It is to see that the portion which will be mounted gets to the taxidermist's hands in the best possible condition, and that the rest of the hide and all the meat receive the care it deserves. Venison is a rare viand which can only be enjoyed by a hunter (and his friends). If it could be had in a meat market (surprising how many anti-hunters are unaware of the fact that no wild meat can be bought or sold), it would fetch a rare price. On the menus of distinguished restaurants, elaborately prepared venison dishes would top the price list. The gourmet columns of metropolitan newspapers would rhapsodize over sauces and wines for venison dinners. That these things don't happen in the United States is directly due to the fact that *sport* hunters long ago put a stop to all commercial traffic in wild meats, and thus to market hunting. They *do* happen in Europe and Central and South America.

Much has been said in this book about *old* bucks, which, in the minds of many people, equates with *tough* old bucks. Nothing could be farther from the truth. The meat of a fine, mature whitetail taken under certain conditions and properly cared for in the field is the best venison available, in my opinion. Does and young bucks are good eating, but their flesh somehow lacks the character of a big buck's, just as veal lacks character in comparison with aged, prime heavy beef. Both are good, but in different ways.

A buck which is shot at or before the peak of the rut, it must be admitted, is inferior to one shot either before or after the rut. With any species of animal on earth, including domestic breeds raised explicitly for their meat, the quality of the meat depends very greatly on the animal's condition at the time of death. If he was lean, and especially if he was *losing* body condition, the steaks and roasts will not be as tender and delicate as they might be. But if the old boy was on the mend, his body condition *improving*, his age has little if anything to do with the meat quality. Some of the best venison I've ever eaten came from a buck so old that he was no longer participating in the rutting frenzy; you could almost cut it with a fork, although he was probably about ten years old. In many states, the hunting season falls either before or after the rut, and in these areas the venison from even a monster trophy buck is likely to be delicious.

We often hear about a "wild taste" in venison, which many people use as an excuse for giving their deer meat away. There is simply no such thing. If venison has a tangy, sharp flavor (except for muleys which have been browsing mostly on sagebrush late in the season), it has been abused in the field, and prime beef given the same treatment would have a tangy, sharp flavor. Venison does not, however, taste like anything else. It doesn't taste like beef, or pork, or mutton. It tastes like venison. It does have a distinctive flavor which identifies it, just as beef or pork or mutton do. That's what I like about it. If you don't like the venison flavor, well and good (I'm not so hot on mutton, either), but don't attribute your distaste to the fact that the meat came from a wild animal. There's more to it than that.

A lot has to do with how the venison is prepared, as well as its treatment in the field. If you cook beef by a pork or lamb recipe and expect it to taste like pork or lamb, you'll doubtless be disappointed. If you cook venison like beef and expect it to taste like beef, you probably won't like it. But if you cook it as *venison* should be cooked and approach it with an open mind, savoring its own distinctive flavor, you may very well come to regard our annual freezerful of deer chops, steaks, and roasts as reserved for very special occasions and not to be given away or shared with any but very special friends.

Venison dinners of *that* quality begin the instant the trigger is pulled. The animal must die instantly, preferably without any premonitions of danger, for the very best meat. Every second his metabolism continues after the bullet strikes him degrades the meat quality. Second and third shots, and even a brief chase of a wounded buck before the *coup de grace*, very noticeably degrade that quality. So expert marksmanship turns out to be not only humane, and the mark of a skillful hunter, but also in your own best gastronomical interests.

Once the animal is dead, he should, of course, be field-dressed at once, and I mean *at once*. All internal organs should be removed, from the jugular, esophagus, and trachea where that bundle of organs enters the chest cavity back to and including the anus. The testicles and the various scent glands can be left in place until later. Some states require evidence of sex attached to the carcass. However, the secretion of the glands can taint portions of the meat if transferred to it on your hands. The meat should not be contacted by

Prompt eviscerating (and sometimes skinning and quartering) at the kill site is essential to quality venison and proper care of the trophy.

bile, urine, stomach contents, or feces, either, so a knowledge of where these sources of contamination are and care to avoid opening them is important. The lower colon and rectum should be removed with the anus itself, intact; the anus can be "cored" out of the skin with a sharp knife, after which the pelvic joint should be separated and the lower tract removed. A good trick here is as follows: once the pelvis is split, with the deer lying on his back, spread his hind legs and put one foot on each hock. Grab the tail and pull upward mightily. The pelvis split will open as if by magic and greatly facilitate removal of the lower digestive tract.

If you're a liver lover, now separate the deer liver and store it in a plastic sack; it's better than the best calf liver you ever ate, and is one of the few parts of the deer which can be cooked and enjoyed immediately. The heart is not bad, either, boiled for several hours in salted water and sliced thin.

With the deer gutted, he should be turned over and the cavity allowed to drain thoroughly. It occurs to me that I haven't mentioned bleeding a deer by opening the jugular. Because I'm a rifle hunter and because a modern rifle bullet through the heart-lung region bleeds a deer more quickly and better than any knife cut, I never even think of it. But if the deer was killed with buckshot, which usually cannot disrupt large veins and arteries, or if he was shot in the brain (for some unimaginable reason), the first step after the hunter arrives at his downed trophy should be opening the jugular, if gutting will not take place at once. However, the thrust should not be made until the cape is peeled back far enough to expose the "sticking spot"; a taxidermist can only do so much in repairing holes in the hide. I presume that any hunter sufficiently far along to be interested in a book with this title already knows better than to cut a dead or dying buck's throat with a transverse slash.

It's axiomatic that the quicker the body heat leaves the meat, the more tender will be the venison. If the carcass can be quickly transported to camp, skinning and quartering can take place there. If not, it should be done at the kill site.

The first consideration in skinning is proper care of the cape, and the most common mistake is cutting it too short. The cape, or headskin, should include not only the entire neck but the brisket and shoulders as well, for the typical shoulder mount. The best way to deal with this most important part of the skin, unless you're an expert skinner and caper, is to make a cut all the way around the buck's shoulders, and then to "case" the skin forward to the head proper. This means simply skinning the neck forward without making any longitudinal cuts at all. Then sever the entire head where the spinal column joins the base of the skull, and lay the head with attached cape aside.

Whether all this is done in camp or in the field, it's done in the same fashion. In camp, the carcass should be hung on a gambrel stick (through the hocks), and the hide removed. Skinning is something of an art, the art being to take the skin only, with no meat attached, but without making any accidental incisions through the hide. If you plan to have the hide tanned into glove-leather buckskin, spread it out, flesh side up, and apply a heavy layer of ordinary table salt all over it. Let it stand in the shade for a few hours, shake off the now-sopping-wet salt, and resalt the whole hide. The hide can now be left, protected from direct sun and moisture, for several days, or until it can be delivered, rolled or folded with the flesh side in, to the tanner, to be made into gloves, a shirt, or whatever. It is one of the finest leathers in the world, exceptionally durable and with the almost unique property of drying soft and pliable after wetting.

By the way, skinning is about ten times easier if accomplished while the carcass is still warm; let it chill, and you just have to whittle it off. While warm, it can almost be pulled off the carcass without the use of a knife or other instrument.

The coat of a deer is made up of hollow hairs which offer a surprising degree of insulation. Leaving the hide on a carcass reduces the rate of cooling materially, and, as mentioned, that makes the venison tougher. Once the carcass is skinned, it will cool rapidly and soon glaze over so that it will keep for a long time in cool, dry weather. However, once you've gone this far, it takes so little additional effort to complete the job that you might as well do it right while you have a knife out. Quartering is simple. The forelegs of a deer have no direct connection with the rest of the skeleton, so the shoulders are easily and quickly removed. The ball-and-socket joints where the large bones in the hams connect with the pelvis must be exposed and disarticulated so that the hams will come free. Now cut out the backstraps, and the smaller, inside tenders. The tenderloin tips are now exposed for removal. Next, with a meat saw (a coarse-tooth hacksaw will serve), cut off the lower legs from hams and shoulders at or above the joints. Sever the spine behind the rib cage, and sever the neck. Most experts saw lengthwise through the spine to separate the two sides of ribs. Bone out the neck and whatever other worthwhile bits of meat remain on the skeleton for stew or chili meat, and the job is finished.

I am now about to reveal to you a secret to tender, sweet venison which I have never seen in print and which you will probably reject instantly—until you try it once. Place the meat in a clean camp icebox and cover it with crushed or cube ice. As the ice melts, do not pour off the water, but keep adding ice. The idea is to soak the venison in water which is only fractionally above the freezing point, and to do it for several days. I've kept venison thus for as long

To do all skinning and butchering jobs right, various knives are necessary, although the second blade from the top is an excellent all-purpose knife. At top is a caping knife by T. M. Dowell for the delicate work of removing a headskin for the taxidermist. Next is a general-purpose blade designed by me and executed by custom cutler Chubby Hueske. At center is an all-out skinner of excellent design by D'Alton Holder. The Morseth is a custom-made butcher knife, and at bottom is a high-quality commercial boning knife.

as nine days, always making certain that the water had plenty of unmelted ice in it. The water will draw the blood out of the meat, which turns whitish on the outside, and this is good. The meat will "age" in the ice water better than in any cold locker, and is easy to transport to your processor, or to your home if you do your own boning, steaking, and trimming for the freezer.

Back to the head with cased cape attached. In any but the warmest weather, it will keep well enough just as it is for the few days normally required to deliver it to a taxidermist, although it may be prudent to remove the tongue. This is easily done from the rear, with the skin left intact on the head. If the weather is warm and humid, and it's a long trip to the taxidermist's, it may be desirable to store the head with cape in an ice house, but it should not be frozen. As a last resort, the head may have to be caped in camp, and there is absolutely no way you're going to learn the fine points of caping from the text or pictures in a book. The best advice I can offer is to hang around your local taxidermist's during the deer-hunting season. Watch him cape out heads for mounting, noting especially the cuts around eyelids, lips, and nostrils, and ask questions. If you're friends, he might even allow you to cape a head or two, under his very watchful eye. That's the way I learned caping.

After the cape is removed, it should be fleshed carefully and salted, then resalted. As you'll learn from the taxidermist, the lips must be split and salted and the ears "turned" and, of course, salted. The salt removes fluids from the skin, and if any spot—say, a fold or wrinkle—escapes the salt, the hair may slip in that area and ruin the cape for mounting. In caping, the novice is well advised to go very, very slowly, making certain of what is being cut before cutting, and the salting must be extremely thorough. As the salted cape dries, it should be rolled loosely and protected from moisture.

When the cape is off, take the saw and remove the skull plate, with antlers attached, by sawing through the cranial cavity from rear to front, guiding the cut so that it passes through the eye sockets. Clean the skull and set it aside with the cape.

There is one more trophy which should be taken at this point, and it is the lower jawbone, or at least one side of it. Cut away all the muscles you can remove with a small, sharp knife, and leave the bone in an antbed where no dogs can get at it. The ants will do a fairly good job of cleaning up the last vestiges of flesh, after which the bone can be bleached either in the sun or with a laundry bleach. The teeth in that jawbone provide a very good index to the owner's age at death.

Although aging by tooth wear may contain as much as a 20 percent error, it's still easy to learn to separate deer jaws into groups as follows: one and a half years and younger, five and a half years and older, and everything between those two ages. Aging to that degree is all any hunter ever needs to do in order to evaluate the bucks he takes. Biologists with your state's game department, and many game wardens, for that matter, can "read" the jawbones for you, as can wildlife-management people at your state university. With a little practice, you can learn to determine age from tooth wear without outside assistance, and this is one of the major keys to

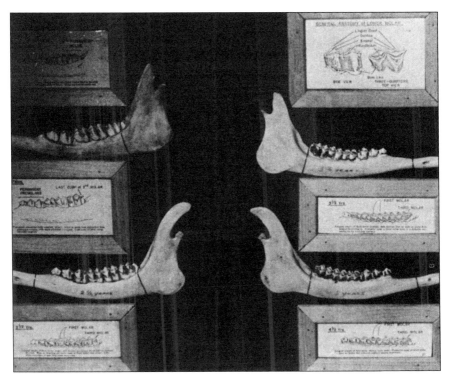

Learning to "age" deer by molar-tooth wear is not particularly difficult, although not easily taught by the printed word. In these pictures, the progressive wear over the eight-year span shown is obvious, even if the finer points of aging are obscure. Any game biologist and many wardens can make those finer points clear in a few minutes with a display of jawbones similar to this one.

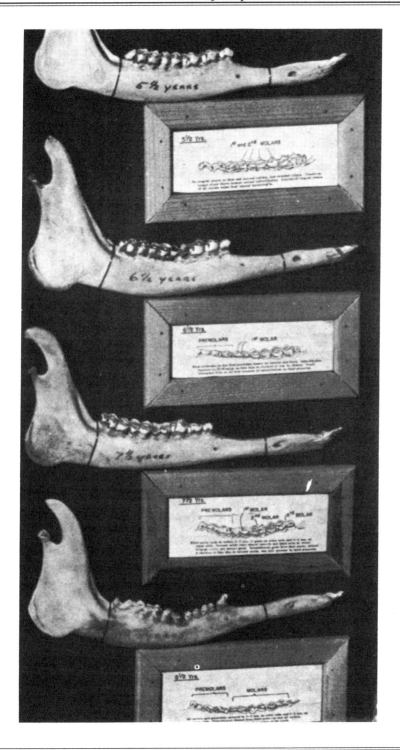

judging the status of the local deer herd. In my camp, we keep careful records of the ages and dressed weights of every deer of either
sex that's collected, just to keep tabs on how our management program is coming along.

Now, with the trophy claimed and safely tucked away at the
taxidermist's and the meat neatly packaged in the freezer, is the time
to enjoy the final reward. Well, not quite the *final* reward; never a
day passes that I don't consciously take pleasure and satisfaction from
the big bucks mounted in my study. The anti-hunters constantly
accuse us of "stuffing" trophy heads to bolster our egos and reinforce
our sense of masculinity. How pitifully wrong they are! The mounted
head of a big buck is a true trophy in every sense of the word, a
genuine memento of a personal accomplishment, and a reminder of a
great day and a high moment. But they will never understand, and
you already do, so we can return to our well-earned venison dinner.

I'm no classic chef, but there are a few hints which may help
you enjoy that dinner. Venison is inherently a fairly dry meat at
best, so every effort to preserve its natural moisture is worth making. I also suggest that venison is juicier and better if not well done;
medium to medium rare is about the best degree of doneness for
most palates. A favorite way of preparing a venison roast is as follows. Build a very small fire in an outdoor charcoal cooker, at one
end of the fuel area. On the grill above it, place a pan of water.
Beside the pan, place the roast, and arrange the draft in such a way
that the airflow enters under the smoldering charcoal and exits
above the meat. In the beginning, and at regular intervals during
the cooking, baste the roast in a mixture of melted butter and bour-
bon. Keep the outside of the meat always moist with this sauce, and
keep the bed of coals very small. Occasionally sprinkle a handful of
watersoaked hickory chips over the coals. Cook for six to eight
hours, adding water to the pan as it evaporates, in effect steaming
and smoking the meat simultaneously. Cook to about medium, when
slices show pink inside. Those slices should be tender and juicy, and
if you prepare this dish for a group of friends I'll bet you don't have
many leftovers!

Another superlative venison meal, even from the oldest buck, is
prepared as follows. Trim the backstraps free of all membranes, cut
in two, and roll like filet mignon. Wrap a strip of bacon around each

roll and tie with a clean cord to make a filet about $2\frac{1}{2}$ inches in diameter and at least that thick. Stuff a few bits of beef suet into the center of the roll. Broil in a very hot oven about twenty minutes on each side, on a trivet in a pan to catch the drippings. While the meat is broiling, baste it occasionally with melted beef suet, and concoct a sauce for it between bastings. Make the sauce in this fashion. Heat a can of consommé to boiling in a saucepan, and melt a stick of butter, preferably unsalted, at the same time. Blend the butter into the consommé and add a couple of serving-spoonfuls of red currant jelly and stir until melted. Add a couple of teaspoonfuls of chopped parsley and allow the whole mixture to simmer until the meat is done. Then, working very quickly, pour some of the sauce mixture into the pan and blend with the meat drippings, working any drippings which have stuck to the hot pan free and stirring the whole sauce thoroughly before serving. Cut and remove the strings and serve with wild rice and apples cooked in wine, with the consommé sauce over everything. Your favorite red wine—cabernet, merlot, burgundy, bordeaux, or even gewürztraminer—will fit right in with this meal; the meat has character and will not be overwhelmed by any of them. But, if you prefer white wines—or, like me, suffer from gout—ignore the wine snobs and drink what you like with venison!

The only drawback to this meal is that each deer has only two backstraps, enough for four to six servings at most. This is a fact which has occasionally caused me to consider a bit of midnight requisitioning of backstraps from other hunters' bucks on the meatpole! If you can eat this dish and still say you don't like venison, then you really *don't* like venison . . . but you'll be unique in my experience.

Backstraps, of course, are the premium meat on any buck. For a good camp meal (after the liver is gone), slice a backstrap diagonally crosswise in disks about $\frac{3}{4}$ inch thick, dredge in seasoned flour, and fry quickly in *very* hot grease. On no account overcook this meat, usually not more than three or four minutes on each side. Place the browned meat on paper towels to drain, pour out most of the grease, and add to the skillet about four chopped onions, and enough milk to make a thick gravy. Simmer to blend, serve with hot buttered biscuits, and stand back!

This great whitetail is not alive, but a life-size mount by Conroe, Texas, taxidermist Mike Simpson for hunter Larry Bailey. Only exceptionally good care of the hide in the field could enable any taxidermist to recreate the animal so perfectly. *(Photo courtesy of Robert Rogers)*

Over coffee, after such a meal, a man can sit back and contemplate the fact that the true trophy hunter of American deer is a somewhat lonely figure in today's world, not because he is a holdover from an earlier day, but because he is ahead of his time. In those earlier days when a successful hunt meant survival, there was no time for trophies, however much a primitive hunter may have admired a big buck when one appeared. The quality-hunting concept is just now aborning, in an age when competent research has given us the tools for professional management of the herds. As we have seen, well-managed herds are herds which include trophy bucks; by definition, a deer herd without any mature males is a badly managed herd. We are beginning to understand that biologically sound big-game management and trophy management are the same thing.

The real holdovers from a bygone day are those who advocate management for *quantity* rather than quality, and those who shout for no management at all, the well-meaning but ignorant preservationists whose philosophy caused 90,000 mule deer to starve in one year in the Kaibab.

The trophy hunter is, in this sense, a pioneer, a sportsman who blazes the trails toward a hunting ethic which can—and must—bring hunting as a wholesome sport into its proper perspective in the public mind and bring the needs of that public (including the non-hunters) and the wildlife of America into a new and more realistic balance.

To do so, he will have to learn how to deal with the media, the bureaucrats and politicians, and his fellow hunters, in addition to the uncanny cleverness of the old bucks themselves. It's a formidable challenge . . . but then, I never said that taking a trophy whitetail or muley—or even having them to hunt—would be easy!

This great whitetail *is* alive, a living symbol of the overall health and balance of the herd of which he is a part, a challenge to every hunter who takes pride in his skills, and a promise for the future of American deer. *(Photo by Jerry Smith)*

Appendix

OFFICIAL SCORING SYSTEM FOR NORTH AMERICAN BIG GAME TROPHIES

Records of North American
Big Game

BOONE AND CROCKETT CLUB®

250 Station Drive
Missoula, MT 59801
(406) 542-1888

Minimum Score:	Awards	All-time
Whitetail	160	170
Coues'	100	110

**TYPICAL
WHITETAIL AND COUES' DEER**

Kind of Deer: _____

Abnormal Points	
Right Antler	Left Antler

Subtotals	
Total to E	

	SEE OTHER SIDE FOR INSTRUCTIONS		Column 1	Column 2	Column 3	Column 4
			Spread Credit	Right Antler	Left Antler	Difference
A. No. Points on Right Antler	No. Points on Left Antler					
B. Tip to Tip Spread	C. Greatest Spread					
D. Inside Spread of Main Beams	(Credit May Equal But Not Exceed Longer Antler)					
E. Total of Lengths of Abnormal Points						
F. Length of Main Beam						
G-1. Length of First Point						
G-2. Length of Second Point						
G-3. Length of Third Point						
G-4. Length of Fourth Point, If Present						
G-5. Length of Fifth Point, If Present						
G-6. Length of Sixth Point, If Present						
G-7. Length of Seventh Point, If Present						
H-1. Circumference at Smallest Place Between Burr and First Point						
H-2. Circumference at Smallest Place Between First and Second Points						
H-3. Circumference at Smallest Place Between Second and Third Points						
H-4. Circumference at Smallest Place Between Third and Fourth Points						
		TOTALS				

ADD	Column 1		Exact Locality Where Killed:
	Column 2		Date Killed: Hunter:
	Column 3		Owner: Telephone #:
	Subtotal		Owner's Address:
SUBTRACT Column 4			Guide's Name and Address:
			Remarks: (Mention Any Abnormalities or Unique Qualities)
	FINAL SCORE		

I certify that I have measured this trophy on _____ 19 _____

at (address) _____ City _____ State _____
and that these measurements and data are, to the best of my knowledge and belief, made in
accordance with the instructions given.

Witness: _____ Signature: _____

B&C Official Measurer

I.D. Number

INSTRUCTIONS FOR MEASURING TYPICAL WHITETAIL AND COUES' DEER

All measurements must be made with a 1/4-inch wide flexible steel tape to the nearest
one-eighth of an inch. (Note: A flexible steel cable can be used to measure points and main beams
only.) Enter fractional figures in eighths, without reduction. Official measurements cannot be
taken until the antlers have air dried for at least 60 days after the animal was killed.

A. Number of Points on Each Antler: To be counted a point, the projection must be at least one
inch long, with the length exceeding width at one inch or more of length. All points are measured
from tip of point to nearest edge of beam as illustrated. Beam tip is counted as a point but not
measured as a point.

B. Tip to Tip Spread is measured between tips of main beams.

C. Greatest Spread is measured between perpendiculars at a right angle to the center line of
the skull at widest part, whether across main beams or points.

D. Inside Spread of Main Beams is measured at a right angle to the center line of the skull at
widest point between main beams. Enter this measurement again as the Spread Credit if it is less
than or equal to the length of the longer antler; if greater, enter longer antler length for
Spread Credit.

E. Total of Lengths of all Abnormal Points: Abnormal Points are those non-typical in location
(such as points originating from a point or from bottom or sides of main beam) or extra points
beyond the normal pattern of points. Measure in usual manner and enter in appropriate blanks.

F. Length of Main Beam is measured from the center of the lowest outside edge of burr over
outer side to the most distant point of the main beam. The point of beginning is that point on
the burr where the center line along the outer side of the beam intersects the burr, then
following generally the line of the illustration.

G-1-2-3-4-5-6-7. Length of Normal Points: Normal points project from the top of the main
beam. They are measured from nearest edge of main beam over outer curve to tip. Lay the tape
along the outer curve of the beam so that the top edge of the tape coincides with the top edge of
the beam on both sides of the point to determine the baseline for point measurements. Record
point lengths in appropriate blanks.

H-1-2-3-4. Circumferences are taken as detailed for each measurement. If brow point is
missing, take H-1 and H-2 at smallest place between burr and G-2. If G-4 is missing, take H-4
halfway between G-3 and tip of main beam.

FAIR CHASE STATEMENT FOR ALL HUNTER-TAKEN TROPHIES

FAIR CHASE, as defined by the Boone and Crockett Club®, is the ethical, sportsmanlike and
lawful pursuit and taking of any free-ranging wild game animal in a manner that does not give
the hunter an improper or unfair advantage over such game animals.

Use of any of the following methods in the taking of game shall be deemed **UNFAIR CHASE**
and unsportsmanlike:

I. Spotting or herding game from the air, followed by landing in its vicinity for the
purpose of pursuit and shooting;

II. Herding, pursuing, or shooting game from any motorboat or motor vehicle;

III. Use of electronic devices for attracting, locating, or observing game, or for guiding
the hunter to such game;

IV. Hunting game confined by artificial barriers, including escape-proof fenced
enclosures, or hunting game transplanted for the purpose of commercial shooting;

V. Taking of game in a manner not in full compliance with the game laws or regulations
of the federal government or of any state, province, territory, or tribal council on
reservations or tribal lands;

VI. Or as may otherwise be deemed unfair or unsportsmanlike by the Executive Committee of
the Boone and Crockett Club.

I certify that the trophy scored on this chart was taken in **FAIR CHASE** as defined above by the
Boone and Crockett Club. In signing this statement, I understand that if the information
provided on this entry is found to be misrepresented or fraudulent in any respect, it will not
be accepted into the Awards Program and all of my prior entries are subject to deletion from
future editions of *Records of North American Big Game* and future entries may not be accepted.

Date: _____ Signature of Hunter:_____
(Signature must be witnessed by an Official Measurer or
a Notary Public.)

Date: _____ Signature of Notary or Official Measurer:_____

OFFICIAL SCORING SYSTEM FOR NORTH AMERICAN BIG GAME TROPHIES

Records of North American
Big Game

BOONE AND CROCKETT CLUB®

250 Station Drive
Missoula, MT 59801
(406) 542-1888

Minimum Score:	Awards	All-time
whitetail	185	195
Coues'	105	120

NON-TYPICAL
WHITETAIL AND COUES' DEER

Kind of Deer: _____

Detail of Point Measurement

	Abnormal Points	
	Right Antler	Left Antler
Subtotals		
E. Total		

SEE OTHER SIDE FOR INSTRUCTIONS			Column 1	Column 2	Column 3	Column 4
A. No. Points on Right Antler		No. Points on Left Antler	Spread Credit	Right Antler	Left Antler	Difference
B. Tip to Tip Spread		C. Greatest Spread				
D. Inside Spread of Main Beams		(Credit May Equal But Not Exceed Longer Antler)				
F. Length of Main Beam						
G-1. Length of First Point						
G-2. Length of Second Point						
G-3. Length of Third Point						
G-4. Length of Fourth Point, If Present						
G-5. Length of Fifth Point, If Present						
G-6. Length of Sixth Point, If Present						
G-7. Length of Seventh Point, If Present						
H-1. Circumference at Smallest Place Between Burr and First Point						
H-2. Circumference at Smallest Place Between First and Second Points						
H-3. Circumference at Smallest Place Between Second and Third Point						
H-4. Circumference at Smallest Place Between Third and Fourth Point						
		TOTALS				

	Column 1		Exact Locality Where Killed:
ADD	Column 2		Date Killed: Hunter:
	Column 3		Owner: Telephone #:
	Subtotal		Owner's Address:
SUBTRACT Column 4			Guide's Name and Address:
	Subtotal		Remarks: (Mention Any Abnormalities or Unique Qualities)
ADD Line E Total			
	FINAL SCORE		

Copyright © 1997 by Boone and Crockett Club®

I certify that I have measured this trophy on _____ 19 _____

at (address) _____ City _____ State _____

and that these measurements and data are, to the best of my knowledge and belief, made in
accordance with the instructions given.

Witness: _____ Signature: _____

B&C Official Measurer

I.D. Number

INSTRUCTIONS FOR MEASURING NON-TYPICAL WHITETAIL AND COUES' DEER

All measurements must be made with a 1/4-inch wide flexible steel tape to the nearest one-eighth of an inch. (Note: A flexible steel cable can be used to measure points and main beams only.) Enter fractional figures in eighths, without reduction. Official measurements cannot be taken until the antlers have air dried for at least 60 days after the animal was killed.

A. Number of Points on Each Antler: To be counted a point, the projection must be at least one inch long, with the length exceeding width at one inch or more of length. All points are measured from tip of point to nearest edge of beam as illustrated. Beam tip is counted as a point but not measured as a point.

B. Tip to Tip Spread is measured between tips of main beams.

C. Greatest Spread is measured between perpendiculars at a right angle to the center line of the skull at widest part, whether across main beams or points.

D. Inside Spread of Main Beams is measured at a right angle to the center line of the skull at widest point between main beams. Enter this measurement again as the Spread Credit if it is less than or equal to the length of the longer antler; if greater, enter longer antler length for Spread Credit.

E. Total of Lengths of all Abnormal Points: Abnormal Points are those non-typical in location (such as points originating from a point or from bottom or sides of main beam) or extra points beyond the normal pattern of points. Measure in usual manner and enter in appropriate blanks.

F. Length of Main Beam is measured from the center of the lowest outside edge of burr over the outer side to the most distant point of the main beam. The point of beginning is that point on the burr where the center line along the outer side of the beam intersects the burr, then following generally the line of the illustration.

G-1-2-3-4-5-6-7. Length of Normal Points: Normal points project from the top of the main beam. They are measured from nearest edge of main beam over outer curve to tip. Lay the tape along the outer curve of the beam so that the top edge of the tape coincides with the top edge of the beam on both sides of the point to determine the baseline for point measurement. Record point lengths in appropriate blanks.

H-1-2-3-4. Circumferences are taken as detailed for each measurement. If brow point is missing, take H-1 and H-2 at smallest place between burr and G-2. If G-4 is missing, take H-4 halfway between G-3 and tip of main beam.

FAIR CHASE STATEMENT FOR ALL HUNTER-TAKEN TROPHIES

FAIR CHASE, as defined by the Boone and Crockett Club®, is the ethical, sportsmanlike and lawful pursuit and taking of any free-ranging wild game animal in a manner that does not give the hunter an improper or unfair advantage over such game animals.

Use of any of the following methods in the taking of game shall be deemed **UNFAIR CHASE** and unsportsmanlike:

I. Spotting or herding game from the air, followed by landing in its vicinity for the purpose of pursuit and shooting;

II. Herding, pursuing, or shooting game from any motorboat or motor vehicle;

III. Use of electronic devices for attracting, locating, or observing game, or for guiding the hunter to such game;

IV. Hunting game confined by artificial barriers, including escape-proof fenced enclosures, or hunting game transplanted for the purpose of commercial shooting;

V. Taking of game in a manner not in full compliance with the game laws or regulations of the federal government or of any state, province, territory, or tribal council on reservations or tribal lands;

VI. Or as may otherwise be deemed unfair or unsportsmanlike by the Executive Committee of the Boone and Crockett Club.

I certify that the trophy scored on this chart was taken in **FAIR CHASE** as defined above by the Boone and Crockett Club. In signing this statement, I understand that if the information provided on this entry is found to be misrepresented or fraudulent in any respect, it will not be accepted into the Awards Program and all of my prior entries are subject to deletion from future editions of *Records of North American Big Game* and future entries may not be accepted.

Date: _____ Signature of Hunter:_____
(Signature must be witnessed by an Official Measurer or a Notary Public.)

Date: _____ Signature of Notary or Official Measurer:_____

OFFICIAL SCORING SYSTEM FOR NORTH AMERICAN BIG GAME TROPHIES

Records of North American
Big Game

BOONE AND CROCKETT CLUB®

250 Station Drive
Missoula, MT 59801
(406) 542-1888

**TYPICAL
MULE DEER AND BLACKTAIL DEER**

Kind of Deer: _____

Minimum Score:	Awards	All-time
mule	180	190
Columbia	125	135
Sitka	100	108

Detail of Point Measurement

Abnormal Points	
Right Antler	Left Antler

| Subtotals | |
| Total to E | |

SEE OTHER SIDE FOR INSTRUCTIONS			Column 1	Column 2	Column 3	Column 4
A. No. Points on Right Antler		No. Points on Left Antler	Spread Credit	Right Antler	Left Antler	Difference
B. Tip to Tip Spread		C. Greatest Spread				
D. Inside Spread of Main Beams		(Credit May Equal But Not Exceed Longer Antler)				
E. Total of Lengths of Abnormal Points						
F. Length of Main Beam						
G-1. Length of First Point, If Present						
G-2. Length of Second Point						
G-3. Length of Third Point, If Present						
G-4. Length of Fourth Point, If Present						
H-1. Circumference at Smallest Place Between Burr and First Point						
H-2. Circumference at Smallest Place Between First and Second Points						
H-3. Circumference at Smallest Place Between Main Beam and Third Point						
H-4. Circumference at Smallest Place Between Second and Fourth Points						
		TOTALS				

ADD	Column 1		Exact Locality Where Killed:
	Column 2		Date Killed: Hunter:
	Column 3		Owner: Telephone #:
	Subtotal		Owner's Address:
SUBTRACT Column 4			Guide's Name and Address:
			Remarks: (Mention Any Abnormalities or Unique Qualities)
	FINAL SCORE		

I certify that I have measured this trophy on _____ 19 _____

at (address) _____ City _____ State _____

and that these measurements and data are, to the best of my knowledge and belief, made in
accordance with the instructions given.

Witness: _____ Signature: _____

                                    B&C Official Measurer

                                                I.D. Number

INSTRUCTIONS FOR MEASURING TYPICAL MULE AND BLACKTAIL DEER

    All measurements must be made with a 1/4-inch wide flexible steel tape to the nearest
one-eighth of an inch. (Note: A flexible steel cable can be used to measure points and main beams
only.) Enter fractional figures in eighths, without reduction. Official measurements cannot be
taken until the antlers have air dried for at least 60 days after the animal was killed.
    A. Number of Points on Each Antler: To be counted a point, the projection must be at least
one inch long, with length exceeding width at one inch or more of length. All points are measured
from tip of point to nearest edge of beam. Beam tip is counted as a point but not measured as a
point.
    B. Tip to Tip Spread is measured between tips of main beams.
    C. Greatest Spread is measured between perpendiculars at a right angle to the center line of
the skull at widest part, whether across main beams or points.
    D. Inside Spread of Main Beams is measured at a right angle to the center line of the skull at
widest point between main beams. Enter this measurement again as the Spread Credit if it is less
than or equal to the length of the longer antler; if greater, enter longer antler length for
Spread Credit.
    E. Total of Lengths of all Abnormal Points: Abnormal Points are those non-typical in location
such as points originating from a point (exception: G-3 originates from G-2 in perfectly normal
fashion) or from bottom or sides of main beam, or any points beyond the normal pattern of five
(including beam tip) per antler. Measure each abnormal point in usual manner and enter in
appropriate blanks.
    F. Length of Main Beam is measured from the center of the lowest outside edge of burr over the
outer side to the most distant point of the Main Beam. The point of beginning is that point on
the burr where the center line along the outer side of the beam intersects the burr, then
following generally the line of the illustration.
    G-1-2-3-4. Length of Normal Points: Normal points are the brow tines and the upper and lower
forks as shown in the illustration. They are measured from nearest edge of main beam over outer
curve to tip. Lay the tape along the outer curve of the beam so that the top edge of the tape
coincides with the top edge of the beam on both sides of point to determine the baseline for point
measurement. Record point lengths in appropriate blanks.
    H-1-2-3-4. Circumferences are taken as detailed for each measurement. If brow point is
missing, take H-1 and H-2 at smallest place between burr and G-2. If G-3 is missing, take H-3
halfway between the base and tip of G-2. If G-4 is missing, take H-4 halfway between G-2 and tip
of main beam.

FAIR CHASE STATEMENT FOR ALL HUNTER-TAKEN TROPHIES

    FAIR CHASE, as defined by the Boone and Crockett Club®, is the ethical, sportsmanlike and
lawful pursuit and taking of any free-ranging wild game animal in a manner that does not give
the hunter an improper or unfair advantage over such game animals.
    Use of any of the following methods in the taking of game shall be deemed **UNFAIR CHASE**
and unsportsmanlike:

    I.   Spotting or herding game from the air, followed by landing in its vicinity for the
          purpose of pursuit and shooting;

    II.   Herding, pursuing, or shooting game from any motorboat or motor vehicle;

    III. Use of electronic devices for attracting, locating, or observing game, or for guiding
          the hunter to such game;

    IV.   Hunting game confined by artificial barriers, including escape-proof fenced
          enclosures, or hunting game transplanted for the purpose of commercial shooting;

    V.   Taking of game in a manner not in full compliance with the game laws or regulations
          of the federal government or of any state, province, territory, or tribal council on
          reservations or tribal lands;

    VI.   Or as may otherwise be deemed unfair or unsportsmanlike by the Executive Committee of
          the Boone and Crockett Club.

I certify that the trophy scored on this chart was taken in **FAIR CHASE** as defined above by the
Boone and Crockett Club. In signing this statement, I understand that if the information
provided on this entry is found to be misrepresented or fraudulent in any respect, it will not
be accepted into the Awards Program and all of my prior entries are subject to deletion from
future editions of *Records of North American Big Game* and future entries may not be accepted.

Date: _____ Signature of Hunter: _____
                                   (Signature must be witnessed by an Official Measurer or
                                   a Notary Public.)

Date: _____ Signature of Notary or Official Measurer:_____

OFFICIAL SCORING SYSTEM FOR NORTH AMERICAN BIG GAME TROPHIES

Records of North American
Big Game

BOONE AND CROCKETT CLUB®

250 Station Drive
Missoula, MT 59801
(406) 542-1888

Minimum Score: Awards All-time
           215   230

NON-TYPICAL MULE DEER

Detail of Point Measurement

Abnormal Points	
Right Antler	Left Antler
Subtotals	
E. Total	

SEE OTHER SIDE FOR INSTRUCTIONS

				Column 1	Column 2	Column 3	Column 4
A. No. Points on Right Antler		No. Points on Left Antler		Spread Credit	Right Antler	Left Antler	Difference
B. Tip to Tip Spread		C. Greatest Spread					
D. Inside Spread of Main Beam		(Credit May Equal But Not Exceed Longer Antler)					
F. Length of Main Beam							
G-1. Length of First Point, If Present							
G-2. Length of Second Point							
G-3. Length of Third Point, If Present							
G-4. Length of Fourth Point, If Present							
H-1. Circumference at Smallest Place Between Burr and First Point							
H-2. Circumference at Smallest Place Between First and Second Points							
H-3. Circumference at Smallest Place Between Main Beam and Third Point							
H-4. Circumference at Smallest Place Between Second and Fourth Points							
		TOTALS					

ADD	Column 1		Exact Locality Where Killed:
	Column 2		Date Killed: Hunter:
	Column 3		Owner: Telephone #:
	Subtotal		Owner's Address:
	SUBTRACT Column 4		Guide's Name and Address:
	Subtotal		Remarks: (Mention Any Abnormalities or Unique Qualities)
	ADD Line E Total		
	FINAL SCORE		

I certify that I have measured this trophy on _____ 19 _____

at (address) _____ City _____ State _____

and that these measurements and data are, to the best of my knowledge and belief, made in
accordance with the instructions given.

Witness: _____ Signature: _____

B&C Official Measurer [| | |]

I.D. Number

INSTRUCTIONS FOR MEASURING NON-TYPICAL MULE DEER

All measurements must be made with a 1/4-inch wide flexible steel tape to the nearest
one-eighth of an inch. (Note: A flexible steel cable can be used to measure points and main beams
only.) Enter fractional figures in eighths, without reduction. Official measurements cannot be
taken until the antlers have air dried for at least 60 days after the animal was killed.

A. Number of Points on Each Antler: To be counted a point, the projection must be at least
one inch long, with length exceeding width at one inch or more of length. All points are measured
from tip of point to nearest edge of beam as illustrated. Beam tip is counted as a point but not
measured as a point.

B. Tip to Tip Spread is measured between tips of main beams.

C. Greatest Spread is measured between perpendiculars at a right angle to the center line of
the skull at widest part, whether across main beams or points.

D. Inside Spread of Main Beams is measured at a right angle to the center line of the skull at
widest point between main beams. Enter this measurement again as the Spread Credit if it is less
than or equal to the length of the longer antler; if greater, enter longer antler length for
Spread Credit.

E. Total of Lengths of all Abnormal Points: Abnormal Points are those non-typical in location
(such as points originating from a point (exception: G-3 originates from G-2 in perfectly normal
fashion) or from bottom of sides of main beam, or any points beyond the normal pattern of five
including beam tip) per antler. Measure each abnormal point in usual manner and enter in
appropriate blanks.

F. Length of Main Beam is measured from the center of the lowest outside edge of burr over the
outer side to the most distant point of the main beam. The point of beginning is that point on
the burr where the center line along the outer side of the beam intersects the burr, then
following generally the line of the illustration.

G-1-2-3-4. Length of Normal Points: Normal points are the brow tines and the upper and lower
forks as shown in the illustration. They are measured from nearest edge of main beam over outer
curve to tip. Lay the tape along the outer curve of the beam so that the top edge of the tape
coincides with the top edge of the beam on both sides of point to determine the baseline for point
measurement. Record point lengths in appropriate blanks.

H-1-2-3-4. Circumferences are taken as detailed for each measurement. If brow point is
missing, take H-1 and H-2 at smallest place between burr and G-2. If G-3 is missing, take H-3
halfway between the base and tip of G-2. If G-4 is missing, take H-4 halfway between G-2 and tip
of main beam.

FAIR CHASE STATEMENT FOR ALL HUNTER-TAKEN TROPHIES

FAIR CHASE, as defined by the Boone and Crockett Club®, is the ethical, sportsmanlike and
lawful pursuit and taking of any free-ranging wild game animal in a manner that does not give
the hunter an improper or unfair advantage over such game animals.

Use of any of the following methods in the taking of game shall be deemed **UNFAIR CHASE**
and unsportsmanlike:

I.   Spotting or herding game from the air, followed by landing in its vicinity for the
     purpose of pursuit and shooting;

II. Herding, pursuing, or shooting game from any motorboat or motor vehicle;

III. Use of electronic devices for attracting, locating, or observing game, or for guiding
     the hunter to such game;

IV. Hunting game confined by artificial barriers, including escape-proof fenced
     enclosures, or hunting game transplanted for the purpose of commercial shooting;

V.   Taking of game in a manner not in full compliance with the game laws or regulations
     of the federal government or of any state, province, territory, or tribal council on
     reservations or tribal lands;

VI. Or as may otherwise be deemed unfair or unsportsmanlike by the Executive Committee of
     the Boone and Crockett Club.

I certify that the trophy scored on this chart was taken in **FAIR CHASE** as defined above by the
Boone and Crockett Club. In signing this statement, I understand that if the information
provided on this entry is found to be misrepresented or fraudulent in any respect, it will not
be accepted into the Awards Program and all of my prior entries are subject to deletion from
future editions of *Records of North American Big Game* and future entries may not be accepted.

Date: _____   Signature of Hunter:_____
                                          (Signature must be witnessed by an Official Measurer or
                                          a Notary Public.)

Date: _____   Signature of Notary or Official Measurer:_____

Index

acorn horns, 30

age, deer, 224, 240-41; and antler size, 19, 50-57, 60; of trophy bucks, 6-9, 19, 57-61

Alberta, Canada, 74, 165, 227

anatomy, deer, 196-98, 235-37

antelopes, Old World, 24

antlers, 24-37, 66, 218; cleaning, 31, 80, 84; color, 31; growing season, 30; growth rate, 27; loss of, 32-33; permanent, 33; shed, 36, 78; size, 56; size, and buck age, 19, 47-57, 60; size, and buck status, 31-32; size, average, and herd condition, 8; size, field judging, 38-49; spread, 10, 12, 42, 45-46, 56; symmetry, 12

Arizona, 225, 228

Arkansas, 75, 113, 154

arteries, 195

bachelor clubs, buck, 56, 66

Barnes bullets, 185

barometric pressure, 100-2

battles, buck: reproduction rivalry, 25-26; status, 25, 32, 66; territorial, 90-92, 155-56, 164

beam lengths, 12, 45-46, 47; estimating, 41

beam massiveness, 10, 12, 46; estimating, 41

bears, 178, 184

beds, deer, 59, 116

binoculars, 130-31

biologists, wildlife, 76, 202, 207, 209, 212-15, 226

blacktail deer, 228

blaze orange clothing, 124

bleeding deer, 225

blinds, ground, 57, 141

blood, tracking, 117-18

blood stain, on antlers, 31

bobcats, 219, 225

Boone and Crockett Club, 9, 11; Records of North American Big Game, 4, 10, 44, 75, 76, 98, 176, 177, 227-28, 229; scoring system, 11-12, 37, 42, 44, 178, 248-55

bowhunters, 125, 177-78

brain, deer, 195

breeding condition, deer, 6-9, 51, 52-56, 92-93. *See also* reproduction, deer

breeding seasons, 56, 66, 85-98

Brister, Bob, 199

British Columbia, Canada, 74, 227

Brothers, Al, 91, 92, 223

Browning rifles: BAR, 186, 187, 189

browse marks, 79, 114

brush blinds, 57

buck/doe ratios, 157, 202, 222-24; high, 95; low, 203-4

bucks, 8, 202-5; dominant, 25, 31-32, 52-54, 63, 85-93, 156;